Marx and the Robots

Marx and the Robots

Networked Production,
AI and Human Labour

Edited by
Florian Butollo and Sabine Nuss

Translated by Jan-Peter Herrmann
with Nivene Raafat

First published 2019 as *Marx und die Roboter: Vernetzte Produktion, Künstliche Intelligenz und lebendige Arbeit*. All Rights Reserved

This authorised translation from the German language edition published by Karl Dietz Verlag Berlin and first published 2022 by Pluto Press New Wing, Somerset House, Strand, London WC2R 1LA

www.plutobooks.com

British Library Cataloguing in Publication Data
A catalogue record for this book is available from the British Library

ISBN   978 0 7453 4438 6   Hardback
ISBN   978 0 7453 4437 9   Paperback
ISBN   978 0 7453 4441 6   PDF
ISBN   978 0 7453 4439 3   EPUB

This book is printed on paper suitable for recycling and made from fully managed and sustained forest sources. Logging, pulping and manufacturing processes are expected to conform to the environmental standards of the country of origin.

Typeset by Stanford DTP Services, Northampton, England

Simultaneously printed in the United Kingdom and United States of America

Contents

Introduction   1
Sabine Nuss and Florian Butollo

1   Automation: Is It Really Different This Time?   12
   Judy Wajcman

I Productive Power Between Revolution and Continuity

2   'Voracious Appetite for Surplus Labour'   25
   Elena Louisa Lange

3   Industrial Revolution and Mechanisation in Marx   39
   Dorothea Schmidt

4   A Long History of the 'Factory without People'   55
   Karsten Uhl

5   The Journey of the 'Automation and Qualification' Project   67
   Frigga Haug

6   'Forward! And Let's Remember'   86
   Christian Meyer

II Robots in the Factory: Vision and Reality

7   High Tech, Low Growth: Robots and the Future of Work   101
   Kim Moody

8   Productive Power in Concrete Terms   120
   Sabine Pfeiffer

9   Drones, Robots, Synthetic Foods   138
   Franza Drechsel and Kristina Dietz

III Digital Work and Networked Production

10 Networked Technology and Production Networks 155
Florian Butollo

11 Computerisation: Software and the Democratisation of
Work as Productive Power 169
Nadine Müller

12 Designing Work for Agility and Affect's Measure 185
Phoebe V. Moore

IV Platform Capitalism under Scrutiny

13 Old Power in Digital Garb? 199
Christine Gerber

14 The Machine System of the Twenty-first Century? 215
Felix Gnisa

15 Digital Labour and Prosumption under Capitalism 228
Sebastian Sevignani

16 Artificial Intelligence as the Latest Machine of Digital
Capitalism – For Now 242
Timo Daum

17 Forces and Relations of Control 255
Georg Jochum and Simon Schaupp

Notes on Contributors 269
Notes 273
Index 316

Introduction

Sabine Nuss and Florian Butollo

Domin: 'What sort of worker do you think is the best?'

Helena: 'The best sort of worker? I suppose one who is honest and dedicated.'

Domin: 'No. The best sort of worker is the cheapest worker. The one that has the least needs. What young Rossum invented was a worker with the least needs possible. He had to make him simpler. He threw out everything that wasn't of direct use in his work, that's to say, he threw out the man and put in the robot.'

Karel Čapek, *R. U. R. (Rossum's Universal Robots)*, Prague 1920

IS IT REALLY ALL SO DIFFERENT THIS TIME?

When the Czech writer Karel Čapek wrote his utopian drama *Rossum's Universal Robots* (*Rossumovi Univerzální Roboti* in the original), he could not have anticipated the kind of global conquest that robots were about to embark on. His play is about a company that sells artificially manufactured humans. Masses of these robots are used as cheap labour in industry until they actually start changing the world economy. Eventually, the artificial humans revolt and destroy humankind. The play is considered to be the origin of the term 'robot'; the utopia of an 'artificial human' in the form of a machine gradually became a reality over the subsequent decades.

Even though human beings have certainly not been removed from the factory entirely, and modern industrial facilities have little in common with the humanoid robots Čapek imagined, automation has had a major impact on the world of work – from the highly automated processes in the automotive industry, the replacement of certain tasks by software, on to the so-called chat bots, text-based dialogue systems which replace or complement telephone service hotlines. The neolo-

1

gism 'Industry 4.0' today suggests another technological leap, given that new, more efficient generations of automated systems equipped with environmental sensitivity (sensor technology) and the ability to learn (artificial intelligence, AI) can be integrated via the so-called Internet of Things.

Although this may allow for progress in robotics, another central question in this context is that of the information flows, enriched with huge masses of data, through which individual companies and entire value chains adapt much faster to changes in consumer demand. The fields in which these technologies are applied have long ceased to be confined to the manufacturing of material goods. Automation through software increasingly refers to 'immaterial' labour such as call handlers in call centres, processing in banks and insurance companies, and even in software programming. Moreover, cloud-based platforms, an IT infrastructure made available via the internet, allow for new forms of division of labour in the 'information space'.[1] The range spans from intensive collaboration between highly skilled scientists in spatially separated innovation processes all the way to the fragmented tasks of precarious clickworkers.

Time and again, 'science fiction becomes reality', Brynjolfsson and McAfee write in their much-discussed book, *The Second Machine Age*.[2] Seemingly sudden or visible developments in technology appear to emerge as something unprecedented, as 'revolution', about which only one thing seems certain: that nothing will remain as it was. Scientists, specialised journalists and protagonists from the digital economy have been warning against technological mass unemployment, the takeover of power by artificial intelligence, or both. The backdrop to these predictions is that while computing performance steadily doubled over the first two decades of the digital age and led to a change in modes of production and consumption, the exponential growth of this technology will likely result in a qualitative sea change in the next few years. Kevin Drum is among the authors who speak of an 'AI revolution'; in his much-praised article, 'You Will Lose Your Job to a Robot – and Sooner Than You Think', he writes: 'In addition to doing our jobs at least as well as we do them, intelligent robots will be cheaper, faster, and far more reliable than humans. And they can work 168 hours a week, not just 40. No capitalist in her right mind would continue to employ humans.'[3]

Such a notion renders technology a fetish. Endowed with higher powers, it both descends on society from outside and revolutionises it – an inescapable technological determinism. Along these lines, Brynjolfsson and McAfee attribute the polarisation of the world of work between high-skilled and low-skilled tasks since the 1980s to technology itself, entirely ignoring the rapid deregulation of the Reagan era. More critical analyses likewise often trace social effects back to technological developments, as, for example, with those warnings of a looming full automation that can supposedly only be countered through the introduction of an unconditional basic income.[4]

Some analyses critical of capitalism and oriented on Marx refer to the famous 'Fragment on Machines', a passage from the *Grundrisse* that Marx himself never titled as such. Here, it is asserted, as early as the mid-nineteenth century Marx already described and clairvoyantly predicted full automation as a way of overcoming capitalism. In these manuscripts, dating to the years of the first global economic crisis in 1857/58, Marx sought to swiftly sum up his years-long economic studies in the face of supposedly imminent revolution. In his treatment of large-scale industry and the impact of machines, he asserted that the 'immediate labour' of humans increasingly ceases to be the source of wealth and that, consequently, labour time also has to cease being the measure of wealth and the exchange value in turn ceases to be the measure of the use value: 'As a result, production based upon exchange value collapses.'[5]

Beside these utopian forward projections of current developments based on Marx, socio-technical dystopias are imagined as well, such as that of a seamless digital control of work or an atomisation of the entire working class into an army of individual self-employed crowdworkers. Such fields of conflict will certainly emerge in the future and are already present in the world of work, as striking Amazon workers or staff at Mechanical Turk, Foodora and Uber will tell you. The generalisation of individual trends and tendencies in automation, digital control or platform-centred work, however, produces a technological fetish that obstructs a differentiated interpretation of contemporary capitalism from which political strategies can be deduced.

DIGITALISATION AND THE DEVELOPMENT
OF THE PRODUCTIVE FORCES

The chapters in this volume paint a no less critical yet differenti-ated picture of the ongoing changes. The point of departure is the Marxian concept of the productive forces and the productive power of labour (or productivity of labour), which represents a helpful tool for making a well-founded assessment of the current socio-technical developments.

Firstly, Marx's use of the term helps draw attention to the fact that the development of productive forces is not an end in itself, but rather a mere means for capital accumulation. The level of the productive forces is not only determined by the current state of technology as such, but 'by a wide range of circumstances; it is determined amongst other things by the workers' average degree of skill, the level of development of science and its technological application, the social organization of the process of production, the extent and effective-ness of the means of production, and the conditions found in the natural environment'.[6]

In the process of competition, each company always seeks to increase the productive power of labour, so 'as to shorten the labour time socially necessary for the production of a commodity, and to endow a given quantity of labour with the power of producing a greater quantity of use value'.[7] The development of the productive forces is not an exogenous factor, but rather inscribed into the capital relation, and the development of new technologies and their use is determined to a large extent by this relation. With regard, then, to interpreting the current boost in technologisation or the accelerated proliferation of technology, this implies the need to understand the use of technology in the context of capital's strategies: to what extent does it serve the increase of relative surplus value and its realisation, for example, when market advantages vis-à-vis the competition are to be secured through product innovation or new forms of interact-ing with customers?

Conceived in this sense, the term 'productive forces' relegates digitalisation, in materialist terms, to a rather modest position. Dig-italisation provides socio-technical solutions which are integrated

4

into historically specific accumulation strategies. It is adapted to tendencies towards flexibilisation, financialisation, precarisation and the systematic rationalisation of entire value chains, all of which are characteristic of the more recent production models. Besides its contribution to the rationalisation of the production of surplus value, digitalisation also serves strategies for accelerating turnover rates of goods, the diversification of supply, and the improvement of product quality – measures designed to achieve competitive advantages in the *realisation* of surplus value.

Secondly, the concept of the forces of production warrants a more precise definition of what is really new and revolutionary and what is not. Marx writes in *Capital*: 'Modern industry never views or treats the existing form of a production process as the definitive one. Its technical basis is therefore revolutionary, whereas all earlier modes of production were essentially conservative.'[8] From such a historical perspective, the current changes appear to be more or less consistent with previous, essentially permanent changes. Although both the theory of long waves put forward by Schumpeter and regulation theory address the fact that capitalism is by all means able to 'shed its skin' through the development of new basic technologies, the question remains as to which degree of change justifies speaking of a qualitatively new stage. A number of 'hyphenated capitalisms' (Sabine Pfeiffer) have been conceived in the more recent discussion, such as the frequently invoked 'digital capitalism' (Nachtwey/Staab), 'surveillance capitalism' (Zuboff), 'platform capitalism' (Srnicek) or 'cybernetic capitalism' (Schaupp).[9] These contributions certainly provide convincing analyses of certain aspects of the digital economy. A comprehensive overview of how they are embedded in the totality of capitalist accumulation and which corresponding conclusions must be drawn, however, is outstanding.

A third aspect is related to a broader understanding of the term productive power of labour that also takes into account the significance of cooperation, qualification, the scientific state of the art, or hierarchies regarding the level of scientific development. The use of new forms of robotics and the corresponding coordination of labour and production processes entail more elaborate, distinct and new forms of cooperation as well as changes in qualification requirements, task designs and forms of control. The methodical error in most predictions of full automation is that this necessary mediation is left unconsidered, which leads to that hastily drawn link between abstract technical potential and labour market development. Yet it can be frequently observed that the use of new technologies is more demanding for the human labour capacity and can hardly be realised without an elaborate restructuring of work organisation.[10] One reason for this is the increasing complexity of manufacturing processes, the extent of which only becomes visible when we take into consideration not only the individual company, but the entire ensemble of 'immaterial' activities such as research and development, marketing, coordination of sub-processes, etc., which make production possible in the first place. New approaches to work organisation such as 'agile work' in the area of white-collar labour reflect the increasing need for flexibility. Furthermore, this is related to higher requirements regarding the capacity for 'social innovation' through which the abstract technical potential can be combined to form a functioning socio-technical organism.

This view of the total organism of value creation opens up a different perspective on the limitations of automation. The abstract possibility of replacing certain work tasks with machines is juxtaposed with the increasing complexity of processes which require constant adaptation to changing environmental conditions. Instead of assuming automation to be a static labour process, the image must be dynamised and the constant change in procedures must be taken into account. Full automation in the automotive industry would likely already be a reality if product development had remained at the level of Ford's Model T, which was relatively simple in its construction and only manufactured in a single version in the early twentieth century. But the automotive industry is marked by rapid innovation and product cycles, a high product variety and complex product architectures. Adding to this is the emergence of entirely new requirements and sectors over the past decades, such as the IT industry, in which labour is deployed in new ways to create surplus value. Marx's chapter on the 'industrial reserve army' provides a formidable point of departure for a 'more dynamic' perspective.[11] Marx does not prioritise the constant build up of an ever-greater base unemployment, but the cyclical integration into, and ejection from, capital accumulation in accordance with the logic of constantly rationalising processes and expending labour 'on an extended scale' in the form of new functions in new sectors to satisfy new consumption demands, which in turn requires more sophisticated manufacturing processes. This interpretation reveals a fourth beneficial perspective for the reading of contemporary capitalism: the relationship between the development of the productive forces and the relations of production. Business federations and market research institutes predict that the use of robotics, the Internet of Things and AI will result in enormous growth – while entirely ignoring the fact that the so-called Third Industrial Revolution, i.e. the introduction of microelectronics in economic processes from the early 1970s, already triggered hardly any economic growth. The current technological thrust is occurring in the context of a long phase of weak economic growth, which both influences the forms of the application of technology and defines its limitations. In his chapter in this volume, Kim Moody points out the current reluctance to invest, which stands in stark contrast to the claim that businesses can catapult themselves into the land of milk and honey through the use of digital technology. On the contrary, digitalisation strategies in fact require higher investment in capital goods and the restructuring of social processes. Their refinancing and profitability are anything but certain in the light of stagnating and highly competitive markets. The so-called Fourth Industrial Revolution is therefore occurring – in contrast to what is suggested in the corresponding discourse – not as radical change, but rather as a tentative search process in which businesses alter selected individual processes in order to increase productivity. Whether they turn out to be profitable remains to be seen. A pump manufacturer from the Westerwald region in Germany embarked on a path of digitalisation in accordance with the concepts of Industry 4.0. Subsequently, although the company was able to diversify its product range – i.e. produce a broader range of pumps for industrial use and become less dependent on a handful of major customers – customers were unwilling to pay a higher price for the customised products. In this example, investment in digitalisation did not lead to higher profits, and Industry 4.0 actually resulted in a decrease in labour productivity.[12]

This case may represent a particularly drastic example, yet it points to a more general problem associated with capitalist accumulation: the theoretically conceivable potential of new technologies comes into conflict with relations of production in which the need for permanent growth is inscribed. The tendency of capital to cut costs through reducing the amount of living labour stands in contrast to the fact that the exploitation of living labour is the only source of capital valorisation. This is expressed not least by the obsession with technical applications aiming at the conquest of market shares through a combination of user data analysis and flexible adjustment of manufacturing processes. Such applications may offer companies competitive advantages, but they do not expand the market volume as a whole. The hope for technology-induced growth thus remains a 'false promise',[13] and the possibilities of further developing those technologies that may actually increase the social benefit remain quite limited despite the hype surrounding Industry 4.0 and AI.

THE CHAPTERS IN THIS VOLUME

This brief outline of a reading of the current technological thrust based on the concept of productive forces hints at a task that is yet to be completed. While the contributions published in this volume represent only components of such a project, together they help produce a more diverse and precise picture that is necessary in order to articulate theoretical generalisations.

The introduction to this volume is a chapter by Judy Wajcman presenting us with a summary review of recently published books that address the effects of automation and robotics with regard to the future of employment. Most texts in this genre predict that the current phase of digital technology will lead to a substantial loss of jobs – a feature that distinguishes today's wave of automation from similar waves in the past. The review critically appraises these claims and puts some of the exaggerations regarding automation, robotics and Artificial Intelligence into perspective, calling for a greater focus on the social dimensions of technological development.

Part I consists of contributions that reflect the phenomenon of automation terminologically and historically. Elena Lange positions rationalisation, and thereby digitalisation, in the Marxian theory of relative surplus production. Dorothea Schmidt draws our attention to the object of study that Marx had in mind and referred to in his day: the nineteenth-century Industrial Revolution and mechanisation. In her fact check, she concludes that Marx in part based his work on somewhat one-sided sources, which ultimately manifests in an exaggeration of the effects of automation. Karsten Uhl addresses visions of twentieth-century automation and demonstrates that the fear of technologically induced mass unemployment as a result of the 'factory without people' is not a new phenomenon.

Frigga Haug takes readers on a journey through time in her report on the research project 'Automation and Qualification' (PAQ), which she headed from 1972 onwards. The project had set itself the goal of carving out an ambitious trade union policy from the perspective of working people in the face of the rapid technological changes of the time. Against the backdrop of this experience, she formulates questions that may provide an adequate orientation for current research. Christian Meyer takes a look at materialist technology debates of the past and postulates that contemporary social science lacks the connecting dots to link up with past discussions and a reception of the Marxian analysis.

The authors in Parts II and III address the use of robotics in the 'hidden abodes of production' (Marx) as well as the effects of digitalisation and computerisation on contemporary relations of work and production. Kim Moody presents the volume's introduction to the analyses of current developments. He investigates how and why robots were introduced at a very slow pace, all futurist hype aside. Ironically, the increased use of information and communications technology (ICT) has led to an increase in employment. Moody describes how both the dynamic of capital accumulation and the turbulences of capitalism have resulted in decreased investment in labour-saving technologies both in the USA and at a global level – an obstacle to the predicted replacement of human labour.

Sabine Pfeiffer takes the use of lightweight robots as an example and analyses how the digital transformation takes effect, or, rather, why it fails to do so in this particular case. Agriculture is also a field of application for robots and digitalisation. How exactly this occurs and what impact it has on employment and the political economy of food production is investigated by Franza Drechsel and Kristina Dietz.

Technically induced rationalisation not only occurs at the level of the individual company, but also between companies, at storage sites and along supply routes. The aim of digitally supported optimisation in this scenario is a more efficient linking up of functionally and spatially separated production processes. In his chapter on the reorganisation of global value chains, Florian Butollo presents the forms this takes and its implications for the geographical distribution of production sites. Nadine Müller addresses the question of how computerisation leads to a loss of a productivity-enhancing effect with regard to industrial cooperation and division of labour, particularly the hierarchical separation of intellectual and manual labour, and with regard to management and task performance, and how this creates a – hitherto unknown – potential for democratisation. Phoebe Moore investigates the use of new sensor and tracking technologies in the workplace, how they feed into new management concepts such as agile work, and what effect this has on the employment conditions for workers.

The last Part of the volume introduces interpretative perspectives on the catchphrase 'platform capitalism'. Christine Gerber presents the findings of a research project investigating labour processes on crowdwork platforms in which the tasks are localised, performed and paid via self-employed workers through an internet portal. Platforms lack traditional workplace structures; instead, they face an anonymous, flexible and globally dispersed workforce. Do these forms of work represent something entirely new, or are we merely seeing the old system of power being perpetuated through new digital technologies?

Based on the examples of Uber, a platform connecting drivers and passengers, and Amazon Mechanical Turk, a crowdsourcing marketplace for a host of computer-based microtasks, Felix Gnisa shows how the real subsumption of work under capital changes in comparison to the classic factory of the industrial age, and which distinct new quality is at play here. According to the author, this analytical concept may serve to gauge the possibility of technological transformation for a democratic organisation of work.

Sebastian Sevignani devotes his attention to the 'prosumers' who use (consume) internet services such as Facebook or Google while leaving (producing) their data, which in turn are used by the tech companies as raw material for their profit-oriented production. In particular, he addresses the much-discussed question as to whether these activities produce value and surplus value, and therefore whether they represent a new form of capitalist exploitation.

Timo Daum addresses the current hype surrounding Artificial Intelligence, confirming that we are currently in the midst of a stage of AI development in which the application technologies are rendered mass-marketable by tech companies, thus becoming everyday technologies. According to Daum, this is facilitating the consolidation of a new social operational mode in which the extraction, evaluation and valorisation of data are at the heart of economic activity.

In the final chapter, Simon Schaupp and Georg Jochum examine what potential the current technological development may hold for fundamental changes to the capitalist mode of production. Based on the concept of the 'control transition' (*Steuerungswende*), they gauge the possibility of sustainable and democratic economic planning in the digital age.

1

Automation:
Is It Really Different This Time?

A summary review[1]

Judy Wajcman

Martin Ford, *The Rise of the Robots: Technology and the Threat of Mass Unemployment*, London 2016.

Richard Susskind and Daniel Susskind, *The Future of the Professions: How Technology Will Transform the Work of Human Experts*, Oxford 2015.

Erik Brynjolfsson and Andrew McAfee, *The Second Machine Age: Work, Progress, and Prosperity in a Time of Brilliant Technologies*, New York 2014.

John Urry, *What is the Future?*, Cambridge 2016.

I have lost count of the number of conferences I have attended on Robots, Artificial Intelligence (AI) and the Future of Work. Predicting the future has once again become big business, a sure sign of which is the plethora of books appearing on this topic – those chosen above are but a tiny sample of the genre.

Such conferences have a common format. A few humanlike robotic heads, often with female nomenclature, are displayed and we are encouraged to interact with them for the wow factor. Then a panel of geeks tells us, the lay audience, about their amazing advances, and how close they are to passing the Turing test (making interaction with social robots indistinguishable from human interaction). This is followed by some economists estimating the dire consequences of advanced technology for job prospects. Finally, a few futurists are also included, some even from the so-called Singularity University.[2] I naively asked one of them where this university was based and was told 'it isn't really a university'! *It's a state of mind, man.*

So let me first sketch out the prevailing predictions about employment, then say something about the hyperbole on automation, robotics and AI, and finally why we need more books like Urry's *What is the Future?* that provide some critical distance on this futurist discourse.

Let's begin with Ford's *The Rise of the Robots*, the *Financial Times* 2015 business book of the year. The book is laudable as a trade book, a pacey read about how an increasingly automated economy will affect modern workers. From manufacturing to services, from higher education to healthcare, myriad developments in AI are addressed that, according to Ford, will leave no occupation untouched. The scope of the book is impressive, not only in providing an accessible overview of the latest advances in automation, but also in comprehensively rehearsing the economic and policy debates about the future of work.

It is a thoughtful book and while history is not Ford's longbow, he does acknowledge that fears of technological unemployment are not new. Even the Luddites get a mention. The crux of his argument, however, is clear. All the books reviewed here say it with one voice: 'this time it is different'. Yes, the masses that were thrown out of agriculture found jobs in factories; yes, there was the expansion of the service sector. But this time it *really* is different. A new future is on its way, and it is *scary*. Ford's book is peppered with words and phrases like 'frightening', 'tipping point' and a 'perfect storm'.

According to Ford, information technology (IT) is the game changer, a uniquely disruptive force that has no historical precedent. This is because it is not only the low-skilled that will be displaced – highly skilled professionals are also at risk of being displaced by machines. Where previous waves of automation ultimately created wealth and new sectors of employment, we are now witnessing a fundamental shift in the relationship between workers and machines. Machines are no longer tools; they are turning into the workers themselves. 'All this progress is, of course,' Ford writes, 'being driven by the relentless acceleration in computer technology' (p. xii). As usual, Moore's Law is invoked to prove the inexorability of accelerating technical progress.

The popular commentators and journalists, not to mention the business consultants, seem to devour this bleak picture with a Frankensteinian relish. It is what Urry calls in his book the 'new catastrophism': we stand in awe – and terrified expectation – of what we have created, awaiting the devastating consequences.

So, what is the empirical evidence for Ford's thesis? Interestingly, Ford pauses halfway through Chapter 2 to eschew a too simple narrative that puts advancing technology 'front and centre' as the explanation for the troubling economic trends he identifies, but then quickly reasserts that IT's relentless acceleration sets it apart. Tellingly, he says, 'I'm content to leave it to economic historians to delve into the data.' Evidence is largely presented in the form of vivid stories about the feats of Big Data and 'deep' machine learning. Here pride of place is given to artificial neural networks – systems that are designed using the same fundamental operating principles as the human brain – that can be used to recognise images or spoken words, translate languages, etc. Such systems already power Apple's Siri and, potentially, could transform the nature and number of knowledge-based jobs. If IBM's Watson can win *Jeopardy!* and Google's AI can recognise cats' faces based on millions of YouTube videos, then, Ford surmises, few jobs will remain.

Like almost everyone else, he cites the Oxford Martin School's Frey and Osborne, whose line about half of US jobs being vulnerable to machine automation within the next two decades is endlessly repeated.[3] This estimate, by the way, is based on an algorithm that predicts the susceptibility to automation of different occupations (rather than on the task content of individual jobs). That this methodology has been heavily critiqued has done nothing to halt its endless citation.[4] They are both nice guys so good luck to them, but the uncritical proliferation of their findings is further proof of the pleasure – even pride – we take in the idea that a man-made, robot-worked utopia/dystopia is on its way.

The hyperbole about AI has reached such proportions that even *New Scientist* (16 July 2016) recently asked 'Will AI's bubble pop?' The author makes the point, familiar to sociologists of science, about the powerful role of metaphors in persuading us that these machines are acquiring human capacities. Yet artificial neural networks do not 'learn' like we do, 'cognitive' computing does not think, and 'neural' networks are not neurons. The language is purposefully saturated with anthropomorphism. Rather than worry about the dreaded moment of Singularity, we should be concerned about the dominance of a small number of corporations who have this computing power and about the social consequences thereof. Such political questions are too often lost in our obsession with the robotic revolution we are set to witness.

In the crystal ball of Susskind and Susskind, this imminent revolution is seen to be even more dramatic than the forecast of Ford. While Ford believes that higher education and healthcare professionals are relatively immune from automation, the authors of *The Future of the Professions* specifically include them in their sweeping diagnosis about the end of the professions as we know them. In the internet society, they argue, we will neither need nor want doctors, teachers, accountants, architects, the clergy, consultants or lawyers to work in the way they did in the twentieth century. Although this will lead to massive job loss, this trend is a positive development as the internet will ultimately democratise expertise and empower people.

With a nod to Abbott,[5] they begin by outlining the historical basis of professionalism as the main way expertise has been institutionalised in industrial societies. Until now there has been no alternative, as only human professionals have had the complex combination of formal knowledge, know-how, expertise, experience and skills they refer to as 'practical expertise'. But now, echoing the books above, we are on the brink of a period of fundamental and irreversible change, driven by technology. The authors envisage increasingly capable machines – from telepresence to AI – that will bring a fundamental change in the way that the 'practical expertise' of specialists is made available in society. These smart machines, operating autonomously or with non-specialist users, will perform many of the tasks that have been the preserve of the professions. The result will be the 'routinisation and commoditization of professional work', an argument much like Braverman's proletarianisation thesis but without the political economy. Here the only actors are the machines themselves.[6]

Richard Susskind has been a leading analyst of the impact of technology on the legal profession for several decades, and he is a firm believer in the positive opportunities for information sharing afforded by the internet. And the book's core moral argument is persuasive. Who would disagree that expensive and exclusive privileged elites need to be overhauled and instead we should promote the widespread distribution of expert knowledge? Indeed, the authors envision a model where most professional advice is delivered by automated IT systems, and is available free to users (just like Wikipedia). Once again, we are told about the unprecedented acceleration in the capabilities of IT, AI, Watson, machine learning, Big Data and affective computing. The nub of the matter here, though, is the premise that intelligent machines, drawing on vast amounts of data, will make better decisions than do mere flawed human experts. The archetypal example is the lack of sound sentencing by tired judges after lunch. Perhaps non-alcoholic lunches would be a simpler solution!

The fundamental problem we have is that technologies are only as good as their makers. There is mounting evidence that machine-learning algorithms, like all previous technologies, bear the imprint of their designers and culture. Whether it's Airbnb discriminating against guests with distinctively African-American names, Google showing advertisements for highly paid jobs primarily to men rather than women, or the use of data-driven risk-assessment tools in 'predictive policing', histories of discrimination live on in digital platforms and become part of the logic of everyday algorithmic systems.[7] Even the much-lauded Wikipedia is skewed, in its representation of male to female scientists for instance. While the Susskinds are right to contest the power of the professions, they seem unconcerned with the rise of an even more powerful elite of male white Silicon Valley engineers whose values and biases will inevitably shape the technical systems they design. Making the politics of algorithms visible, explicit and accountable may turn out to be even more difficult than calling, say, lawyers to account.

I am with Brynjolfsson and McAfee who, in *The Second Machine Age*, argue that the most efficient future lies with machines and humans working together. Human beings will always have value to add as collaborators with machines. For a start, I do not believe that all the knowledge and experience, the 'practical expertise' of professionals, can be conveyed via online intelligent systems. Take the suggestion that even the problem of 'empathy' in delivering bad news in hospitals could be countered through an algorithm using consumers' 'psychological and emotional profiles'. Leaving aside the privacy issues this raises, the Susskinds do not grasp the nature of the 'unrecognised' emotional work that is already delegated to largely female para-professionals such as nurses.

Indeed, the social character of skill and expertise, let alone the way that the professions have traditionally been structured around a gendered division of labour, gets no mention in this book (or in any of the others for that matter). We may be 'suckers for the wide eyes and endearing giggles of affective robots', but to advocate the use of robots for empathetic care of the elderly mistakes the appearance of care with real empathy and genuine personal interaction. And anyway, as any roboticist will tell you, there is a huge chasm between the current claims about what these affective, sociable robots can technically feasibly do and what they really can do. Perhaps if eldercare was revalued and remunerated like, say, coding work, the putative labour shortages in this sector that robots are designed to alleviate would disappear. As they would if, more radically, housing and cities were redesigned so that the elderly were not relegated to separate places but were integrated into the wider civil society. But such thoughts are way beyond the scope of any of these books.

The Second Machine Age is the best of this bunch. While covering similar ground, Brynjolfsson and McAfee provide a much more balanced account of the pros and cons of automation on work. The book has been extremely influential, spawning a number of imitations (viz the Chair of DAVOS Klaus Schwab's *The Fourth Industrial Revolution*). The titles of these books are themselves worthy of an article. Here, the history of technology starts with the Industrial Revolution ('the first machine age') and our interest in AI dates from the 1950s. If you want to remind yourself of how much older our obsession with the vitality of machines actually is, I suggest a quick visit to the webpage for the 2017 exhibition on Robots at London's Science Museum.[8]

Brynjolfsson and McAfee are ultimately optimistic about the jobs that will be created as a result of the digital revolution. Although agreeing that many jobs will be swept away by innovations like the driverless car and 3D printers, they argue that, with the right policy levers, such advances can bring forth a bountiful future of less toil, more creative work and greater human freedom. Intervention is crucial given the worrying trends they identify: the polarisation of the labour market, the rise in income inequality and the 'winner-take-all economy'. But, if we 'race with machines, instead of against them', we can take advantage of the uniquely human qualities of creativity, ideation and communication to create more high-quality jobs such as those of creative writers, digital scientists and entrepreneurs. While Brynjolfsson and McAfee also reify technology, treating it as a neutral inevitable force driving these changes, they are strong advocates of government investment in education and infrastructure to deal with its effects. For them, unlike Urry, the effects of technology are political but the causes are not.

Interestingly, like Ford, they propose a guaranteed basic income as one practical solution to the problem of technological unemployment. That this idea has once again become popular across the entire political spectrum makes me a little wary. It immediately conjures up a vision in which the Silicon Valley tech crowd continue to thrive on 24/7 working hours, while those left behind are paid to watch TV and sleep. This idea has a long and sound history and I am watching with interest the trials taking place in Finland and the Netherlands, for example. But in the current context, it is as well to focus on the huge unmet needs we have and the plentiful work that needs doing. Notwithstanding all these books, there is little convincing evidence that large-scale technological unemployment is actually happening or will happen in the immediate future. The real issue is the unequal distribution of work, time and money that exist already.

All these authors shy away from addressing the extent to which the pursuit of profit, rather than progress, shapes the development of digital technologies on an ongoing basis, and the ways in which these very same technologies are facilitating not less work but more worse jobs. This is the proverbial elephant in the room. They seem blind to the huge, casual, insecure, low-paid workforce that powers the wheels of the likes of Google, Amazon and Twitter. Information systems rely on armies of coders, data cleaners, page raters, porn filterers, and checkers – subcontractors who are recruited through global sites such as Mechanical Turk and who do not appear on the company payroll. Even Brynjolfsson and McAfee overlook such classed, gendered, racialised data-processing work as if algorithms trained, tuned and augmented themselves like magic.[9] While these kinds of jobs may well in turn be automated, other novel forms will be created in unexpected ways as capital seeks new ways to accumulate. As Suchman argues, the enchantment or magic of artefacts (such as AI and robotics) is brought about through the masking of labours of production in precisely this way.[10]

As someone immersed in these debates, I have been wondering for some time why this perennial anxiety about automation has come to the fore now. What is the cultural significance of all this breathless talk about AI? No amount of economic history shakes the certainty: *This time it really – really – is different.*[11]

In this context, Urry's astute reflections in *What is the Future?*, published posthumously, could not be more apposite. The social sciences must reclaim the terrain of future studies, he argues, because future visions have enormously powerful consequences for society, carrying with them implicit ideas about public purposes and the common good. Thus, a 'key question for social science is who or what owns the future – this capacity to own futures being central in how power works' (p. 11).

The book begins with a comprehensive overview of the history of 'past futures', from More's *Utopia* (which depicted a six-hour working day half a millennium before Keynes) to the remarkable explosion of new dystopian futures that emerged in the early years of this century. This new catastrophism in social thought is contrasted with the global optimism of the 1990s, especially the digital utopianism that accompanied the emergence of the World Wide Web. Haraway's upbeat 'manifesto for cyborgs', for example, celebrated the positive potential of technoscience to create new meanings and new entities, to make new worlds.

So it is all the more striking that the Zeitgeist within the rich North so radically changed from 2003 onwards. Urry makes this point starkly by simply listing, on pages 36 and 37, the astonishing number of English language texts, films, art exhibitions and research centres within this catastrophic mode. As he rightly argues, such dystopian writing induces a fatalism about the future, helps mobilise powerful interests to promote planetary technological fixes (especially for climate change), and is as much performative as analytic or representational. As I have already intimated, I share this same unease about the rash of books on technological unemployment.

While much of this is familiar territory – viz. the sociology of expectations and Jasanoff's writing on sociotechnical imaginaries[12] – Urry goes further in specifying how futures thinking as a 'method' is a way of bringing back planning, but under a new name. Planning, he says, has become an ideologically contaminated term from the era of organised capitalism and social democracy. So this is a new form of planning, one that brings the state and civil society back in from the cold, and planning is crucial given the long-term wickedness of many problems such as climate change. Only by insisting that futures are always social can public bodies, rather than autonomous markets and endogenous technologies, become central to disentangling, debating and delivering those futures.

Urry was a leading figure in British sociology and, given the sheer range and magnitude of his outputs, it is hard to exaggerate his influence. He was wholly committed to the discipline, always energetically pursuing new ideas, and often prescient in identifying key under-explored social issues of the day. What many will be less aware of are his direct contributions to policy, both to the climate change area and transport. He was appointed to the UK Government's Foresight programme on transport and policy futures, which in turn led to his research on social futures, as well as his setting up an Institute for Social Futures at Lancaster University.

The book therefore builds on long-standing research projects, with substantial chapters on mobilities in the city, 3D printing and the future of manufacturing, and the futures of energy and climate change. Throughout, Urry manages to explain in clear, accessible prose how social practices are constitutive of technology, stressing how technological systems are always socio-material, that the process of innovation is complex and unpredictable, the importance of concepts such as path dependency and lock-in, and the need for what is often termed 'responsible innovation'. For him, these features are best captured by complexity theory, which emphasises how systems are dynamic, processual and unpredictable.

While I found the claim for the distinctiveness of this notion not altogether convincing, perhaps because the recent scholarship on infrastructures in science and technology studies is wholly compatible with his approach,[13] this is a minor quibble. I wholeheartedly agree with the spirit of his argument. The point of these scenario-building exercises is precisely to authorise the participation of a broad range of relevant actors typically excluded from processes of deliberation about the future. And this turn would entail democratising the whole organisation of the making of technology and, with it, society.

The cover of *What is the Future?* features Antony Gormley's 'Another Place'. This work, located on the foreshore in Crosby Beach, Merseyside, consists of 100 cast-iron sculptures of the artist's own body facing out to sea. It is a fitting metaphor for a book that asks us to take seriously our role as sociologists in crafting the future. Evoking Walter Benjamin's Angel of History, we need to conjure up our own Angels of the Future, which stand on the shore of society, their gaze fixed on the horizon, alert to the winds of change. They must be both several and diverse. The homogeneity of the Silicon Valley creators is a more dangerous threat to the future than any perceived robotic apocalypse. Too often these purveyors of the future have their backs to society, enchanted by technological promise and blind to the problems around them. It will require more than robots to ensure that the future really is different this time.

I

Productive Power Between Revolution and Continuity

2

'Voracious Appetite for Surplus Labour'

Understanding the digital revolution
through Marx

Elena Louisa Lange

Only a few years ago, automatic self-checkout points started appearing at local supermarkets like misplaced objects from outer space. To the annoyance of many customers already stressed out by work and family life, automatic checkouts demanded 'proactive' behaviour from grocery shoppers: each item has to be scanned by consumers themselves, holding the barcode of the product above the scanner in the right way and so forth. And as if that were not enough, these checkout points bred mistrust particularly among more 'conscious' consumers: the principle of the self-checkout gave the impression of an insidious yet nonetheless apparent job killer. The initial wave of distancing, or downright rejection, even symbolic boycotting, however, quickly turned into acceptance and eventually a kind of indifferent sympathy. Today, the self-checkout has simply become an everyday object – a normal part of grocery shopping. No one really wants to know the exact workings of such machines. The scanning of items by customers is, as it were, nothing but a *cost-saving measure* on the part of the supermarket owner, chain or parent company. For example, one of the selling points for Russian firm SFOUR's *Automatic Cash Register* – alongside the 'monitoring of all payment operations', the automatic generation of data regarding the sales stock, market research and 'increased customer loyalty' – is, first and foremost, 'the complete replacement of a cashier'.[1]

The productive forces under the form of social production known as capitalism seem to have developed to a point where labour – or, more precisely, wage labour – is redundant, or at least becoming continuously cheaper. The development of the productive forces in this sense permeates society as a whole, impacting consumption, production and distribution. What the self-checkout points represent in the sphere of consumption becomes industrial automation in the realm of production: the dream of a completely autonomous, self-learning and self-optimising factory – the 'factory out of the 3D printer'. And when it comes to social distribution, over the past two decades so-called online platforms have started to occupy the space between production and the 'end customer'. Amazon, Uber, Airbnb, Google and Facebook do not produce anything, but instead generate their profit from commission (e.g. for goods, taxi rides, apartments) and advertising. Even in those cases where the accumulation of data, on which the platforms' entire business model is built, still requires something resembling labour, production forms such as crowdsourcing and clickwork outsource work to individual platform 'microworkers' whose income per *Human Intelligence Task or 'HIT'* is usually measured in cents rather than euros.[2]

Although labour is not eliminated entirely here, it is more decentralised and individualised – and therefore cheaper. In short, over the course of the development of capital's productive forces, human labour is increasingly leading a shadowy existence, while specialised machines and robots are taking over social production. That is not necessarily a problem per se. It only becomes one under the valorisation conditions of capital as robots do not produce value. The crisis is – to use a fitting term – *preprogrammed*. This chapter seeks to understand – with the help of Marx – how the destruction of living labour and its replacement with machines and robots, the development of the productive forces and the crisis of capitalism are linked. The focus is thus placed on the question of why robots do not create any value or surplus value (profit): surely they work too? As we shall see, this notion is owing to a 'fetishist' view of the capitalist mode of production.

Regardless of all the excitement about the 'digital revolution' and its technological potential (to which public broadcasters dedicate entire prime-time programmes) – all the advanced education and training, promotional events and taster workshops (for we are all supposed to be made 'fit for digitalisation') – it is only the 'technical-material' aspects that are addressed in the debate. The 'socio-economic' or 'material-social' elements are largely ignored. As Felix Klopotek points out, this leads to the discussion of 'socio-economic relations in light of their dependence on technical-material processes, which, in turn, and precisely as a result thereof, are stylised as a fetish'.[3] This 'stylisation as a fetish', however, is itself part of a mode of production which declares not only the 'material objectification' of self-learning machines a 'fetish', but even that of seemingly simple yet highly complex and *socially* mediated 'things' such as commodities and money. As a result, all the social *prerequisites* for the dizzying development of the productive forces we are currently witnessing involuntarily are blanked out. The stylisation of the technical-material component of digitalisation as a 'fetish' is therefore the result of an absolutisation of the material appearance of complex social relations in which the question is no longer how it is possible that money can actually represent 'value', how capital yields profit or – and this is particularly relevant for the discussion in this chapter – how it is possible for machines and robots to 'create value'.

The basic aspects of the social – historic, but mainly systematic – prerequisites for explaining the phenomena of automation and digitalisation were already taken up and criticised by Marx in his analysis of the capitalist mode of production. For it was only through his magnum opus, *Capital*, and his *Critique of Political Economy* that he created the theoretical backdrop against which we can understand and criticise the problems and contradictions of digitalisation and the development of the productive forces that confront us today: labour being 'made superfluous' while the class relation between capital and labour persists, the 'cheapening' of production costs with a simultaneous continuity of proneness to crisis, the 'valorisation' of capital alongside ever-lower profit margins. Marx not only identified these contradictions, but indeed provided the *context of justification* which reduces them to a common denominator and illustrates their validity in reality – namely through the heuristic centrepiece of his analysis, the theory of value and surplus value.

In the following, I seek to substantiate the basic features of the validity of the Marxian theory of value and surplus value – a theory through which terms such as the development of the productive forces and the concrete phenomenon of digitalisation can be grasped in the first place. Only an understanding of the expenditure of abstract-human labour in the production process as the source of value and surplus value makes the essence of the capitalist mode of production – valorisation, expressed in the value form of profit – comprehensible. Given that, according to Marx, capital has the 'vocation to approach, by quantitative increase, as near as possible to absolute wealth'[4] – which is why the *postulate of valorisation* constitutes the central motive of the capitalist mode of production to be satisfied through the 'voracious appetite for surplus labour'[5] – it is the relentless drive to 'pump out'[6] increasingly more surplus value from the productive process, the 'boundless thirst for surplus labour',[7] that propels the development of productive forces, as we shall see below, in a way that is highly contradictory both for capital and its own logic of valorisation.

WHY ROBOTS PRODUCE NO VALUE: AN OUTLINE OF THE MARXIAN THEORY OF VALUE

For Marx, 'production is the actual point of departure and hence also the dominant moment [of consumption and distribution]': without an analysis of production it is impossible to understand consumption and distribution.[8] Marx's theory of value, commonly referred to as the *Labour Theory of Value*, establishes the objective relationship between human labour within the production process and the value substance and magnitude of value that emerge from it. Hence, it does not exhaust itself in a 'price theory',[9] but represents the foundation for an understanding of what actually constitutes the social relationship – and how it *appears* – in the first place. For 'value in itself' never appears as such, but is attached to certain manifestations, the forms of value. These are commodities, money, capital, labour wage, price, profit, interest, ground rent, etc. These value forms, or forms of value appearance, all rest on abstract *human* labour – more precisely, on the unpaid labour of others. In fact, the source of value, i.e. abstract-human labour in the production process, is no longer recognisable in its 'objectified' forms of appearance – the value forms – and essentially commands today's fetishist attitude towards technology and supposedly profit-producing robots. In order to elucidate Marx's explanation as to why robots produce no value or surplus value, the theory of value and surplus value will first be outlined.

But before we begin, let us take a step back and ask what 'abstract labour' actually means. Marx distinguishes between the individually produced capitalist commodity's use value and its value: 'The usefulness of a thing makes it a use-value.'[10] Here use value is the result of a certain purposeful, useful and concrete labour. In contrast to value, it is the result of *abstract-general* labour. However, it does not manifest itself in a single commodity: 'An apple is worth one apple' is not an expression of value. The value of a commodity appears only in the *exchange of commodities*, even though this is not where it originates. An individual commodity can express its value only through another commodity. Marx therefore considers the social exchange relation of two distinct commodities and shows that the exchange of, say, a quarter of wheat and 50kg of iron is possible only on the condition of a 'common element of identical magnitude', which is itself neither the use value of wheat nor that of iron. Rather, '[b]oth are therefore equal to a third thing, which in itself is neither the one nor the other. Each of them, so far as it is exchange-value, must therefore be reducible to this third thing.'[11] Consequently, 'the exchange relation of commodities is characterized precisely by its abstraction from their use values.'[12] To Marx, it is clear that the abstraction from the commodities' use values and the concrete labour that went into their production leaves little more than 'the same phantom-like objectivity; they are merely congealed quantities of homogeneous human labour, i.e. of human labour-power expended without regard to the form of its expenditure.'[13] This 'phantom-like objectivity' is the *value* of the commodity and it emerges in actual commodity exchange via an exchange relation which asserts itself with quasi-natural regularity. Correspondingly, at least under normal circumstances, two mid-range cars will commonly be exchanged for more money than will a normal bar of chocolate, and twelve pairs of shoes will be traded for less than three single-family houses. The assertion of certain exchange relations, however, cannot be deduced from the use value or the need of those involved in the exchange: commodities with a high use value, such as water (or oxygen), have a low value, whereas those with a relatively low use value (diamonds, works of art) have a high value.[14] The *quantitative* definition of the exchange relation between two commodities thus rests on the magnitude of their value, which in turn is determined in *qualitative* terms through 'the quantity of the "value-forming substance", the labour, contained in the article. This quantity is measured by its duration, and the labour-time is itself measured on the particular scale of hours, days, etc.' Given the possibility that one may assert that a particularly slow worker could produce a greater value than one who works faster, Marx adds that '[w]hat exclusively determines the magnitude of the value of any article is therefore the amount of labour socially necessary, or the labour-time socially necessary for its production'.[15] What is decisive for the magnitude of value is the labour time under *socially average production conditions*. This reduction of labour to 'the quantitative proportions in which society requires them' in turn depends on a commodity production that rests on a general division of labour, in which the relations of exchange assert themselves through the socially necessary labour time objectified in the commodities, just like 'the law of gravity asserts itself when a person's house collapses on top of him'.[16]

The 'twofold nature of the labour contained in commodities' – that is, rather than being two distinct 'kinds of labour', it is the exact same labour, considered under the two mutually exclusive aspects of use value and value – is for Marx the 'point [which] is crucial to an understanding of political economy'[17] and which represents the foundation for the Marxian analysis. After all, the 'crucial point' is that the commodity product has a use value, but the *motive of production* is not the creation of use values but the production of (surplus) value and its value forms of capital and profit. This is immediately evident: if the use value or the benefit for people were the motive of production, not a single person on the planet would have to go hungry. Consequently, it is not supply and demand that regulate production under capitalist conditions, but monetary, that is, *solvent*, demand. It is the value form of money that attracts commodities, not the need for certain use values. The way in which value and surplus value become the motive driving production will be shown in the following outline of the Marxian theory of surplus value.

THE BASIC FEATURES OF THE MARXIAN THEORY
OF SURPLUS VALUE

The theory of value may be the *theoretical foundation* for the theory of surplus value – Marx's revolutionary scientific insight into the exchange of capital and labour under unequal conditions, and simultaneously the centrepiece of his entire analysis[18] – but capitalist exchange relations can only be explained on the basis of the theory of *surplus value*. For the commodity produced under capitalist relations is a bearer not only of value, but of *surplus value*. If capitalists gained only value, but no surplus value, from the sale of a commodity, there would be no reason for the capitalist mode of production to exist – and hence no reason for the capitalist to exist either. Here we also find the reason why robots and other machines do not produce any *value*: robots produce no *value* because they produce no surplus value. When defining living abstract labour expended in the production process as the only source of (surplus) value, Marx simultaneously addressed the relation between wage labour and capital, without which there would be no capitalist mode of production.

As we have seen, Marx considers abstract human labour to be the source of value. This labour force is traded like a commodity on the 'free market', i.e. it is bought and sold. The worker, who depends on her wage for daily reproduction, sells her 'capacity' to work as a commodity. The capitalist buys this commodity for a certain period of time, be it a working day or a month. The value, or sales price, of labour force is the wage. As we have seen, however, the value of a commodity corresponds to the socially necessary labour time that 'it contains'. The labour wage or value of the commodity of labour therefore corresponds precisely to that part of the working day in which the worker performs the *necessary* labour, i.e. produces a value sum, which corresponds to her wage and thus ensures her own reproduction (food, clothing, housing, etc.). In principle, production could be organised this way: workers only work the number of hours it takes to reproduce themselves as workers. *Capitalist* production, with its postulate of valorisation, however, would be made impossible as a result given that it requires the production of surplus value, the production of *capital*. That is why the money owner or capitalist is indeed pleased

31

to be 'lucky enough'[19] to find the workers' labour power as a commodity on the market, because the capitalist, like the buyer of any other commodity, pays for the *value* of labour power – not for its *use value*. And yet it is the *use value* of the commodity of labour power, that is, its consumption or application by the capitalist in the production process for a certain amount of time, which has the peculiar property of producing *value* that is *greater than its own value*, the labour wage. The capitalist is thus 'lucky' in the sense that he (or she) does not violate the principle of the exchange of equivalents: the commodity of labour power is bought at its value: the wage. The capitalist, as the legitimate buyer, is entitled to own the full use value of this commodity. The fact that this commodity has a use value that itself creates value – indeed *beyond the actual value* at which it was purchased as it produces *surplus value* – is therefore not the result of fraud. The capitalist does not permit the worker to perform labour only for enough time as to allow her to reproduce the labour wage; she must work longer. The wage labourer thus works not only for herself, but also performs unpaid labour for the capitalist. This way, the capitalist appropriates 'alien unpaid labour' without infringing on any principle or law.

NEW VALUE AND SURPLUS VALUE

According to Marx, the whole secret of value and surplus value production rests on the temporal difference between necessary and surplus labour within the production process. Regarding robots and machines, however, there is no point in distinguishing between necessary and surplus labour. Robots neither have to reproduce themselves nor do they work for a wage. Most notably, they are unable to produce any new value, i.e. to preserve their own value while creating surplus value.

Robots, assistance systems, self-checkout points, supercomputers, etc. are *means of production*. As such, they constitute 'constant capital' (c) and a component of 'productive capital'. The latter also includes the wage for workers advanced by the owners of money – i.e. the owners of the means of production for the production process – which Marx terms 'variable capital' (v). Productive capital is the starting point of the production process. The choice of terminology is no coincidence: constant capital transfers either all or a part of its value to the value product during production. It thus becomes part of the value product c + v + s, in which s denotes surplus value and v + s is the *new value* created during production. This new value, however, is only created by the expended living labour v, the use of which (for the one applying it, i.e. the capitalist) consists precisely of not only *preserving* the value of the means of production (i.e. transferring the value, but not the use value, to the new product), but also creating an *additional new value*, a new product, a new commodity. In this sense, the value of the commodity of labour power only flows into the final product of a commodity as long as it creates new value, that is, *only in terms of* the preservation and new creation of value. It is therefore variable: the capital component advanced in v, then, not only reproduces its own value, but *changes* the value of the product over the course of the production process (becoming greater in proportion to the intensity and duration of expended labour power), while the part advanced in c remains constant. In other words: a change in the value of c has a direct impact on the value product in the formula c + v + s. A change in the value of v, however, has no direct impact on the value product: the creation of new and surplus value depends not on the worker's wage, but on the intensity and duration of labour expenditure. The 'valorisation of capital' thus results 'exclusively from its variable component'.[20] Marx refers to the relation between surplus labour and variable capital, i.e. the relation in which living labour creates surplus value, as the 'rate of surplus-value', or s / v, which at the same time is an indicator of the degree of exploitation of labour power.

Machines (and therefore robots as well) may represent important factors for the *efficiency* of production and the *compression* of labour from the perspective of valorisation. Yet they are bought by the unit and as such merged into the value product: they are really *paid* for and form part of the value product as *purchased* products. Labour, however, which produces new value, i.e. which reproduces its own value while simultaneously creating surplus value, is *not paid for*. Only here can we meaningfully speak of surplus labour, which constitutes the foundation of valorisation. Given that the valorisation process is not only a process of value creation but also of value *preservation*, and capitalist production produces use values only as bearers of value and surplus value, value production must essentially be understood as a *part of surplus value* production, and not the other way around. If no surplus value is produced, there is no value. Consequently, then, as robots produce no surplus value, they do not produce any value either.

This is where the fetish phenomenon can be brought full circle. The fact that the value form called 'labour wage' appears as if it paid for the labour of one working day or month is part and parcel of the 'stylisation' of capital as fetish. It makes it seem as though 'labour' and 'means of production' contribute *equally* to the process of value creation – as though 'dead' labour, i.e. already objectified labour such as machinery, robots and *self-learning algorithms*, produce value as well. In truth, however, the 'production of value and surplus value' can only be understood in a meaningful way as the expenditure of *living* human labour. The development of the productive forces in this sense occurs under the precept of achieving the most effective valorisation of this labour. From the perspective of capital, labour actually really seems to be valorised more efficiently through the use of increasingly specialised innovative technology in terms of the means of production – after all, it is precisely the goal of using the invested capital in the *most productive* way, i.e. gaining a surplus value or profit from the sale of commodities, which propels the technical-technological development and thus the development of the productive forces. Yet it is precisely this logic of valorisation at all costs, which is the engine driving the development of productive forces, that is undoing the valorisation postulate. An important component of this undoing is the 'capital fetish', that is, the notion that means of production, or 'dead' labour – which includes all material-technological factors of production – contribute to (surplus) value creation. It is therefore clear to Marx that

With the development of relative surplus-value in the specifically capitalist mode of production, involving the growth of the productive forces of social labour, these productive forces and the social context of labour appear in the immediate labour process as *shifted from labour to capital.* Capital thereby already becomes a very mystical being, since all the productive forces of social labour appear attributable to it, and not to labour as such, as a power springing forth from its own womb.[21]

This fateful undoing, which manifests itself for all those involved as a *crisis of valorisation*, or simply a crisis of capitalist production, is subsumed under the analytical category of relative surplus value. For it is the production of relative surplus value that essentially characterises the wholly capitalist mode of production. Here, capital not only finds the conditions of production and appropriates an already existing mode of production, but indeed *changes* it and thus sets in motion the development of the productive forces. The category of relative surplus value accounts for the dynamic of value production under the conditions of real and progressive application of the latest technological development and innovation in the form of constant capital accompanied by the simultaneously decreasing use of living labour: in other words, it explains the *crisis* proneness intrinsic to the development of capitalist social productive power. The validity of the term 'relative surplus value' must certainly not be underestimated. To conclude, we shall therefore take a look at how Marx introduces this term.

THE DEVELOPMENT OF PRODUCTIVE POWER, RELATIVE SURPLUS VALUE AND CRISIS

As we have seen, surplus value is based on the difference between socially necessary and surplus labour, measured in labour time. The greater the proportion of surplus labour vis-à-vis necessary labour there is in a working day, the greater the surplus value and profit. In the early stages of capitalist production, there was a given technical state which required workers to work for a certain ratio of the working day on average – say, six hours – for themselves. The socially necessary labour time for their own reproduction was given. Six hours per day allowed for an unimpeded reproduction of labour power. Hence, in order to 'pump out' as much surplus labour as possible from the production process, *surplus labour had to be extended.* Marx calls this extension of the working day beyond socially required labour the production of *absolute surplus value*. Unfortunately for capital, there is a 'maximum limit' to this form of production that cannot be exceeded for physical and social reasons: no one can work 24 hours per day. People have to satisfy 'intellectual and social requirements, and the extent and the number of these requirements is conditioned by the general level of civilization'.[22] Capital, however, in its drive towards valorisation, seeks and finds, over the course of its development, ways of increasing the production of surplus value, i.e. of extending surplus labour without consideration for natural limitations. Given that this cannot be done simply through prolonging surplus labour due to the natural limits of the working day, the only option for increasing the production of surplus value is the 'contraction of the necessary labour-time',[23] or the *shortening* of the part of the working day during which the worker works for themselves. Correspondingly, the 'respective lengths of the two components of the working day'[24] change as well. If the necessary labour is contracted, surplus labour and thus the production of surplus value expands. Marx refers to this form of surplus value production as the production of *relative surplus value*. Yet, as this obviously entails a reduction in wages, too, and the reproduction of labour power becomes very difficult without a certain 'standard of living', capital itself must change the conditions of production under which it valorises itself. It is forced to produce greater volumes faster, more efficiently or, in short, in a more cost-saving way. By reducing production costs, particularly with regard to variable capital, and increasing the use of constant capital, it is able to produce a greater mass of commodities in a shorter period of time, resulting in a corresponding 'cheapening' of the value of the goods the worker necessarily has to consume (in addition to other goods). The production of relative surplus value reduces the value of the commodity of labour power along with the production costs because the shopping cart – or what we might refer to today as consumer price index (CPI) – becomes cheaper. It is this dynamic change in production conditions with the aim of lowering the price of the commodity of labour power which drives forward the development of the productive forces under the directive of surplus value production, i.e. under capitalist conditions. The

36

means for achieving this is the replacement of living labour with technical auxiliary apparatuses, computers, machinery, robotics, etc. Seeing as the prevalence of specialised private production and competition between individual capitals continues, any use of capital is considered with a view to saving costs – while each individual capitalist simultaneously seeks the utmost efficient valorisation of their own capital. The individual capitalist by no means makes a conscious decision to shorten the necessary labour time and reduce the value of labour power, '[b]ut he contributes towards increasing the general rate of surplus-value only in so far as he ultimately contributes to this result'.[25]

The valorisation postulate, then, is seriously disturbed by this ever-faster development of the productive forces. Here, the 'necessary tendencies' become manifest, namely as a contradiction of the capitalist mode of production. Marx termed this tendency the 'Law of the Tendency of the Profit Rate to Fall' (LTPRF).[26] For if constant capital is increased in relation to variable capital while the rate of surplus value remains unchanged – Marx calls this the 'increase in the organic composition of capital' – the part of capital which creates new value, or v, becomes smaller. As a result, less surplus value is created in the production process. This in turn is expressed by the 'gradual fall in the general rate of profit',[27] as Marx illustrates with a number of simple equations. This 'necessary tendency' is rooted in a mode of production which develops the forces of production only for the purpose of an ever-greater self-valorisation: 'The progressive tendency for the general rate of profit to fall is thus simply the expression, peculiar to the capitalist mode of production, of the progressive development of the social productivity of labour.'[28] After all, capital is what it is only because of its quantitative expansion, as accumulation of abstract wealth or 'value', measured in money. Expanded accumulation in particular, however, requires cost saving and the replacement of living labour, or 'expensive labour costs', through 'cheap machinery', thus inevitably producing less surplus value: it is a vicious circle or, rather, a 'contradiction-in-process', because capital strives

to reduce labour time to a minimum, while, on the other hand, positing labour time as the sole measure and source of wealth [...]

On the one hand, therefore, it calls into life all the powers of science and nature, and of social combination and social intercourse, in order to make the creation of wealth (relatively) independent of the labour time employed for that purpose. On the other hand, it wishes the enormous social forces thus created to be measured by labour time and to confine them within the limits necessary to maintain as value the value already created.[29]

In the same passage, however, Marx also describes the development of the productive forces as a means to abolish the domination of (material or) objectified relations as well as the dominance of capital and its valorisation postulate over human beings and their real needs. Once the development of the social forces of production were no longer subject to the directive of surplus value, the human liberation from labour would actually be possible. 'The productive forces and social relations [...] appear to capital merely as the means, and are merely the means, for it to carry on production on its restricted basis. In fact, however, they are the material conditions for exploding that basis.'[30] Whether this possibility will come to fruition one day will crucially depend on whether the pretence of the 'objectified' or 'material-technical' foundations of digitalisation is revealed and overcome, and social prerequisites of these foundations are reflected.

3

Industrial Revolution and Mechanisation in Marx

A fact check

Dorothea Schmidt

In the first half of the nineteenth century, England, Scotland and Wales underwent radical changes. New machines like the spinning jenny and the self-acting spinning mule revolutionised spinning, while the mechanical loom did the same for artisanal weaving. Large factories sprung up everywhere, and the population of Manchester multiplied within only a few decades, turning a small town into the second-largest city in England, henceforth to be known as the *workshop of the world*. At the time, the endless stacks of smoking chimneys provoked feelings of both fascination and fear among people – including Karl Marx, who had meticulously studied questions pertaining to machines and the overall technological development since the mid-1840s. Later assessments often asserted that Marx had been a machine fetishist – a theoretician of the relentless mechanisation of production and the inevitable degradation of the labour force.[1] Was this really the case, and did it in fact correspond with the development of industrialisation in Great Britain at the time? And on what sources were his studies based?

MECHANISATION AND LABOUR FORCES IN MARX

Marx presented his first lengthy deliberations on the significance of machines in his *Grundrisse* of 1857/58, which also contains the so-called 'Fragment on Machines':

Once included into the production process of capital [...] the means of labour passes through a series of metamorphoses until it ends up as the machine, or rather as an automatic system of machinery (system of machinery: automatic merely means the most complete, most adequate form of machinery, and alone transforms machinery into a system). That system is set in motion by an automaton, self-moved motive power; this automaton consists of a large number of mechanical and intellectual organs, with the workers themselves cast in the role of merely conscious members of it.[2]

These passages are not primarily concerned with the historical significance of mechanisation in the production process so much as with more general reflections on machinery as fixed capital and its use value in the production process. In his *Economic Manuscript* composed between 1861 and 1863, Marx was somewhat more specific, presenting the following compelling sequence: 'The large-scale *industrial system* has been put into effect: 1) in factories proper; 2) in manufactories, which all now employ machines to some degree; 3) in agriculture. In all these one finds a *system of production on a large scale*.'[3] This development appeared unstoppable and seemed to encompass all areas of material production, including agriculture. Its impact on the labour forces is described as follows:

[T]he industrial revolution first affects the part of the machine which does the work. The motive force here is at first still man himself. But operations such as previously needed the virtuoso to play upon the instrument, are *now brought about by the conversion* of the movement directly affected by the simplest mechanical impulse (turning the crank, treading the wheel) of human origin into the refined movements of a working machine.[4]

Similarly, further on it reads:

Once the tool is itself driven by a mechanism, once the tool of the worker, his implement, of which the efficiency depends on his own skill, and which needs his labour as an intermediary in the working process, is converted into the tool of a mechanism, the machine has replaced the tool.[5]

In Chapter 15 of the first volume of *Capital*, the chapter on machinery and large-scale industry, Marx proceeds from Stuart Mill's question on whether mechanical inventions had ever 'lightened' the work of a human being. His succinct response – and, moreover, the motif for the following 140 pages – is:

> That is, however, by no means the aim of the application of machinery under capitalism. Like every other instrument for increasing the productivity of labour, machinery is intended to cheapen commodities and, by shortening the part of the working day in which the worker works for himself, to lengthen the other part, the part he gives to the capitalist for nothing. The machine is a means for producing surplus-value.[6]

In diagnosing the 'Transition from Modern Manufacture and Domestic Industry to Large-Scale Industry'[7] for his own present, Marx returns to the stage theory already postulated earlier:

> The principle of machine production, namely the division of the production process into its constituent phases, and the solution of the problems arising from this by the application of mechanics, chemistry and the whole range of the natural sciences, now plays the determining role everywhere. Hence machinery penetrates into manufacture for one specialized process after another.[8]

Marx saw three specific forces at work that were driving the increasing mechanisation. First, the relations between the distinct sectors of what today would be referred to as the value chain: 'The transformation of the mode of production in one sphere of industry necessitates a similar transformation in other spheres.'[9] Correspondingly, machine spinning necessitated machine weaving due to increased productivity; the two combined revolutionised bleachery, cloth printing and dyeworks, but had repercussions for the previous production stage, mechanical engineering: 'Large-scale industry therefore had to take over the machine itself, its own characteristic instrument of production, and to produce machines by means of machines.'[10] Likewise, the downstream sectors of the garment industry were subordinated to the need for mechanisation and factory production: 'The decisively revolutionary machine, the machine which attacks in an equal degree all the innumerable branches of this sphere of production, such as dressmaking, tailoring, shoemaking, sewing, hat-making and so on, is the sewing-machine.'[11]

Marx considered social reforms to be a second driving force. For the first time, legal limits were placed on the production of absolute surplus value by shortening the working day, which had, in the past, been repeatedly prolonged. Once the standard working day was introduced, 'capital threw itself with all its might, and in full awareness of the situation, into the production of relative surplus-value, by speeding up the development of the machine system'.[12]

Ultimately, he argued, the development of machinery would depend on class struggles: 'It would be possible to write a whole history of the inventions made since 1830 for the sole purpose of providing capital with weapons against working-class revolt.'[13] As a case in point, he referred to the self-actor and machine engineering, and referenced James Nasmyth, the inventor of the steam hammer, who had boasted before a government commission in 1851 that the introduction of 'self-acting tool machinery' had allowed him to get rid of the skilled workers who had initiated a strike.[14]

Marx apparently saw one of the crucial dynamics in the efforts on the part of capital to make itself independent from the knowledge and capabilities of trained staff, on whom it still greatly relied in the manufactures, and he assumed that this was entirely successful through the introduction of machines. Relevant passages – which were gladly and frequently quoted subsequently – can be found in both the *Grundrisse* and in *Capital*, in which Marx eloquently denounces the destructive impact of the machine system on the workers, or, more precisely, the destruction of their erstwhile virtuosity: 'Along with the tool, the skill of the worker in handling it passes over to the machine', which is why, in the 'automatic factory', there is no longer, as there was in manufacture, a 'hierarchy of specialized workers', but rather 'a tendency to equalize and reduce to an identical level every kind of work that has to be done by the minders of the machines'.[15] Later in the text, it reads:

> Factory work exhausts the nervous system to the uttermost; at the same time, it does away with the many-sided play of the muscles, and confiscates every atom of freedom, both in bodily and in intellectual activity. Even the lightening of the labour becomes an instrument of torture, since the machine does not free the worker from the work, but rather deprives the work itself of all content.[16]

In Marx's view, this development was accompanied by a new 'composition of the collective labourer' and the novelty that mechanisation increasingly allowed for the employment of women and children. The expertise of the erstwhile skilled workers became dispensable, as their work tasks no longer required their previous levels of qualification: 'In handicrafts and manufacture, the worker makes use of a tool; in the factory, the machine makes use of him.' The worker was now being transformed into an 'automaton': 'The special skill of each individual machine-operator, who has now been deprived of all significance, vanishes as an infinitesimal quantity in the face of the science, the gigantic natural forces, and the mass of social labour.' In short: 'The instrument of labour strikes down the worker.'[17]

THE INDUSTRIALISATION OF GREAT BRITAIN FROM A TWENTIETH-CENTURY PERSPECTIVE

In the depiction of developments in Britain, even bourgeois historiography mostly toes the line pursued by Marx in *Capital*, most prominently of all David Landes in his definitive book, *The Unbound Prometheus*. According to him, the decisive innovations facilitating the emergence of the factory system include 'the substitution of machines – rapid, regular, precise, tireless – for human skill and effort' and 'the substitution of inanimate for animate sources of power' which opened up 'a new and almost unlimited supply of energy'.[18] Only rarely has this view been contradicted, most vocally perhaps by Raphael Samuel, an influential and original Marxist British historian who, like David Landes, criticised Karl Marx.

Samuel pointed out that industrialisation was not only a process of substitution – as Marx's prime example, the replacement of hand weaving by machine weaving, suggested – but also engendered a series of hitherto unknown trades and activities: 'The fireman raising steam in an engine cab, or the boilermaker flanging plates in a furnace, were engaged in wholly new occupations which had no real analogy in previous times.'[19] Moreover, the assertion of the capitalist economy signified not only the expansion of the factory system: 'Capitalist enterprise took quite different forms in, for instance, cabinetmaking and the clothing trades, where rising demand was met by a proliferation of small producers. [...] In metalwork and engineering – at least until the 1880s – it was the workshop rather than the factory which prevailed, in boot and shoemaking, cottage industry.'[20] Consequently, there was no sequence of development stages in the sense that each stage – simple commodity production, manufacture and modern industry – neatly and entirely replaced the previous one. Rather, the nineteenth century saw a lasting coexistence of distinct forms, in which older ones, such as workshop labour or cottage industry, partly remained in place, partly emerged anew.[21] The different forms of production were frequently closely linked to one another. The individual segments of the value chains did not automatically evolve into large mechanised firms, such as in the following case: 'Timber was sawn at the saw mills, where steam-driven machinery was, by the 1850s, very general; but it was shaped at the carpenter's bench, on the cabinet-maker's trestles, and at the cooper's cokefired cresset.'[22] Similarly, the primary products for knives and cutlery were produced in rolling mills and then subsequently further processed by hand in Sheffield; Lancashire's major textile industry provided the cloth which was then sewn into garments in thousands of small workshops and the cottage industry. Likewise, the use of the steam engine was distributed highly unevenly between individual industries: while it was very common in cotton factories and in iron manufacturing in 1871, it was a marginal phenomenon in the garment industry, saddlery and glove-making, boatbuilding and in food production.[23]

Hence, Samuel emphasised that the capitalist growth of that time did not rest on *one* but on several technologies. This was true even in individual industrial branches when, say, some tasks were mechanised and others remained traditional handicraft, performed as in the past, such as in mining, one of the nineteenth century's growth industries, where the use of steam-driven pumps allowed workers to reach even greater depths than before: 'But there was a total absence of mechanisation at the point of production, where the coal was still excavated by shovel and pick – "tools of the most primitive description, requiring the utmost amount of bodily exertion to render effective".'[24] In the textile industry, which served as Marx's prime example of mechanisation, the use of the machine loom and the emergence of factories also occurred very unevenly: they appeared more frequently in spinning than in weaving, and more often in the processing of cotton than in that of linen or silk. Adding to this was the fact that, given the volatility of fluctuating sales, many entrepreneurs were reluctant to risk any greater investment in self-actors and preferred traditional manual spinning, which resulted in both means of production existing simultaneously.[25]

With regard to the production of food, a diverse picture emerges: 'There was more machinery in jam-making, where by the 1880s steam-jacketed boilers reduced the fruit to pulp, but the preparatory stages were performed by hand' – i.e. the sorting, peeling, cutting and cleaning.[26] The traditional bakeries by no means disappeared, and attempts to set up large-scale bakeries foundered almost every time. Given that cities were growing very rapidly during this time, the number of manual producers of foodstuffs increased accordingly. In the brewing industry, for example, large-scale breweries began appearing in London, whose kettles were fired by steam, but there were countless small-scale and micro-breweries as well: in Birmingham alone, there were 1,800.[27]

One of the most important industries to be bypassed by mechanisation was the construction industry: the labour force grew more than threefold over the second half of the nineteenth century, and there was twice as much investment capital in this sector than in the cotton industry: 'But the scale of enterprise was characteristically small, and investment, whether by master-builders or sub-contractors, went on labour and materials, not on plant. The main thrust of technical innovation, such as it was, came in the direction of labour-saving materials rather than of mechanical devices.'[28] The splendour of Victorian architecture was displayed in bank buildings with columns of all imaginable styles, neo-Gothic churches, administrative buildings, train stations and town halls with little towers and gables, ledges and statues, that is to say, with a vast variety of ornamentation and decoration, offering plenty of work to masons and stuccoers. The tools used included hammers, pliers, hatchets and soldering irons, with wheelbarrows being the only means of cargo transport. Only very few building materials – such as marble for chimney pieces – were produced with the use of machines, whereas bricks, roof tiles, clinkers, stone window lintels and other building components were crafted and – if needed – polished by hand.[29]

Concerning the investment goods sector, it is primarily the production of raw materials that merits closer attention. 'In metallurgy steam power was massively harnessed to the primary processes of production, notably in puddling and rolling; but at the same time new fields were opened up for handicraft skills' in the foundries and finishing shops.[30] Mechanical engineering – the industry which produced, among other things, the machines for the textile industry – continued to be dominated largely by handicrafts. With the exception of sewing machines, most machines were made in individual make-to-order production, in which each component was produced to fit precise specifications and refinished subsequently as required. Workers possessed manual skills, and their precision work at the turning lathe was considered more important than the speed at which it occurred. The situation was similar with regard to steam locomotives, which generally consisted of more than 5,000 individual components. Even steam boilers were produced manually, seeing as hydraulic riveting, although known at the time, was deemed unreliable for the boilers' durability. Make-to-order manufacturing was also common practice in the world-leading British shipbuilding sector, with a company's reputation depending on the quality of work. Here, hydraulic riveting was used in some individual production steps, but even in the larger shipyards, manual riveting was common. Parallel to the growth of steam locomotives, the construction of railway lines also expanded at the same rate, employing around 300,000 workers by the mid-nineteenth century. For the most part, the tools of their trade were the pick and shovel, regardless of whether they were building railway embankments, shafts, tunnels or viaducts.[31]

Overall, Samuel concluded: 'In manufacture, as in agriculture and mineral work, a vast amount of capitalist enterprise was organised on the basis of hand rather than steam-powered technologies.'[32] He listed several reasons why mechanisation was implemented in only a minority of trades.

Firstly, there was a relative abundance of skilled and unskilled labour forces. Entrepreneurs were therefore less interested in labour-saving so much as in capital-saving innovations. This situation was specific to the United Kingdom; the United States, on the other hand, suffered from a lack of labour forces. Here, railway construction occurred with the use of steam-driven diggers, lock manufacturing relied on processed cast iron, and nail machines were implemented for nail production, while handcrafted products were still common in Victorian England.[33]

Secondly, mechanisation was not the only way of increasing productivity. Another was to improve tools or use new raw materials. In British agriculture, there was an increased use of scythes instead of sickles; in mining the steel pickaxe came to replace the iron pickaxe. Simultaneously, products were often redesigned and individual work steps were simplified; for example, in shoemaking the soles were no longer sewn, but nailed on.[34]

Thirdly, there was often a significant 'gap between expectation and performance. In many cases the machines failed to perform the "self-acting" miracles promised in the patents, and either needed a great deal of skilled attendance, or failed to execute their appointed tasks.'[35] It took decades before, say, the needle machine built by Wright, which was supposed to produce a 'perfect needle' in a single operation, or the steam-powered Jolly wheel, which was to replace manual pottery making, were actually operational and provided satisfactory results. Many materials in fact resisted machine processing: 'In the leather trades, every process of production, from the preparatory work to the finishing, depended on manual dexterity and strength.'[36] The situation was similar in shoemaking and saddlery.[37]

Fourthly, companies often faced unsteady and limited demand. This could change on a weekly basis or according to the seasons, and was, moreover, subject to cyclical economic fluctuations, which were preferably countered with the hiring or firing of labour forces instead of leaving expensive machinery idle. Demand was limited in the sense that there were no standardised products in many areas, which required the production and sale of many distinct types of product – there were around 45 types of axe and 500 different hammer variants.[38]

WHAT WAS THE BASIS OF MARX'S VIEW ON BRITISH INDUSTRIALISATION?

We do not know whether Marx, who had lived in London with his family since 1849, attended the Great Exhibition in London's Hyde Park in 1851, the very first World's Fair. It was regarded as a particularly glamorous showcasing of British capitalism, and he could have marvelled not only at the 'self-active machines' and other brilliant technical achievements there, but at handcrafted products as well: 'even in the "Machinery Court" many of the exhibits were assembled from hand-made components'.[39] What cannot have eluded him, however, was the abundance of construction work that was taking place in London at the time: the 1850s saw the construction of most of the major railway stations, the underground, countless administrative buildings – among others, the vast Palace of Westminster in neo-Gothic style, not far from the British Museum, the library of which he used from 1850 onwards. The number of London's inhabitants grew from 2.7 million in 1850 to 3.9 million by 1870.[40] He either did not notice that countless bricklayers, masons and stuccoers, joiners and lathe operators were using tools, and not machines, or he classified this as a transitional state, in order to then immerse himself in his preferred sources for the development of industrialisation, seeking to grasp the characteristic features it would have in terms of future developments.

In his time in Brussels from 1845 to 1848, Marx already engaged with and wrote up extensive excerpts, particularly with regard to steam engines, from the *Technical Dictionary* by Andrew Ure, which explains their construction logic and functional principles, as well as presenting inventions towards their improvement. He also read Ure's *The Philosophy of Manufactures*,[41] and although he regarded the author to be a 'shameless apologist of the factory system', he credited him with 'being the first to grasp its spirit correctly [...] with its accompaniment of absolute discipline, regimentation, subjection to the clock and the rules of the factory'.[42]

Ure was a Scottish professor of the natural sciences and chemistry who, in *The Philosophy of Manufactures*, treated the textile industry as the prototype of the factory system, describing in great detail the most recent manufacturing processes and machines used for the different types of cloth. He proved to be a fervent optimist of progress who saw salvation in the general proliferation of the machine system and claimed that factory labour was easier than any pre-industrial activity: the workers earned more money and were much healthier as well. In this sense, the factory system represented a 'grand palladium'; that is, a large protective space for the labour force.[43] Although Marx regarded Ure as a vile apologist, he also considered him an expert on existing conditions at the time. Yet the false, rose-tinted image Ure painted of the miserable working conditions was also reflected in Marx's depiction of the 'automatic' factories he described anecdotally by drawing on selected cases. What eluded Marx was the fact that Ure did not provide an accurate description of work in the factories, but instead frequently simply fell for the propaganda spread by the machine producers.

As William Lazonick has shown, Ure echoed, for instance, the rather grandiose promise of a company from Manchester that the new self-actor would make skilled spinners redundant. The machine moved entirely automatically, so the argument went, and all that was needed were a few adolescent workers who sporadically tied strings to one another and stopped the machine on a bell signal. Yet in practice the machines were used quite differently. In most spinning mills, the skilled spinners kept their jobs, because they had to be able to intervene in the machine's operating process given that knots could form and the thread could get tangled up in the machine; they were also responsible for the careful treatment and maintenance of the machines and, moreover, acted as subcontractors who each hired, instructed and supervised two apprentice spinners. Performing these functions made them indispensable to the factories.[44]

While residing in Brussels, Marx also read *On the Economy of Machinery and Manufactures* by Charles Babbage, published in 1832, which he used excerpts from at the time and would return to at a later point.[45] Babbage, a London-based mathematician and astronomer, is famously known for having constructed a calculating machine regarded as a precursor to the computer, but also – in allusion to Adam Smith and his famous example of pins – for having studied the productivity advantages of an operational division of labour: the division of a production process into various suboperations, which allowed for workers to be paid less and develop highly specialised skills. In this study, Babbage continually spoke of tools *and* machines, considering traditional and modern forms of production simultaneously, and was also interested in the improvement of tools.[46] As shown by Raphael Samuel, these changes in the labour process of nineteenth-century capitalist practice were very significant. Marx, however, made reference to Babbage in *Capital* only in Chapter 14, which deals with the division of labour and manufacture, asserting that he may be 'superior in mathematics and mechanics' to Ure, but that he 'treated large-scale industry from the standpoint of manufacture alone'.[47] In his analysis of the factory system, Marx did not take up the reflections on the changes in the organisation of labour but simply assumed the replacement of tools by machines.

In London in 1851, Marx engaged with the writings of German technologists (which at the time was the term used for researchers who documented the history of technologies), especially the *History of Technology* by Johann Heinrich Poppe, which was published from 1807 to 1811. Through reference to such works, he sought above all to systematise technical developments. In said works, technical development was regarded as a continuous process of steady evolution driven forward by (preferably German) inventors, leading to premium products; one significant flaw, however, is that they commonly failed to mention which of the introduced innovations was actually in use.[48]

Another important source that Marx referenced extensively in *Capital* were reports by factory inspectors. They pertained to the industries in which certain laws concerning working hours and the employment of women and children were applicable, which was initially the case only in the textile industry before being extended to several other industries from 1867 onwards. In his *Economic Manuscript* of 1861–63, Marx lists page after page of figures and numbers on factories and weaving looms as well as on the children, women and men employed in factories producing wool, cotton, worsted yarn, flax and burlap in England, Ireland and Scotland.[49] In the chapter in *Capital* on the 'working day', he does indeed also describe industries in which no regulations were in place, and provides dramatic descriptions of the labour carried out by children and adolescents as well as the miserable conditions to which they were exposed in the potteries, match factories, wallpaper factories, bakeries and millineries.[50] Yet he ignored typically male-dominated industries, such as mining and construction, shipbuilding and mechanical engineering, as well as structural and civil engineering, just as much as the common labour in backyard workshops and the cottage industry. His specific set of references therefore contributed to his overestimation of the spread of 'modern' industrial operations and their advanced mechanisation, as well as to his neglect of all craft-like areas or new industries in which tool-based labour dominated.

MARX: A MACHINE FETISHIST?

Although Marx did study the catastrophic conditions in the textile industry particularly thoroughly, his interest was by no means confined to it. In his *Economic Manuscript* of 1861–63 he examined mills, crushing and hammer mills, the production of steel springs, paper and envelopes, and the casting of type letters.[51] In *Capital*, he establishes that, apart from the actual new industries, there were expanding industries and trades related to the construction of canals, docks, tunnels and bridges. He goes on to mention the establishment of gas works, telegraphy and railways. Furthermore, he was quite aware that the 'servant class', i.e. the number of handmaids, lackeys and maidservants, increased significantly during his day and age (in London, employing a maidservant was quite common, even for the Marx family – theirs was the legendary Helena Demuth, or '*Lenchen*'). These 'servants' constituted a far larger group than the workers in the textile industry. Finally, Marx notes that a 'modern domestic industry' had emerged, for example, in lace-making and straw-plaiting, as well as a 'modern manufacture', which employed women, adolescents and children in particular, such as in 'brass foundries, button factories, enamelling, galvanizing and lacquering works', bookbinderies and brickyards.[52] But none of this seemed to change his view that all of these represented mere transitional phenomena on the path to large-scale industry.

And yet we find comments in Marx that point in a different direction. There was, after all, no one who knew better than he that capital was ultimately not simply interested in the most cutting-edge technology and the highest possible level of mechanisation, but above all in maximum profit, which in part depended on wage costs, which is why the limits to mechanisation were determined 'by the difference between the value of the machine and the value of the labour-power replaced by it':

> Hence the invention nowadays in England of machines that are employed only in North America; just as in the sixteenth and seventeenth centuries machines were invented in Germany for use exclusively in Holland, and just as many French inventions of the eighteenth century were exploited only in England [...] The Yankees have invented a stone-breaking machine. The English do not make use of it because the 'wretch' who does this work gets paid for such a small portion of his labour that machinery would increase the cost of production to the capitalist.[53]

Marx the theoretician emphasised that the main interest of capital – be it with the use of machinery or without – was the valorisation of capital, while Marx the polemicist often tended to demonise mechanisation as a descent into hell. This also applies to his remark that labour forces would inevitably be deskilled and degraded.

As Donald McKenzie emphasises, Marx has often been interpreted as implying that the destruction of skills and qualifications represented an entrepreneurial objective in its own right, yet since the nineteenth century there has been evidence that *skill* as such is by no means necessarily an obstacle to the valorisation of capital with regard to quality products, sophisticated manufacturing processes or the flexibilisation of production.[54] Marx was apparently aware of this as well. Although he did assert that the traditional duration of apprenticeships had been abandoned by large-scale industry, he also noted the following:

> Modern industry never views or treats the existing form of a production process as the definitive one [...] But if, at present, variation of labour imposes itself after the manner of an overpowering natural law, and with the blindly destructive action of a natural law that meets with obstacles everywhere, large-scale industry, through its very catastrophes, makes the recognition of variation of labour and hence of the fitness of the worker for the maximum number of different kinds of labour into a question of life and death [...] the partially developed individual, who is merely the bearer of one specialized social function, must be replaced by the totally developed individual, for whom the different social functions are different modes of activity he takes up in turn.[55]

He saw the beginnings of this 'totally developed individual' not only after the overcoming of capitalism, but even in the present, as polytechnical or agronomic schools, or *écoles d'enseignement professionnel*, i.e. vocational schools for working-class children, were set up.[56]

Marx's hints that the mechanisation of production does not necessarily have to occur everywhere and evenly, and that capital itself may have an interest in skilled labour forces, ought to be incorporated and refined in today's diagnoses of allegedly relentless automation. Similarly, we should keep in mind the findings of Raphael Samuel concerning the nineteenth century, which also posit relevant considerations for current debates.

Rationalisation may also occur through other forms than the mere use of machines – such as through new versions of Taylorist concepts (as in the warehouse labour occurring in mail-order companies), but also via other forms of labour organisation such as teamwork (in the automotive industry), performance-based remuneration (as in investment banking) or project-based contracting (as in software development).

Machines do not always work as promised – the number of failed innovations is abundant, although the public may not be quite as aware of this as they are of the 'new generation' of countless IT products. For years, the Standish Group has published figures according to which some 70 per cent of all IT projects fail. These numbers are often deemed dubious and exaggerated, and yet recent years have seen a whole series of spectacular failures in (among others) the introduction of SAP projects, which saw several companies lose millions; in Germany this includes the Otto corporation, Deutsche Bank and Deutsche Post, along with the supermarket chains Edeka and Lidl.[57]

Given the objective of financialisation, companies often shy away from costly investment in their machine equipment, preferring instead to invest their money in the takeover of other firms or on financial markets. The Mannheim-based Leibnitz Institute for European Economic Research (ZEW) has monitored the innovation activities of German companies for years and recently found that the innovator rate, i.e. the ratio of those firms who implement innovations, decreased from 60 per cent in 1992 to 36 per cent by 2015.[58]

Hence, what remains true is that, in contrast to what we are presented with in the glossy brochures and imagery of business associations, it is not always cutting-edge machinery that characterises the economy and labour under capitalism, but strategies of profit maximisation, designed to make flexible use of the opportunities on the markets for the means of production and labour.

4

A Long History of the 'Factory without People'

Visions of automation and technological change in the twentieth century[1]

Karsten Uhl

The ongoing debate concerning the digitalisation of work is being defined to a great extent, at least in the German-speaking world, by the term 'Fourth Industrial Revolution'.[2] The synonymously used 'Industry 4.0' already reveals the essence of the phrase: the notion of a linear development. On the one hand, the most recent digital developments in industry are being embedded in a long history of industrialisation which began in late eighteenth-century England; on the other hand, the fourth stage, just as the preceding three, is said to mark the advent of a new quality, a sea change in the industrial system.

In the context of this debate – mainly among social scientists and engineers – the underlying stage model of the Industrial Revolution has been criticised for ultimately reducing the changes, in the sense of technological determinism, to new propulsion and manufacturing technologies while failing to take into account the respective forms of work organisation.[3] Like the processes of change in the past, the current changes are not determined by the potential requirements of new technologies but rather marked by a certain openness. Hence, with regard to ongoing developments attributed to the fourth stage of the Industrial Revolution, there are various scenarios concerning the changes in skill requirements. It is generally conceivable, firstly, that digital technology is used as a tool in the labour process, resulting in skilled workers remaining important. A second scenario proceeds

Karsten Uhl

from the assumption of an all-encompassing automation and a corresponding process of deskilling. A third possibility being discussed is a development in which human beings and machines work together essentially as partners in the production process, which would engender new skill profiles altogether.[4]

The question is frequently raised as to whether we are really witnessing a new development. In this sense, certain parallels can be drawn with the debates of the 1980s – although at the time the issue was not discussed under the term *digitalisation*, but as *computer-integrated manufacturing* (CIM) – or even those of the 1950s and 1960s, when automation and its social consequences were for the first time publicly addressed.[5] One of the most high-profile participants in the current discussion, the sociologist Hartmut Hirsch-Kreinsen, emphasises, all scepticism about potential exaggerations aside, that there are certain indications of a surge in technological development today. According to Hirsch-Kreinsen, the level of digital development has reached a point where applications are taking on a new quality, although 'diverging development perspectives of digitalised work' are becoming apparent and any hasty inference of a general cross-industrial trend should be avoided.[6]

What the discipline of history can contribute to this question concerning the relationship between continuity and change is the positioning of certain developments within long-term historical processes. First, it is crucial to find out which exact concepts of industrial labour automation dominated in the twentieth century. It is also relevant to explore the extent to which utopian hopes or dystopian concerns were associated with new technologies and which new visions of automation emerged over the century. The historian of technology Martina Heßler has demonstrated that, since the mid-1950s, the automation discourse has been marked by a surprising continuity of consistent arguments. The debate was nonetheless characterised by a certain range of views and generally moved between two extremes: on one side, automation was linked to the notion of removing human beings (as the source of errors) from the production process. This was often associated with the liberation of humans from monotonous tasks. On the other side, there was the fear of technology-induced unemployment and, ultimately, the 'expendability of

56

human beings in the labour process'.[7] Even though the fear of unemployment consistently dominated the debate, the notion of a limited automation, which incorporated human skills rather than replacing them, became increasingly influential from the 1980s onwards.[8]

This chapter will seek to look even further into the past, namely to the beginning of the twentieth century. The different political systems in twentieth-century Germany indeed reveal visions of automation which generally confirm Heßler's findings. Yet the sources also suggest that we are dealing with a much older debate which set in long before the postwar era. The current argument surrounding a supposed Fourth Industrial Revolution is mistaken in inferring any new quality, at least with regard to the hopes and fears associated with the automation of production: most of it is in fact old wine in new bottles. A glimpse at the printing industry of the 1960s and '70s, moreover, shows that even the more specific topic of computerisation has for decades been linked to the hopes and fears we also find dominating the current debate about the alleged Fourth Industrial Revolution.

EARLY VISIONS OF AUTOMATION

The prospect of a fully automated factory took shape before the twentieth century. The early factory experts of the nineteenth century – that is, the contemporaries of the first stage of the Industrial Revolution according to the four-stage model – already shared this vision. In his influential 1835 treatment of the textile factories of his time, the natural scientist Andrew Ure painted a picture of a near future in which the automated organisation of factory labour would gradually make skilled labour redundant. In this automated factory of the future, skilled workers would be replaced by workers who merely minded the machines.[9] Karl Marx likewise followed this vision in the first volume of *Capital* fifty years later, remaining quite close to Ure's description and vision of the factory more generally, contradicting only Ure's political assessment. Just like Ure, whom he mockingly referred to as 'the Pindar of the automatic factory', Marx himself expected an 'automatic system of machinery' in the not-too-distant future, which would largely do without human labour and require 'only supplementary assistance from the worker'.[10] What mattered to Marx was the question of whether 'machinery [rests] in the hands of capital': for then 'the same worker receives a greater quantity of machinery to supervise or operate'.[11]

In the early twentieth century, the methods of increasing efficiency associated with the American engineer Frederick Winslow Taylor raised the expectation that such 'rationalisation' denoted an increasingly self-dynamising process of optimisation in the organisation of work. The image of an automated factory played into this as well, although to Taylor the physical labour of the worker remained central. In this specific anticipation of automation, the otherwise quite distinct hopes of Taylor's followers and the fears of his opponents converged. In 1913, an article in the French trade union newspaper *La Vie Ouvrière* painted a picture of skilled workers who were transformed into 'submissive automatons', or 'arms without brains', by rationalisation measures.[12] Taylor's German translator, the Aachen-based engineer and professor Adolf Wallichs, in a presentation delivered during the war in 1917, concurred with such an assessment only with respect to looming automation. Yet Wallichs associated this technological vision with the hope for an 'elimination of monotony': the 'particularly monotonous tasks' could soon be 'taken over by the machine in what is called self-acting operations'.[13]

The interwar period in Germany was marked more by debates surrounding automation than by actual change.[14] The discussion about the future of work continued to move between the familiar extremes: fear of the redundancy of human beings on one side, and the hope of liberation through technological progress on the other. The scenario of fear was additionally reinforced by the world of entertainment: at the end of the 1920s, supposed robots, as simulations of artificial humans, were widely displayed in major exhibitions across the western world.[15] An article in the German trade union newspaper *Metallarbeiter-Zeitung* in 1929 voiced the concern that such developments would soon find their way into industrial processes. In that case, all rationalisation measures seen up to then would have been no more than the beginning of an 'even farther-reaching revolution in production and distribution'. The author expected that such 'machine-humans' would soon be found 'in a considerable number

of trades, tasks and services', making mass unemployment a permanent feature of society.[16] The other stance, the belief in progress, is
exemplified in a 1930 publication by the bestselling popular science
author Hanns Günther about 'automatons': in his view, technological
progress was already on the brink of engendering the 'self-condi-
tioned automaton' which would relieve humans of the most difficult
tasks and thus become the 'liberator' of humankind.[17] The fear of
technology-induced unemployment, according to Günther, had
been fuelled ever since the seventeenth century by the enemies of
progress; and yet it was unfounded as long as technology was used in
the correct political way, i.e. in pursuit of the common good.[18]

THE 'FACTORY WITHOUT PEOPLE'

Following the Second World War, the debates around automation
intensified; firstly due to technological developments in industry,
and, secondly, because of the impact of cybernetics. An article by
Canadian physicists John Brown and Eric Leaver, published under
the title 'Machines Without Man' in a consumer publication in 1946,
is generally seen as marking the beginning of the discussion on the
factory without people. The two physicists' approach proceeded from
a certain unease with the developments in industrial rationalisation
up to then. In their view, the degradation of the worker, i.e. their
having to perform unskilled tasks, could only be prevented through
comprehensive automation because only in that scenario would
highly skilled staff be required. This new automated industrial order
would thus entail a push towards a more highly skilled labour force.
At the same time, a shorter working week would become possible and
indeed – due to the technologically induced redundancy of labour
forces – necessary. In this vision, the automated work-centred society
of the future was characterised by an increase in leisure time.[19]

This conception of the future of industry was by no means confined to liberal North America. A surprisingly similar, albeit less
scientifically substantiated, image of looming automation was
presented by an article titled 'Factories without People' ('*Menschenleere Fabriken*') published in the official paper of the Nazi Party,
Völkischer Beobachter, in 1944. It was authored by Helmut Stein,

engineer and plant manager at the Cologne-based engine manufacturer Klöckner-Humboldt-Deutz. His starting point was the same as the one adopted by the Canadian physicists two years later: Stein generally favoured rationalisation, but believed the current level of mechanisation, shaped by mass production, entailed the 'danger' of a 'degeneration of work'. The two visions were also similar in terms of their proposed solution: for one, Stein also called for more 'distraction and relaxation' in workers' free time as compensation, although this took on a markedly National Socialist tone, as the article explicitly intended one's after-work free time to be devoted to the Nazi organisation 'Strength through Joy' (*Kraft durch Freude*). At the same time, Stein also proposed resolving the technology-induced problem through further mechanisation: only 'full automation' could lead to the 'liberation of humans from monotonous and soulless work as such'. This concept sought, paradoxically, to salvage skilled labour: although all of the new tasks would 'be simple and require less training time', workers could (in terms of consciousness and self-validation) consider themselves to be the 'master of the machine forces', thereby experiencing 'spiritual satisfaction'. In this sense, they would remain 'skilled workers' and continue to sit enthroned, 'regulating and supervising', above the machine world. This vision of the 'factory of the future – the factory without people' was based on the expectation that this future would become reality very soon: that its realisation was imminent.[20]

The reduction of the problem to the inanimation of industrial labour and the supposed solution of a 'spiritual satisfaction' was not specific to National Socialism: the influential American architect Moritz Kahn emphasised as early as 1917 that the factory of the future would indeed be efficient, but by no means inanimate or soulless.[21] During the Weimar era this topic was addressed – needless to say, with very distinct political objectives – by both the political left and right.[22]

After 1945, the discussion on the factory without people continued in both East and West Germany; in both the capitalist West and the communist East it was claimed (albeit with differing emphasis) that the imminently anticipated technological change would initiate revolutionising transformations.[23] The debate turned particularly euphoric between the mid-1950s and early 1970s.[24] In West Germany, the discussion among experts was quite differentiated: during this period, engineers expected the onset of full automation, i.e. factories without people, only in large-scale mass-producing factories, while the target set for small and medium-sized enterprises was partial automation.[25] The West German trade unions, too, were prominent participants in the debate surrounding automation early on. Trade union actors consistently considered both sides during this debate: on the one hand, there was the fear of unemployment; on the other, the hopes associated with the social and political effects of technological progress which the labour movement had harboured ever since its inception.[26]

In East Germany it was emphasised that fully automated factories could be both a promise and a threat, depending on the state of production conditions. Correspondingly, in 1960, the popular non-fiction book for young readers, *Unsere Welt von morgen* ('Our World of Tomorrow'), which was widely distributed mainly as a gift on the occasion of the *Jugendweihe*, a coming of age ceremony,[27] stated that automation in capitalism signified above all the danger of unemployment, while in socialism it would lead to the upskilling of workers because it would require significantly more and new knowledge about the production process.[28] What seemed clear, at any rate, was that 'fully automated factories [would] determine the face of future industrial work'. The illustration accompanying this vision of the future is almost void of humans; in this draft version of the factory 'of tomorrow' there are only two people standing in the control room.[29] It would still be a 'major step' to reach this point, but reference was made to an experimental automatic factory which already existed in the Soviet Union.[30]

Even after the wave of automation euphoria receded, the debate by no means fell silent. In 1982, in an article titled 'The Factory without People Will Be a Reality in Ten Years', the *Frankfurter Rundschau* newspaper reported on a study conducted by a market research institute which considered the technological preconditions for the factory without people, or at least the 'factory with hardly any humans', as given. It was expected that by 1990 half of all industrial assembly processes in West Germany would be automated. This referred not to the familiar robotic arms which had long been implemented for welding and similar tasks in the automotive industry, but to unspecified new flexible 'systems'.[31]

THE COMPUTERISATION OF THE PRINTING INDUSTRY

At first glance, these expectations by all means seem to corroborate the diagnosis made by the engineering scientist Brödner, according to which the 'cyber-physical systems' of the early twenty-first century must be understood as a mere continuation of the digital process control of the 1970s.[32] In terms of technology and work organisation, this assessment remains controversial, as mentioned earlier. There is some indication that the systemic character of current industrial digitalisation may entail a shift in the organisation of the labour process. That said, the discursive continuity is remarkable: notions of a factory without people and innovative digital systems have dominated the debate for decades.

One industry that was confronted with the more concrete advent of computer technology early on was the printing industry. During the second half of the 1970s, the first print shops in West Germany switched to computerised phototypesetting, and in 1978 there were fierce contract negotiations around the new 'computerised text systems'.[33] During a labour conflict in March of 1978, the printing union (*Industriegewerkschaft Druck und Papier*, or IG DruPa) prevented the production of many daily newspapers, while the union itself published so-called strike or emergency papers during the dispute. On 6 March one of these 'emergency papers' (*Notzeitung*) wrote about an incident that took place on the street during a strike rally in Wuppertal. Any potentially fictitious editorial amendments to this depiction aside, the passage certainly testifies to the future expectations of the striking workers: a worker from a different industry, a patternmaker, quite bewildered, asked the picketer from the IG DruPa why on earth the striking workers were opposed to this new technology. The picketer, a shop steward with the union, replied to the sceptical joiner:

'Imagine there is an order for a new workpiece, and your employer also has these cheeky computerised systems. Then all you do is take the wood, the glue and the drawing of the model and enter that into the computer, which then produces the finished piece. Also, you won't be needed any longer to press the button for the machine to start, that'll be done by someone else. How do you like that?'

According to the report, the joiner was quite shocked, responding, 'Oh, my God, that can't be true', and donating five Deutschmarks to the strike fund.[34]

This account underscores the differences in perception regarding the computerisation of the printing industry: while large parts of the population merely assumed another stage of manageable rationalisation, the striking typesetters and printers expected a process of comprehensive technological transformation. If we transfer this scenario to the trade of the joiner, it would not only be that of a gradual technological development – the rejection of which could be substantiated only with great difficulty given the tradition of the German labour movement – but indeed a new quality, threatening to change the world of work entirely. From a modern-day perspective, the picketer essentially sketched out the reality of a 3D printer *ex ante*; albeit a 3D printer which, in contrast to the existing models currently available, would be suitable for broad industrial use.

Ever since the 1960s, there had been a widespread awareness within the industry of the automation process already underway as well as its related far-reaching implications. A starting point for this awareness and the corresponding debates were remarks by John Diebold, an influential American expert on automation, who asserted in 1963 that the printing industry would be more profoundly affected by technological changes than any other industry over the following decade, and that those in charge were not even aware of this.[35] Diebold's hypotheses quickly reached the German craft union as well: while Richard Burkhardt, the printing union's expert on technical matters, had still assumed in the late 1950s that the pace of automation was generally being exaggerated and that typesetting would remain a haven of skilled human labour for years to come,[36] he corrected his position by 1964 in explicit reference to Diebold. In fact, it did not stop there: not only did he anticipate the computerisation of typesetting, but he expected the end of the print age as such – albeit not in the manner that eventually became manifest in the twenty-first century, but rather in the sense that 'a TV will print a newspaper electrostatically'.[37]

Both the computer experts in the printing industry, who convened in London for the very first 'Computer Typesetting Conference' in 1965, and the trade unions nevertheless largely agreed on the presumed impact on the workforce: the fear of a comprehensive replacement of human workers was unfounded. In their view, there would only be partial automation; human skills would always be needed to a certain extent.[38] Correspondingly, the union's strategy was maintained despite the change in its expectations for the future: in the 1970s, the assumption that skilled labour would be required even after the implementation of computerisation was still dominant.[39] During the industrial dispute of 1978, the trade union regarded the new technology itself as 'neutral'. In this sense, its task was to influence the social design of new technologies.[40] It was not until they were confronted with the 'cheeky computerised systems' that some workers in early computerised print shops felt compelled to reject the new technology or even developed Luddite fantasies. One worker, who attended the specialised trade fair 'Drupa' with several of his colleagues to inform visitors about the anticipated dreadful consequences of computerisation, pointed out that he would 'gladly like to grab and smash up' these machines 'because they are taking away my job'.[41]

The introduction of the new technology did in fact entail a decisive caesura for the industry, although the changes did not occur abruptly in every respect. On the one hand, the widespread introduction of computer typesetting caused the traditional trade of the typesetter to disappear. On the other hand, a specific provision in the labour contract of 1978, which was valid for eight years and concerned the introduction and application of computer-aided text systems, served to slow down the typesetters' replacement as it stipulated that they should remain employed even after the introduction of technological innovations. Furthermore, many of the countless small print shops based on manual labour maintained the same modus operandi well into the 1980s. Total employment in the printing industry in West

Germany between 1976 and 2000 in fact remained remarkably stable, hovering around 225,000: the reduction of the number of typesetters was offset by an increasing number of unskilled workers in the continuously growing sector. Despite this loss in skilled labour, the picture of deskilling through computerisation deserves a more nuanced assessment. Firstly, because a set of specialised tasks was preserved and, secondly, because a number of new skill profiles were introduced after the profound changes of the 1980s.[42]

One consequence of the computerisation shock in the printing industry was that trade union predictions now significantly exceeded the actual pace of technological change, overestimating the speed of imminent automation. In this vein, an internal paper by the printing union invoked allegedly 'unlimited rationalisation possibilities'. Against the backdrop of computer-based voice recognition and the associated redundancy of manual text entry, which at the time was expected in the near future, even the more recent technological changes appeared 'negligible'.[43]

CONCLUSION

The prospect of industrial automation so extensive that it will lead to factories without people in the immediate future is not unique to the early twenty-first century. Rather, it has accompanied all stages of industrialisation ever since the Industrial Revolution in the late eighteenth century. The anticipation of automation generally spanned the different ideological camps, although it was of course linked to varying social and political visions. One recurring feature throughout all the distinct political systems of the twentieth century, however, was the belief that technological progress – manifested through automation – could be shaped socially.

This form of mental continuity was also apparent during the computerisation of the printing industry that occurred around 1980 – albeit with some initial cracks emerging, particularly at the grassroots level. The new technologies could not be seamlessly integrated into a history of linear change. The computerisation of typesetting quite obviously caused a rupture in the history of the printing industry, especially from the perspective of skilled workers. Furthermore, the entire chronology of a four-stage industrialisation process seems questionable, given that the alleged fourth stage in this industry occurred during a period still associated with the third.

What can be established more generally, then, is that the technological change induced by the digitalisation of industrial labour has not been embedded in a new narrative of automation thus far. Instead, the traditional narrative, which during the twentieth century was already oscillating between distinct extremes and comprised both the hope of liberation from monotony and the fear of human beings being replaced, persists to this day. Current indications that technological transformation may be taking on a new quality in the present, as well as signs of associated political challenges with regard to the shaping of skill profiles, thus remain to be confirmed. Proceeding from Fernand Braudel, a number of distinct temporal levels of automation can be identified: on the one hand, major changes at the technological level and, related to this, at the social level; on the other hand, a continuity in terms of mentality (*longue durée*),[44] that is to say, concerning the perception and classification of computerisation. In order to do justice to any new quality of technology in the present, the automation debate should not merely continue on its well-trodden paths, but must take into account the specific challenge of hybrid human–machine labour relations as well. Here, the starting point could be the same as it was for those approaches whose gradual emergence Heßler already ascertained for the automation debate of the 1980s: whenever the limitations of automation became obvious, the significance of human skills also came into view again more strongly.[45] It therefore appears that a contemporary automation narrative would more adequately account for the challenges of digitalisation if it abandoned the old narrative of the replacement of humans. Instead, the focus should be on the specific forms that a combination of technology and human beings in the organisation of work may take, including the potential social consequences.

5

The Journey of the 'Automation and Qualification' Project

Frigga Haug

The 'Automation and Qualification' research project (PAQ) was launched at the (independent) Institute of Psychology at the Free University of Berlin in 1972 and lasted for 16 years, despite the scattered locations of the research group's members. The first volume compiled by the PAQ, *Automation in der BRD* ('Automation in West Germany') was published in 1975, and the last, *Politik um die Arbeit* ('Politics around Work'), in 1988. The project group had set itself the goal of devising an assertive trade union policy from the perspective of wage earners that would embrace the opportunities of ongoing technological change. It benefited and learned from its historical grounding, relied on its own empirical studies and critical theory, and proceeded from a critical psychology oriented towards the world of work. Marx's studies on the transition from manufacture to large-scale industry served as a model for writing about the development of the productive forces – not simply as a history of technology, nor to neglect it in favour of human subject research, but to proceed in an utmost comprehensive manner when engaging with struggles to shape society. In our work, we applied the tested methods of theory appropriation and empirical procedures through field visits, questionnaires and interviews with experts as well as with workers and employers in factories in the countryside, at fairs and international daily newspapers, and were oriented, pursuing our own method, towards working with contradictions and inconsistencies in both our questions and assessments as sources of new insights.

There are a number of reasons why the journey of this research group should be retraced today: the collective approach to research;

the courage to continue working in the face of resistance; the methods of seeking out what is to be preserved while simultaneously treading new pathways; grasping contradictions as a driving force for understanding, intervention and change; the inclusion of dimensions of gender relations and culture in the evolving research in industrial sociology; the necessity to doubt ourselves through the questions of the present while always proceeding from the relation between humans and their natural environment, thereby pursuing a critique from an emancipatory perspective. We never followed any kind of master plan. Rather, the questions forced themselves upon us during the research process, which itself was a learning curve in terms of methodology and guiding theory. From the outset, this process consisted of us feeling our way forward; it was an experiment in a densely populated, dynamic and embattled field of reality. One should not imagine a large-scale study, only feasible when conducted by a collective and in the context of a large research institution, where the required tools are available in a neatly arranged and well-preserved form: you simply dash into the library and select the appropriate books, which you are already familiar with, and set to work. Ours was not commissioned, well-resourced, bespoke research. Our reality was entirely different: it was full of idealism and carried by the unquestioned assumption that science must serve humanity and that we, who had studied Marx in the context of the student movement, wanted to make use of our acquired knowledge on behalf of working people.

The urgent questions demanding answers are clearly audible in our current society that is changing so rapidly but at the same time does not yet embody these changes as a whole. It seems incidental as to which of these questions one chooses to tackle first. In our case, it was the major education reform programme of the 1970s, which inundated the nation with reports of a continuous and calamitous shortage of teachers, followed by horror stories about a lack of schools and universities and outdated curricula, and a subsequent major – and veritably hectic – campaign to build new universities, including a host of newly created professorial posts, the corresponding allocation of funds, and, in our case, the establishment of the discipline of educational economics with a post I was appointed to at the newly established Institute of Critical Psychology. It was the result of the government's attempt to channel the awakening of the 1968 movement in a way that would isolate the troublemakers from mainstream academia, including the provision of funds to give them their own institute.

As a Marxist, I assumed that the sudden demand for education in society had to be rooted in changes in the world of work or, more precisely, in the development of the productive forces. I had been assigned a student tutor and, together with him, identified interested and potential new members of the institute in order to set up a research group which would investigate and prove precisely this link between a socially recognised and necessary qualification of the labour forces and the processes of automation, and to do so, from day one, with the unequivocal intention of serving as advisors for a trade union policy concerning automation.

In developing our research, we chose to embark on a critical approach based around doubt: we challenged what everybody thought or assumed they knew. This entailed constantly pursuing a path that went beyond the respective mainstream, including that of the left. The best way to learn a lesson from our particular path of research – to build on it and to avoid mistakes – is to reconstruct the multifaceted battles that took place.

THE GROUP – READING – DISCUSSING

One advantage of the collective was that we were able to boldly take on vast amounts of literature. There were eleven members, which meant that familiarising ourselves with 20 new titles, for example, would involve each one of us reading and preparing two essays or books in a given period of time. At our weekly meetings, we could then present and discuss at least one report, for which we had worked out a focus grid.

Given that, as Marxists, we were convinced at the time that research in the interest of workers was most developed in the GDR (East Germany), we started off by studying the advanced research that was being conducted there on the development of the productive forces. Indeed, the research of that time[1] turned out to be a great resource and welcome nourishment for our desire for knowledge. However, it dealt exclusively with the past, not the present. We learned, for example, from Jürgen Kuczynski[2] that automation existed only in the socialist countries. Capitalism had long entered a state of decay and could no longer develop the productive forces.

This made it necessary for us to first present evidence of automation in West Germany. It was here that the path of our research forked for the first time: we wrote to the relevant companies in industry and administration, asking about their production equipment – a study that may have begun in quite a naive manner, but which nevertheless laid the foundation for the subsequent empirical study of 67 companies in which we pursued an investigation of the concrete changes in the forms of work, that is, in the actual tasks people were performing. This was one of the paths which led us to publish the comprehensive study *Automation in der BRD* ('Automation in the Federal Republic of Germany') in 1975, with an initial circulation of 3,000 copies (and two subsequent editions with 2,000 copies each in 1976 and 1979). The aim of the volume was to identify relevant driving forces and development tendencies in order to predict the further development of automation. We included a register and an index, and, referencing the most diverse sources, meticulously indicated the current state of play in all the different industries, as well as the invested capital, turnover, the workforce and the changes it was undergoing (or had undergone), the new professions and, of course, the specific ways in which automation had been introduced.

In order to do so, we had to study the genesis of automation as a result of the government-commissioned arms industry, the full implementation during the war, all the way to nuclear energy, a research path which brought us closer to the violence underlying the driving forces of this development, even though none of this appeared to be directly linked to the education reform. The book not only represented a justification for our research, but was in fact useful and earned us recognition as an 'Interdisciplinary Project at the Institute of Psychology at the Free University of Berlin'. These were not merely words and titles, but actually helped us obtain the resources that allowed us to travel for our research and, inside the university context, the entitlement to adequate funding, offices and an additional tutor position.

On the other hand, we had to familiarise ourselves with the discipline of educational economics. In line with our assumption that the government's educational reform was linked to the changes in the world of work, it seemed only natural to ask employers about their assessments and common practices. This path also proved productive. It contributed considerably to ascertaining our knowledge, for it showed that the employers, who had long launched their own educational reform – Siemens, for example, even went as far as to found its own university – were very informative, supplying us with a vast range of material. We wrote a lengthy article, 'Bildungsreform vom Standpunkt des Kapitals' ('Educational Reform from the Perspective of Capital'),[3] and not only publicised our findings in lectures, but also unveiled them to our own faculty during a major event, through which we gained additional staff and further acceptance. The path became broader, better paved and longer, expanded in time and soon forced us to study the many other theoretical schools which occupied the field.

THE ANTHROPOLOGICAL AND PSYCHOLOGICAL GROUNDING OF WORK

At first, we had to ground our methodological toolkit historically. In order to grasp the changes in work tasks caused by automation, we required more than just a questionnaire and a guideline on how our comprehensive empirical study should proceed in the field. And, once again, we needed several approaches to the subject: what are the criteria on the basis of which one studies and speaks about specific tasks or work activities? How can particularities in their execution be recognised? What interviews must be conducted, and how are such activities to be monitored? Once we have studied the existing research and analyses of a specific task execution and work activities, we need to decide which aspects we want to focus on – which, in our experience, usually differed from those commonly studied by others.

Engagement with numerous studies in the field of the sociology of work – some of which were contradictory or unable to even justify why they had raised a question in the manner they had – led us to begin, with almost carefree rigour, by positing the question in a far

71

more general manner. Given that it was a project in the context of critical psychology, we naturally assumed that *work*, as an engagement with nature for the sake of improving the conditions of life, is the very activity which distinguishes humans from other living creatures with which they otherwise have much in common. The question as to what changes these activities undergo over the course of automated production first required an understanding of what exactly is human and what constitutes work. This question confronted us with the need to expand our knowledge of the development of human labour, not only in general terms, but, even more difficult, regarding the question: how does work develop under the conditions of exploitation throughout the historical process?

We had assumed that a *history of work* already existed and we could simply find it in libraries. Quite surprisingly, this turned out to be wrong as well. Although there were books with corresponding titles, they dealt with the development of machinery and engineering, not with that of the work performed by the mass of ordinary people. The changes this work underwent as a result of the development towards automation constituted the object of our study, which, from an engineering perspective, essentially only becomes interesting from the point at which humans are excluded from the process: when the work is divided into its basic operative components and handed over to the machines. Our work-oriented scientific stance intervenes, so to speak, before this handing over takes place; it requires knowledge about the deployment of humans and is interested in the future work in automated systems and in the question of what is gained in humanness and what is lost. The history of the evolution of work was another issue we had to study – at least in its basic features – in order to build upon it.[4]

The question about the progress of work becomes a question about the progress of humanity as such, at least as long as humans perform work. Consequently, anthropology becomes an underlying basic discipline of the science of work, seeing as we always, at least in the medium to long term, also speak about what *human* work actually is in an evaluative sense. The aim is to substantiate, in a scientific manner, what the objective of truly human life is and to decide what must be regarded as *non-human*. And it does not stop there: the task at hand is about taking the analysis of the animal–human transition as a starting point to formulate criteria by which work is no longer defined in terms of unaccounted, external, ultimately random ideals, and instead making possible, through the analysis of the development of work as such, a sober, watertight critique of contemporary work. As a result, one relevant – albeit underexamined – aspect which determined the study's questions, in line with the objective (i.e. the scientific substantiation), was that of what human labour is supposed to be, and thus what the relationship between intellectual and physical work ought to look like in the long term.

Our cooperation within the broader critical psychology community – which has in fact analysed the driving forces underlying the development of work and all of its intermediate stages over millions of years since the beginnings of life, starting from the monad[5] – allowed us to identify historical development stages.[6] From this body of knowledge we deduced – in terms of guidelines or basic concepts for our own project of analysing labour in automated production processes in a capitalist society – what the effective inner driving forces are, establishing the following criterion of human work: the realisation of specific human development potentials entails a certain objective, from the perspective of which the forms of work existing throughout the long history of humankind develop in sequential order. The ultimate objective is the all-round development of human potentials; Marx calls this 'fully developed human beings', while Lucien Sève refers to it as: 'setting oneself the task of the full psychological development of all human beings'.[7]

Our engagement with the history of work, moreover, led us to the insight (not least in critical distinction to Marx and Engels) that the juxtaposition of physical and intellectual labour, from which most analyses in the sociology of work proceeded, is itself an idealistic notion. From the perspective of capital, it is applied for the naturalisation of hierarchy, yet it obstructs the research on the reflection of work just as much as the recognition of unpaid work performed largely by women. It was therefore – in the truest sense of the word – highly impractical for our research.

In our understanding, the question had to be how individuals within the collective gain control of their life circumstances in the production process. Breaking this down for an empirical investigation means taking a closer look at the form and practice of cooperation, including the relationship between the individual and the collective, the individual's 'autonomy' vis-à-vis the others involved in the work process. The more tasks are delegated to machines, the more important the question of determining the end of work and the beginning of play, music and art becomes in the investigation of high-tech labour processes. Furthermore, it is a matter of workers' entitlement to participate in determining the development of social labour, which takes us into the realm of politics.

Correspondingly, the question of work and its organisation immediately confronts us with that of private ownership of the means of production. For example, I was once invited to a conference of the Association of German Engineers (VDI) to speak about our research on the automated production process. I began my presentation with the question: 'Why not allow workers to take charge of the production process?' The question was intended as a provocation, but just as much as a research question, linked to the hope that the gathered engineers would be able to envisage the superiority of their knowledge and skills. But one after the other, they stood up and silently walked out of the room. I had barely begun my lecture and I was left speaking to an audience of two.

A CRITIQUE OF THE DESKILLING THESIS

Without critical and careful reflection, we, as the Marxists we were, had assumed – not least in order to criticise the assumptions made by critical psychology[8] – that the development of the productive forces bore great opportunities for workers, and that we had to carve these opportunities out at all costs in order for workers to be able to truly seize them. Correspondingly, we thought, based purely on our own belief, that our research proceeded not only from the perspective of labour, but indeed represented a necessary support for the work of trade unions. In short, we pursued our project both in the sense of a subject science, which is how critical psychology conceives of itself, and with a clear orientation towards the unions. Indeed, we were also invited to trade union conferences to speak about our work. In fact,

I do recall some degree of agreement from within these circles. Yet the engagement with the research and the theoretical approaches of others entailed various surprises and also took us in new directions.

On the one hand, we found that the trade union field in particular was under the interpretational sovereignty of Horst Kern and Michael Schumann (at the Göttingen based Sociological Research Institute, or SOFI), who advocated this central focus: automation transforms workers into mere button pushers. Wherever manual skill was required, in the future only those tasks would be needed which could just as well be executed by a monkey.[9] Automation should therefore be rejected as far as possible, and its implementation ought to be resisted – in a similar way to the Luddites, who started resisting the introduction of machines through destruction and sabotage. In short, the trade unions were oriented towards defence. Indeed, this line dominated the union mainstream and prevented the pursuit of an interventionist automation policy from the perspective of workers and their skills in due time. We travelled up and down the country to propagate our main counter-argument, which we had condensed into a short slogan: *automation leads to upskilling*. It was a mantra we sang at train stations, waiting for the trains to arrive. It was an open confrontation that brought us many enemies and little honour, for even the Industrial Sociology section of the German Sociological Association, of which I was a member, had long been under the hegemony of the deskilling thesis, which was subsequently refined into the polarisation thesis: a few gain, many lose out. Several years later, there was a rehabilitation process in this section, and our works, which we had continued tirelessly, were recognised as ground-breaking – albeit very late on (with regard to trade union policy, recognition came far too late).

At the same time, we adapted an ever-greater, fascinating host of intriguing research which had, unjustly, been largely forgotten. We delved into this literature and wrote our third book about it (*Theorien über Automationsarbeit* ['Theories on Work in Automated Processes'], Berlin 1978; the bibliography included seven densely printed pages in tiny footnote font). Around this time, we also produced a considerable number of articles, one of which dealt with trade union-oriented research ('Thesen über das Verhältnis von Wissenschaft und Gewerkschaftspolitik' ['Theses on the Relationship between Science and Trade Union Politics'], in *Das Argument*, No. 112, 1978), as we were entirely consumed by our urge to study the development of the productive forces on behalf of workers and outline an interventionist trade union policy. Our book on the various theories was simultaneously an attack on the deskilling thesis, only this time with the support of a generation of industrial sociologists who had preceded us. We compiled a table which illustrates at a glance how many of our predecessors assumed a positive development of upskilling, or whose research suggested as much, and how few of them actually believed in the prediction of workers becoming mere button pushers. Up to then, we had proudly accepted our lonely stance regarding the upskilling thesis, yet we were even prouder now that we felt part of a larger community.

FIELDWORK

Finally came the long-prepared, eagerly anticipated and much dreaded visit to a factory. We had arranged a discussion and a guided tour led by engineers that included the opportunity to speak with the workers at the plant. We walked into a large hall; lights were flashing on a large control board which covered almost the entire wall. A worker was standing in front of the towering apparatus, staring intently at what appeared to me to be just a confusion of unintelligible symbols. Perhaps I should have taken an introductory course in the technology used at this new production facility. I was hoping the others had a better grasp on all this, while at the same time reminding myself that we were not engineers, nor did we want to become control room workers ourselves, but were here to find out more about the work of others. With a somewhat diffident researcher's confidence, I stepped forward and asked the worker: 'So what is it you are doing here?' He immediately responded, muttering: 'I'm acidifying.' It was clear to me that we did not speak the same language. To my ear, he was talking jargon and the gulf between us widened. Of course, that was not the end of it, and in fact there were others in our group who did understand a great deal more about what was happening. In short, we simply wrote down what we were being told, made light conversation with the senior managers accompanying us, studied beforehand which processes were occurring in each of the visited factories and never gave up. Our overview survey aimed at hearing the representatives of capital as well as the production managers, observing and speaking with the workers, and, subsequently, discussing our observations among ourselves.

We quickly learned that the production managers had a very different understanding of the workers' tasks than the latter themselves, which might have been due to the superiors' ignorance, the language barrier between us and the workers, or our long-prepared and elaborate ideas about what requirements automated production systems held for workers. As a result, we developed a corresponding method which, as the innovation that it was, ought to be preserved for this kind of research: the triad of *requirements, tasks* and *operations*. By *requirements*, we understood the human practice or input which the automated systems needed, while *tasks* pertained to the way in which the employers introduced these requirements into the operational structure of the company and translated them into tasks for the workers. Finally, the *operations*, which the workers executed, were in turn a translation of the tasks demanded of them, potentially with a better understanding of the machine equipment, a kind of secret knowledge, allowing also for deceit and avoidance or reduction of work. Tasks were thus directed not so much at individuals but at the collective of workers and their cooperation.

The breaking down and simultaneous merging of the distinct practices of both superiors and workers in the outlined triad provided a major tension in our study from the outset, which in turn helped expand the scope of our research. The analysis of work attitudes, according to the methodological guideline, was *management-critical, contradiction-minded* and *cooperation-oriented*.

For example, we asked employers about their ideal image of a worker in their automated factory. This constitutes a short chapter of its own in the first of the three books we wrote about the empirical investigation. It was rather instructive for us, since it was precisely this insight that ultimately shifted our subsequent research: the employers indicated that the requirements with regard to skills and attitude which they were looking for in workers – and considered essential – were the very same qualities one could find in the skilled workers who had been working in the factory thus far. This retrograde utopia in fact not only determines Marx's style of writing in many instances in which he examines the development of industry, but also determines those studies which interpret the automation process as leading to deskilling; moreover, it influences, in a quite surprising way, the skilled workers themselves. The latter, whose attitudes and skills, as it turned out, were very much wanted, that is, needed, fell into a major crisis. They obviously felt threatened by the changes in the work processes, which we had readily regarded as opportunities, namely the reduction in hard physical labour with a simultaneous increase in intellectual demands. This ultimately did not pertain to the proverbial virtues of skilled workers such as conscientiousness, quality and responsibility. But the identity of skilled workers also entails a kind of physical grounding conceived of and lived in combination with masculinity, which is why the inclusion of women in the jobs affected by automation changes the familiar gender relations in their natural hierarchy between the sexes, a hierarchy potentially extending unchallenged from industrial labour processes into the private home. This contradiction between feeling threatened and the reality of being needed shifted our research in several regards.

Which of the skilled workers' abilities and attitudes were still of any use to the automated systems? After all, the skill requirements of these systems were entirely different from those of the workers' previous tasks – i.e. more theoretical and challenging to the general intellect. We received one surprising answer to the question of what the greatest challenges for the workers in the labour process were: they unanimously responded that this was when operations had to be 'run by hand', that is, when the process which ran automatically failed to do so and they had to return to the previous development stage of the productive forces. This step back not only demanded the (stored) knowledge needed in the previous stage of the productive forces, but, beyond that, the ability to juggle with both, going back and forth as needed, as if they had constructed the machine themselves. It appears that the crisis awareness of skilled workers continues to be owing largely to the chatter of industrial sociologists, but also to the actual replacement of humans by machines, that is, to the production of unemployment on an ever-increasing scale.

At the same time, such discrepancies and contradictions between our expectations and the workers' attitudes forced us to include the dimension of work climate and, as in the example given here, the *culture of skilled workers*; it reveals the crisis and opens up a layer of labour policy. Automation destroys work collectives and, with them, forms of resistance. Rituals and *habits* such as drinking, oral *tradition*, and *male physical strength* as an ability determining skilled workers' pride and their *self-confidence*, are partly destroyed, partly shifted, because some of the tasks are replaced by office work and take on a rather *academic* character, including within production itself. While we saw the opportunity for skilled work for many workers increasing, we had not taken into account the fact that the old qualifications are linked to traditions of consensus and resistance, and that politics versus capital and the dissociation from other groups of workers are interconnected.

GENDER RELATIONS

We encountered further contradictions, rooted in – at first sight, downright insane – perceptions, yet which turned out to be a far greater problem during the investigation and entailed a radical shift in our own research. As a pre-stage to electronic typesetting in the printing industry, there was the introduction of phototypesetting, which, according to the industrial sociology of the time, would have no future. Phototypesetting prevailed, and the difficult, protracted and proud work of these formerly most qualified and progressive, strongly unionised skilled workers was given to women – the 'typists', with their clattering typewriters, who skilled workers were used to looking down upon. Subsequently, there was a fierce discussion about whether automated work constituted technical work, and thus had to be male labour organised in the corresponding union, or female office work, and therefore unskilled work for typists with 'naturally agile' fingers. It is a known fact that this reality ended when the further development of automation occurred in favour of the masculinity of such work. Indeed, the entire further development of these tasks, whereby they are completed by numerically controlled machines, and their interlinking into integrated systems right up to the new stage of Industry 4.0, involves primarily men. Yet, in this report, I would like to return to the introduction of phototypesetting and thus to the question of what happened to the affected individuals, that is, the erstwhile typesetters and all the other 'forces' who were hired in their droves.

Not only was the control room attendant by himself at his work station – an experience that necessarily, and strangely, placed the question of cooperation on the agenda – but we also met the typesetter alone in the case room equipped with photocomposition machinery. When asked about the changes he had experienced, he lamented above all the great feeling of loneliness, the loss of all his colleagues. And he did so while being surrounded by women who were feeding large quantities of data into the typesetting machine. Given that they had what he considered the 'wrong' gender, he was unable to perceive them as colleagues. Moreover, he denied them the very ability which in the history of typesetting had constituted the skill and pride of the typesetter, indeed even their intellectuality and ability to think in context: the typesetter's mastery of language. The lonely typesetter assumed that all these typing women had no clue about what they were doing. The legitimate pride in the typesetting profession, working with language and its objectification in writing and reproduction for the many, had turned into blind arrogance. This misogyny blurred his perception to the point that he essentially denied them the status of human beings. A heated argument with the chairperson of the print union (which took place via the members' paper) forced us to study the history and development of the union, leading to the rather surprising insight that the pride of this left-wing trade union was based on the fact that it was a men's union, and the exclusion of women had essentially been a natural given ever since its founding days right up to the introduction of phototypesetting. The automation of this field of work thus had to be perceived as an utmost threat and was responded to with resistance on all levels as a result, raising our awareness of the role gender relations play in the deployment of the developed productive forces in the workplaces.

At this point, somewhat in hindsight, we realised that our assumptions with regard to the possibilities and opportunities of automation rested to a great extent on our ignorance regarding the historical forces of the workers' movement. We had naturally assumed (as had Marx) that the reduction of hard labour, brawn and the hazardous deployment of human life would be fortunate and an enrichment, not least because this would allow women to be welcomed into the production process as equal partners. This expectation, which turned out to be utterly and entirely mistaken, had led us to overlook very visible signs.

For example, there was the introduction of belts that automatically moved the individual pieces for processing. In the factories we visited, they were initially not in operation at all because they had been dismantled by the workers, who showed us that they were, of course, able to lift heavy loads using their own physical strength. This group of workers was notorious for having back problems and taking early retirement due to disability, leading us to include the question of the relationship with one's own body in the interviews we were conducting. Initially, we had not taken into consideration the fact that one element that workers – whose 'strong arm halts all wheels' – took pride in was the fact that women were unable to perform men's work simply because of their physical constitution. Once this is falsified in practice, say, by women moving into these areas of work, the men's self-confidence is fundamentally challenged. The disrespect for women, as we learned, with some difficulty, at this point of rupture where automation intervenes in the work practice, represents a dimension in its own right, the flip side of which is the alleged female need for protection which belongs to the core of the male worker identity as a provider; it forms the foundation of the breadwinner's wage, which must suffice for him and, as Marx put it, his 'replacements, i.e. his children'.[10] This sudden dawning at the fault line that constituted the revolutionising of the productive forces of labour essentially meant we had to start over. Wherever we had gone, we had come across peculiar behaviour as well as silence towards and an acceptance of untenable situations on the part of both sexes.

In short, we had to include the *cultural dimension* of the relationship, which had evolved over time, to one's own work and to the other gender. We studied the research conducted by the CCCS (Centre for Contemporary Cultural Studies in Birmingham), which had – simultaneously to our own research and based on Antonio Gramsci – begun studying the potentials for and reality of resistance and the practices of acceptance of exploitation, i.e. the tolerance of an inhuman division of labour. Subsequently, we launched a new empirical investigation guided by the question of *what changes occur in the life of workers as a result of automation*, the results of which we published in the book *Zerreissproben* (Hamburg 1983) as Volume 4 of the empirical studies, our seventh book.

THE CONTRADICTION LOGIC IN THE METHOD

Our experience with the workers in the factories and with ourselves in our attempt to understand what we had seen and heard – and that which we had failed to comprehend – showed us something that we had so far only been aware of on an abstract level: the contradiction between the productive forces and relations of production not only substantiates the crisis proneness of the system as a whole, but, moreover, constitutes a contradiction in real life, permeating and thoroughly rattling the lives of human beings in society – a circumstance which the research method itself must take into account. Once again, the corresponding clues can be found in Marx, firstly in his depiction in *Capital* of the capitalist production process and its development, and, secondly, in his broader perspective more generally. For there is no total belief in progress in Marx, as is often insinuated. Instead, his entire dialectical thinking is essentially determined by the search for the driving forces of development which contradict each other, either demanding an alternative of social coexistence or leading to society's downfall. Trapped in its own logic of restless growth, capitalism floats from one crisis to the next, the solution to which is always merely temporary, simply unscrewing the safety valve only to end up in the next, more severe crisis. Throughout history, global society has witnessed this on a grand scale: capitalism limping onwards. At the same time, this trajectory is borne and lived by the individual members of society, who see it as being marred by ruptures and not simply as continuous growth and self-development to the point of comprehensive agency. This must be taken into consideration in our search for the beneficial use of high tech, while also opening up the space, methodically and critically, for the perception of the effects on culture and way of life, its forms and the familiar identities in the balance of forces and the togetherness of the sexes. In most of the studies in industrial sociology, and even in Marx, we found the critique and perspectives neatly ordered around an ideal of craftsmanship which, on the one hand, inevitably had to lead to reports of loss (of employment and skills) in the face of automation and, on the other hand, precisely to this yes/no logic, which obstructed the nullifying perception of the required skills and possibilities of intervention, planning and development. The logic of contradiction helps avoid the merely conservative retrospective view by posing questions in such a way as to reveal the shackles and restrictions which obstruct the desired perspective. Such research, which seeks not merely to preserve the old and thereby maintain the dominance of the few over the subjected many, would thus have to be guided by the following questions:

- Which of the barriers obstructing a horizontal division of labour are being removed?
- Are the forms which stabilise long-standing divisions for the sake of domination – such as that between intellectual and physical labour, or male and female labour – being dissolved?
- Where is the ossification of horizontal, mutually independent labour being dissolved?
- Where are forms of a vertical division of labour being dissolved?
- Are hierarchies, and thus class rule and control from above, being challenged?
- Is mere experience-based knowledge being replaced by science and theory-guided observation?
- Is there a subversion of forms of training which entrench privileges and a dissociation from the unskilled?
- Where and in what way(s) is the old order entering into crisis?

We expect that the custodians of the old order will seek to structure a new order in their favour. They are aided in this by the fact that the blasting apart of old shackles is not automatically perceived as liberation by workers as long as the old conditions persist. It is far more natural for them to unite, reinforced by habit, with the backward forces than to seize the potential agency without any kind of 'revolutionary *realpolitik*' (Luxemburg) in the form of an interventionist automation policy, say, on the part of trade unions. Overcoming this state would require significant collective efforts in all areas of life. The particular task of academia consists of pinpointing the strategic points of intervention. This was our understanding of how to substantiate an interventionist trade union automation policy.

OUTLOOK

What was the outcome of these two decades of optimistically contending that automation would lead to upskilling? Essentially, it has at least become clear that this 'up' itself needs to be specified and defined in a very general manner. Firstly, in a negative sense: there is no doubt that automation, as well as Industry 4.0, destroys jobs on a large scale. It has long been rendering physical strength obsolete. In positive terms, automation is geared towards eliminating malfunctions, identifying improvements, developing the potential for the optimisation of processes, changing products, and planning, constructing, researching and developing process targets. The specifically human contribution to this is the ability to criticise and change existing reality, that is, to process contradictory findings and revise objectives. Human input must be economical with regard to material, energy, time, security, etc., as well as oriented by use value and the safety of both humans and the natural environment. In this regard, we wrote:

> The theoretical form of work in automated processes, the planning of the unplanned, the correspondingly required intensification of communication and cooperation, demands a new stage of the socialisation of workers, the development of a new culture of work in which decisions are increasingly made collectively, in the form of self-management of production and administrative processes. The realisation of this prospect, which emerges alongside the evolution of automation, requires the democratic restructuring of social

84

relations extending into the workplaces in a way that everyone can participate in important decisions and is able to develop and affirm their self-responsibility for the whole, for nature and society.[11]

As is obvious, this perspective goes well beyond the boundaries of capitalist relations of production, yet there are major areas remaining on the agenda which, thanks to the unleashing of force(s), that is, of time and life, would have to be urgently tackled without further ado: these are the questions of how to interact with a non-human natural world – in terms of the ecology debate – and, ultimately, the question of relationships and relations which humans enter into with each other and themselves. In more solemn terms, the matter at hand is the development of one's own capacities and the countless capacities inherent in human individuals, and the tremendous task, which may sound both utopian and worn out, of building loving, caring, friendly and lasting relationships with one another – relationships which fall by the wayside in times of war, misery and under capitalist relations of production geared towards private profit. This, above all, is what must be developed. In short: it is high time that humanity transits from its prehistory into its history.

6

'Forward! And Let's Remember'

A review of materialist technology debates of the past

Christian Meyer

When attempting to gain an understanding of technological developments in the world of work, it is certainly worth briefly looking at the
technology debates taking place within the critical social sciences,
where, time and again, Marx has been referenced. However, this begs
the question as to whether returning to texts that date back two centuries is necessary in order to understand digitalisation. Can we really
continue to base ourselves on Marx? The argument put forward in the
following pages is that, firstly, we can and should continue drawing
on Marxian theory, but, secondly, that we are by no means doomed
to keep reinventing the wheel and should instead learn the lessons
from past debates.[1]

RETURNING TO MARX

The approaches to Marx's works and the resulting analyses and theoretical traditions have always been very diverse. One reason for this
lies in the Marxian work itself.

Over the decades, three of Marx's texts became key reference points
for understanding the mutual influence of technology and society,
and three distinct notions of technology can be extrapolated from
these works. In the first volume of *Capital*, the application of technology in society takes centre stage:

> And this is the point relied on by our economic apologists! The
> contradictions and antagonisms inseparable from the capitalist

application of machinery do not exist, they say, because they do not arise out of machinery as such, but out of its capitalist application! Therefore, since machinery in itself shortens the hours of labour, but when employed by capital it lengthens them; since in itself it lightens labour, but when employed by capital it heightens its intensity; since in itself it is a victory of man over the forces of nature, but in the hands of capital it makes man the slave of those forces; since in itself it increases the wealth of the producers, but in the hands of capital it makes them into paupers, the bourgeois economist simply states that the contemplation of machinery in itself demonstrates with exactitude that all these evident contradictions are a mere semblance, present in everyday reality, but not existing in themselves, and therefore having no theoretical existence either.[2]

Here, Marx criticises bourgeois economics and defends the tremendous potential mobilised by the capitalist mode of production. Similarly, only a few pages before this passage, he accuses the Luddites of failing to distinguish between machinery and its capitalist use:

The large-scale destruction of machinery which occurred in the English manufacturing districts during the first fifteen years of the nineteenth century, largely as a result of the employment of the power-loom; and known as the Luddite movement, gave the anti-Jacobin government, composed of such people as Sidmouth and Castlereagh, a pretext for the most violent and reactionary measures. It took both time and experience before the workers learnt to distinguish between machinery and its employment by capital, and therefore to transfer their attacks from the material instruments of production to the form of society which utilizes those instruments.[3]

Based on this and similar text passages, it is often alleged that Marx harboured an instrumental notion of technology, according to which technology as such may be ultimately neutral, but, under capitalist conditions, is not used for the satisfaction of needs. Braverman refers to this as the 'Marxist view' and emphasises the dual function of technology in terms of productivity increases and control over workers.[4]

The instrumental stance, which insinuates technology's neutrality, sparked some criticism. Marcuse regards 'technology as a form of social control and domination', a circumstance already inherent in natural-science rationalism. Ullrich attributes to the natural sciences an 'affinity for capital' and exposes precisely the problems associated with their supposed 'neutrality' and indeterminate potential application.[5]

A passage from *The Poverty of Philosophy*, often reduced to a kind of mnemonic, suggests a different reading of the relation between technology and society.

> In acquiring new productive forces men change their mode of production; and in changing their mode of production, in changing the way of earning their living, they change all their social relations. The hand-mill gives you society with the feudal lord; the steam-mill, society with the industrial capitalist.[6]

The last sentence of this quote has contributed to an understanding according to which technology determines society. From this perspective, commonly referred to as technological determinism, it is deduced, for example, that nuclear energy must necessarily lead to an authoritarian state (Jungk) or that information technologies bring us post-capitalism (Mason).[7] The reference to the mode of production adds the historical factor to the equation. In this sense we may ask: does the steam mill actually precede capitalism in temporal terms? According to Kuczynski, historical research has shown that it took centuries before capitalism bore its own technological basis, namely in the form of the steam-powered mill, which provided it with a degree of stability. Marcuse likewise cites the example of the steam mill, but specifies Marx's statement regarding the defining effect of technology. '[W]hen technics becomes the universal form of material production, it circumscribes an entire culture; it projects a historical totality – a "world".'[8]

The third text is the so-called 'Machine Fragment' contained in the *Grundrisse*:

The *productive forces and social relations* – two different aspects of the development of the social individual – appear to capital merely as the means, and are merely the means, for it to carry on production on its restricted basis. In fact, however, they are the material conditions for exploding that basis. [...] *Nature does not construct machines, locomotives, railways, electric telegraphs, self-acting mules, etc.* [...] *They are organs of the human mind which are created by the human hand*, the objectified power of knowledge. The development of fixed capital shows the degree to which society's general science, knowledge, has become an *immediate productive force*, and hence the degree to which the conditions of the social life process itself have been brought under the control of the general intellect and remoulded according to it.[9]

In this instance, Marx tends towards a social-constructivist position, emphasising how social knowledge becomes the most important productive force. This knowledge, the *general intellect*, is often linked to so-called immaterial labour,[10] a theme which more recent texts on digitalisation have often proceeded from. Hardt and Negri describe algorithms as 'fixed capital, a machine that is born of social, cooperative intelligence, a product of "general intellect". Fixed capital today, they continue, is the human being, carrying in him or herself the knowledge which allows for more autonomy vis-à-vis capital.[11] Mason, too, refers to technology's potential for emancipation and crisis that surfaces in this passage, and infers that the contradiction between market mechanisms and technology must ultimately lead to the downfall of capitalism because it is unable to accommodate shared knowledge.[12]

In sum, Marx certainly did not leave behind a coherent theory of technology, and it is hardly surprising that the references to his work reach such a vast range of different conclusions. In what follows, Marxist perspectives on technology will first be reconstructed in the context of the given historical conditions and the development of the social sciences as a discipline in order to subsequently place the focus on relevant stages of development through the lens of different authors. To conclude, current debates around digitalisation and their connecting points with the outlined discussions will be critically assessed.

THE DEVELOPMENT OF THE TECHNOLOGY DEBATE
IN THE CRITICAL SOCIAL SCIENCES

Since the 1950s, the approach to technology among Marxist authors in Germany has oscillated between technological determinism and social constructivism, often failing to grasp the dialectics of the relations of production and the productive forces (the latter of which include technology). After all, '[m]en make their own history, but they do not make it just as they please; they do not make it under circumstances chosen by themselves, but under circumstances directly encountered, given and transmitted from the past'.[13]

A rough historical trajectory can at least be outlined. The 1950s were characterised by a strong faith in progress and an evolutionary understanding of technological development. This optimistic belief in progress, which saw the new society as emerging from the productive forces,[14] was often criticised or called into question.[15] A reduction in physically demanding labour and arbitrary workplace regimen could, however, be corroborated empirically.[16] Furthermore, machine wrecking was frowned upon among the workers' movement[17] – not least in the sense of a 'dissociation from [the] elitist contempt for technology' characteristic of conservative cultural criticism.[18]

As mechanisation and automation progressed, the assessments put forward in the 1960s became increasingly sceptical, seeing as semi-skilled and physically demanding labour were far from being a thing of the past for all wage earners. This marked the starting point for the thesis on the polarisation of occupational groups, which is still asserted to this day.[19] The deployment of new production technologies, the thesis claims, leads to deskilling for some while allowing for a greater degree of self-determination and an expansion of the range of tasks for others.

The 1970s and '80s can be regarded as the heyday of Marx-oriented technology research. The most relevant institutes of the time each developed their own distinctive research approaches. The SOFI in Göttingen[20] (Kern and Schumann, among others) understood production technology as a framework for the organisation of work which, despite certain intrinsic logics, allows some leeway for shaping the labour process. That said, this leeway is very limited due to capitalist constraints.[21] Even though technology was thought to offer a wide range of possibilities for new production concepts and a less strict division of labour, there were no illusions that a far-reaching social transformation might be underway as long as technology exclusively served the production of profit.[22] Works produced at the ISF in Munich (Hirsch-Kreinsen, among others) emphasised the autonomy of operative strategies for the deployment of technology vis-à-vis political-economic constraints. The IfS in Frankfurt (Bergmann, Brandt, among others), by contrast, interpreted production and information technology as powerful elements of basic capitalist socialisation. Brandt does admit, however, that 'the Frankfurt researchers did not always resist their traditional tendency of adopting a totalising and apocalyptic version of subsumption theory'.[23] The works of all three institutes are based on an instrumental understanding of technology, according to which technology is studied in its capitalist application.

The approaches listed here are frequently referred to as the *subsumption model* (IfS) and the *production model* (SOFI, ISF). The focus on work pursued by both approaches is based on Marx.[24] The subsumption model places emphasis on the subjection of the productive forces, in particular the formal and real subsumption of human labour, and regards abstract labour as the specific 'result of capitalist socialisation'.[25] In a shorter, more pointed definition, the production model regards productivity increase as the main motivation for the deployment of technology, while in the subsumption model the motivation is domination.

The 'Automation and Qualification' research project (PAQ) eludes this distinction altogether, proceeding instead from the question of how the contradiction between productive forces and relations of production is expressed at the level of the individual.[26] Although the principle of profit drives the development of the productive forces, so the argument goes, this does not account for the specific implementation of automation because the concrete make up thereof also includes issues of domination and interests in relation to the social balance of forces.[27]

Parallel to this, a public awareness of the problems of 'the risks of technological-scientific civilisation' emerged during the 1970s.[28] The critique of environmental and technological rationality put forward above, e.g. by Marcuse and Ullrich, falls under this category. Apart from addressing social and ecological limits to growth, it was also accompanied by the abandonment of technological determinism, while societal interests in the construction and implementation of technology took centre stage.[29]

The critical social sciences, of course, only rarely argued in a strictly deterministic manner in the sense that they viewed technology as an independent variable. Technology was always considered under capitalist conditions. Lutz summarises the prevailing technological determinism of the time as follows:

> Social modernisation and social change are thus ultimately nothing other than the adjustment – of course, often delayed by inertia, bigotry or short-term interests – of the socioeconomic and socio-psychological structures to the conditions, constraints and opportunities which are either directly created and opened up by technological progress or are the consequence of its implementation in the form of productivity increases and economic growth.[30]

Correspondingly, technology has a certain intrinsic logic and rigidity but is deployed for specific purposes. In this sense, the instrumental and the technological-deterministic notion do not necessarily contradict one another.

At the same time, there was a thrust of rationalisation and mechanisation in the world of work that had only rarely occurred throughout history, and which received a 'specific social dynamic' through simultaneous mass unemployment. Additional pressure to rationalise was placed on capital by a more closely interconnected global market and economic stagnation.[31]

Over the course of the 1980s, questions of work organisation increasingly replaced those of technology.[32] The Labour Process Debate, proceeding from the work of Braverman (1974), which emphasises the domination in the workplace and the political sub-stance of the labour process, henceforth served as a point of reference for many authors.[33] Adding to this is the fact that, from the late 1980s onwards, a German-language sociology of technology was constituted as an independent subdiscipline[34] in contrast to the Marx-oriented sociology of work and industry, and terms such as capitalism and industrial society were called into question within sociology itself.[35] Some of the protagonists say in hindsight that the sociology of work never really did involve that much Marxian theory. Nevertheless, that theory did help explain many of the conflicts and crises that mani-fested themselves from the late 1960s onwards (e.g. labour conflicts, the 1968 revolt, the economic crisis of 1974/75). Yet the more the work-centred society's institutions proved flexible, the more Marx was removed from industrial sociology, while system-theoretical and neo-institutionalist approaches became increasingly popular during the 1980s. Moreover, 'Social Democracy and trade unions, who were implementing corresponding government reform programmes', were no longer available as addressees and strategic allies.[36]

Just as interest in technology receded in the sociology of work and industry, so too did references to the Marxian legacy. It was not until the advent of comprehensive digitalisation that Marx-oriented research, appearing over recent years, increasingly returned to focus on technology once again.

THE DEVELOPMENT OF THE PRODUCTIVE FORCES
FROM AUTOMATION TO INFORMATION

Marx envisaged large-scale industry, machine tools and steam power, and the image of the capitalist mode of production was undergo-ing dramatic changes. Yet the essence was the change of productive forces this process institutionalised. 'Modern industry never views or treats the existing form of a production process as the definitive one. Its technical basis is therefore revolutionary.'[37]

Along with the productive forces, the production paradigms change as well, not consistently but sporadically, and in a fundamental, 'revolutionary' way. This also found expression in the correspond-ing research, and the bulk of materialist analysis was dedicated to automation – until the technological base was once again revolutionised with the advent of computers and information technologies. Sporadic, dynamic periods of major advances were identified over the course of several decades, which the research sought to conceptualise. Digitalisation was not the first buzzword designating novel production paradigms and technologies, and the terms used in the past turned out to be just as vague.

As early as 1956, Pollock had pointed out that there was no coherent definition of automation. In his view, some saw it as denoting genuinely new production methods, while others simply understood it as a certain stage of an evolutionary development of mechanisation. In Pollock's view, however, the consequences for society, namely the threat of economic instability as a result of underconsumption, centralisation and job cuts, nevertheless justified using the term 'automation' to depict the historical stage in the industrial countries. Pollock predicted the emergence of an 'automation hierarchy' which would privilege 'people working on all levels in automated factories and offices', whose qualification levels, self-confidence and standard of living would be higher and whose jobs would be more secure. The rest would become a mere *surplus population*, that is, a reserve army, while those whose jobs were not being substituted would at the very least be aware of the threat of their potential replacement. Pollock can thus be regarded as an early proponent of the polarisation thesis. However, 'when applied in a sensible way, automation could once again make humans the masters of the economic process on all levels'.[38]

The PAQ, in turn, challenged the polarisation thesis, asserting that automation fostered the atomisation of workers on the one hand, while also demanding forms of self-management and democracy in the workplace, ultimately requiring higher qualification levels, seeing as more decision-making competencies were needed on the shop floor.[39] Braverman suggests a scenario in which the possibility of external control and universal applicability allows people to increasingly return to dominating the machines. But because management remains in control, he contends that the domination of the labour process by humans would turn into the domination of humans by the labour process.[40]

Many consider the rectification of malfunctions and corrective interventions as characteristic of work in automated workplaces.[41] The question is whether the bulk of the workforce is granted the possibility of 'planned action in uncertain situations' (PAQ), or whether living labour simply fills the gaps in automated processes, as Braverman argues. The integration of tasks, in Bergmann's view, can only be achieved through pressure from the trade unions, and 'shop floor programming (SFP) is practised far less than would be technically feasible'.[42]

In this perspective, women working in office jobs are particularly threatened by technologically induced unemployment.[43] In industrial workplaces, they are given easy sub-tasks such as converting technical planning sheets into machine-readable formats.[44] Beyond that women have a hard time finding employment in automation, according to this view. What remains are those jobs which are continuously threatened by replacement and characterised by a lack of flexibility and low qualification levels, such as data entry roles.[45]

The increasing relevance of computers in the production process and their broad range of application have been a topic of discussion at least since the 1980s.[46] Capital, it is argued, responds to the crisis of Fordism and Taylorist production by devising flexibilisation strategies – pertaining to both humans and machines – via microelectronics. Given that rationalisation and the decreasing purchasing power of wage earners come into conflict with one another and obstruct the realisation of profits, the problem of the '"microelectronic" accumulation strategy' is not a technological one.[47] Kern and Schumann also see the development 'not as a technological phenomenon, but as a complex sea change in the industrial structure'.[48] According to Kern and Schumann, this change of thinking is further fuelled, on the one hand, by the application of new technology, while, on the other hand, the latter can be applied more effectively when qualifications and the design of work organisation correspond.

In the 1990s, Schmiede turns to information and communication technologies and embeds their dissemination – in terms of the concept of *informatisation* – in the historical development of the capitalist mode of production. In his view, the 'control over the relevant information' becomes the necessary basis, particularly for the domination of workers under increasing capital intensity, for the control of machines and an increase in the turnover rate.[49] Schmiede thus follows the tradition of the subsumption thesis. The prominent role of information as abstraction and digital symbolisation has far-reaching implications, and abstract labour changes from being an analytical concept to a sensually palpable reality in the workplace, as Braverman already argued. The result is a 'de-qualification' of work, not in the sense of deskilling, but in the sense of a loss of distinct qualities. More and more tasks resemble one another in terms of working with symbols on a screen. The level of qualification may rise or fall in the process, but the separation of manual from intellectual labour continues – frequently even within the same individual. Schmiede regards the computer as the embodiment of a transferral of Taylorist concepts to intellectual processes, the latter of which can likewise be subdivided this way. Management itself thereby becomes the object of Taylorism.

Schmiede asserts that increasing storage capacities and ever-greater communication networks have made complex autonomous machine systems technologically feasible. And even though these systems essentially no longer require any human control, they are not uncontrolled: 'The anonymous constraints of the law of value [...] continue to determine the purpose.' Although the possibilities of information and knowledge acquisition have greatly increased, 'the veil of domination that lies over the capitalist mode of production has only become thicker'.[50]

'*DIGITAL IST BESSER*':[51] BETWEEN HYPE AND REVOLUTION

The proliferation of digital technologies is a process that affects all of society. Summarised by the buzzword Industry 4.0, the debate in Germany focuses mainly on industrial production, which, against the backdrop of the 2008 crisis, is attributed a new relevance.[52] The discourse on Industry 4.0 must be seen largely as hype and a public relations effort on the part of capital. Apart from the concern about where production is located geographically, it reveals a technological determinism that also characterises the international debate.[53] Technology often appears as the agent, or *subject*, of change, to which work and society then have to adapt, while social processes are ignored. The range of what the diagnosed technological revolution[54] is supposed to encompass changes almost on a daily basis: the Internet of Things, cyber-physical production systems, the Smart Factory, Big Data… the diversity of terms, however, is hardly able to conceal the lack of orientation. For example, a precise definition of technology or an exact description of its role in society is absent from mainstream discourse.

Yet questions of technology are also back on the agenda of Marx-oriented social science. In the international discussion about digitalisation, decentralised company models – variably referred to, with differing emphasis, as *platform capitalism* or *surveillance capitalism*[55] – often take centre stage.

The engagement with the digitalisation of work frequently resembles the debates on automation: technologically induced unemployment is regarded as a risk just as much as the polarisation within workplaces.[56] More extensive control as one possible outcome of the introduction of new technologies marks a prominent theme in current debates – namely in the sense of the direct surveillance of workers, consumers and users. It ranges from pretend participation to authoritarian access through detailed data collection and on to the manipulation or downright control of behaviour. However, the subsumption thesis in its more apocalyptic version seems to no longer play any greater role. While some indulge in fantasies of total automation, such as Srnicek and Mason, others warn against neglecting human labour power and experience in scenarios of digitalisation.

The critics' camp has not yet made up its mind as to whether to confirm an historic sea change or to state that we are simply witnessing more of the same. From this perspective, it is far from clear that a Fourth Industrial Revolution is indeed looming. While Haug speaks of an 'epochal threshold', Fuchs stresses that the proliferation of information technologies cannot be understood as a radical break because it does not by itself indicate relations of production, exploitation and modes of production.[57]

At the beginning of the new millennium, a left-wing, emancipatory project with regard to digital technologies was nowhere to be seen, and the ruling power bloc was able to assert its own concept. The example of cybernetics shows that technologies have always been linked to oppositional political visions, which asserted themselves in an interplay of 'material and ideological development'.[58] One paradox of the current debate is that a social alternative to the capitalist model is being expressed most clearly in terms of a relatively uncritical enthusiasm for technology. A left-wing project, then, is also taking shape where questions of democracy are raised and the potential of digital technologies for economic democracy is being explored.[59]

Digitalisation is a process that affects society as a whole, but analyses of platforms and digitalised industrial companies mostly appear unconnected to each other, let alone to analyses of culture, gender relations, ecology and politics. To Marx, it was clear that '[t]he transformation of the mode of production in one sphere of industry necessitates a similar transformation in other spheres'.[60] That said, most scholars all too often make no attempt to take the mode of production as a starting point. In this regard, the question of whether the relationship between productive forces and relations of production can still be grasped in a digital scenario, in an attempt that echoes Marx, remains to be resolved.

Indeed, it is generally to be welcomed that technology in the context of digitalisation is once again acquiring a greater role in the critical social sciences. Unfortunately, there is a lack of mutual referencing among contemporary contributions, of a connection with past discussions, and also of an engagement with Marx's ideas as such. Critical research today can certainly benefit from critical scrutiny of his fragmented work on questions of technology. More frequently incorporating Marx into the discussion once again would mean taking contradictions, the knowledge about social contingency and the critique of capitalist society as natural starting points for analysis.

II

Robots in the Factory: Vision and Reality

7

High Tech, Low Growth: Robots and the Future of Work[1]

Kim Moody

In the last few years, works by such techno-futurists as Martin Ford, and Brynjolfsson and McAfee, both *New York Times* bestsellers, have contributed to the revival of the recurring debate about technology and the future of work, dazzling the public with mountains of information on new technology, artificial intelligence, robotics, self-driving cars and trucks, 3D printers, and their projected destruction of jobs and, hence, the inevitable vanishing of the working class – and perhaps managers and bean-counters as well.[2] Confronted with such overwhelming accounts of technical progress, we tend to respond like the deer frozen in the headlights. The disaster rushing towards us appears unstoppable.

This generation of technophiles, however, is by no means the first to describe and analyse the evolution of technology and its 'inevitable' impact on employment. As Ford himself notes, the 1964 report *The Triple Revolution* catalogued rising automation and predicted the inevitable loss of countless jobs.[3] Inevitability, however, failed to materialise as the US workforce grew apace even in manufacturing and despite the big recession of 1974–5. The turning point came with the bigger recession of 1980–2 that did the sort of job-destroying work automation had not.

The 1990s saw another wave of popular techno-scare analyses, one of the most substantial of which was Jeremy Rifkin's 1995 *The End of Work*.[4] The title, of course, is the message. Rifkin compiled an array of examples of the latest developments in work-related technology and the new practice of 'reengineering', predicting the massive and permanent loss of jobs. Yet, a quarter of a century later, there are more, not fewer, jobs in the United States and the world. Work did not end, it just changed official statistical categories and got worse, as we will see below. Like today's projections, Rifkin's were based on a lot of information, much of it anecdotal, and a lot of predictions, most of them off the mark.

For example, Rifkin cited a 1993 Andersen Consulting study that predicted the loss of 700,000 jobs in 'banking and thrift institutions' over the next seven years as a result of re-engineering. Between 1990 and 2000 commercial banking did lose jobs, 111,700, about a sixth of the prediction, and this is likely due to industry consolidation. By 2010, commercial banks had gained back half of those lost jobs despite consolidations and better computers, and by mid-2017 they had reached 97 per cent of the 1990 level. Computers destroyed jobs, but nowhere near on the scale imagined by Andersen Consulting or Rifkin.[5]

Even more off-base was a 1990 prediction from the US Department of Labor cited by Rifkin that automation of various sorts could reduce warehouse 'labour requirements' by 25 per cent. Instead, warehouse production and non-supervisory jobs grew by 27 per cent from 1990 to 2000 and by another 83 per cent from 2000 to mid-2017, despite recession and technological advances.[6] One reason why this prediction was so far off is that not only are there many more warehouses, but, as we will see below, they are much larger and hence require more rather than less labour.

Typically, the projections of techno-futurists, while looking at some big economic trends, do not really grasp how capitalism works in relation to investment, whether in structures, machines, IT or robots. Rifkin's predictions fell short not just because the technology was not always up to the task or the tendency of futurists to project from limited evidence, but because of the economic times in which they were made and the underlying contradictions of capitalist accumulation that gathered force even in the late 1960s and have asserted themselves since the 1970s. Writing in the mid-1990s, when the economy seemed to be on an upward course with high-tech investment on the rise, he could be optimistic. But, in fact, capitalism was having deeper problems, investment would halt, and the dot-com boom go bust within a few years.

METHOD AND SUMMARY OF ARGUMENT

The approach taken here will be different from the techno-futurists, many academics, and major institutions of capitalist thought and regulation. This study employs the dynamics of Marxist political economy in order to assess the past, current and likely future progress of job-destroying automation. The underlying context of this examination is the turbulent reality of actually-existing capitalism as it has unfolded since the 1970s and is projected to continue for the foreseeable future. The major contention here is that the susceptibility of any job to automation is secondary to the potential profitability of its actual application. This is a view of the prospects of the 'Fourth Industrial Revolution' that poses a different question than those assumed by most of the predictions, projections and estimates cited above, and many others like them. The question is not that of the susceptibility of various jobs and occupations to automation, but the practicality of their application through actual investment.

The article will next empirically examine the surprisingly slow introduction of industrial robots in manufacturing due in part to their persistent limitations, relative costs and the problems of profitability; the real forces behind manufacturing job loss since the early 1980s; the irony that the increased use of information and communications technology (ICT) to track and guide goods in supply chains and within and between warehouses has actually led to rapid growth in employment in this sector; and, finally, the ever-delayed promise of 'driverless' cars and trucks.* In conclusion, it will be argued that the dynamics of capital accumulation itself, as well as the turbulence of capitalism globally and in the United States, have led to a slowing-down of investment in work-related technology which remains a barrier to the sort of dramatic replacement of human labour by machines projected by the techno-futurists.

SUSCEPTIBILITY VERSUS PROFITABILITY

In addition to popular works such as those of Ford or Brynjolfsson and McAfee, there have been academic attempts to measure the like-

---

* Editor's note: Although the two sections on supply chains and 'driverless' vehicles are not included in this edited version, they are well worth reading in the original.

lihood of massive job loss due to automation or other technological advances. A frequently cited recent study by Oxford academics Carl Frey and Michael Osborne, for example, attempted to rank the susceptibility of 702 detailed occupations to computerisation, broadly defined, using data and descriptions from the Bureau of Labour Statistics (BLS). They conclude that '47% of total US employment is in the high-risk category', meaning that associated occupations are potentially automatable over some unspecified number of years, perhaps a decade or two'.[7] While they assume the accelerating progress of such key elements of automation as 'machine learning', 'Big Data', and robot dexterity, they make no effort to assess the economic feasibility or practicality of applying various forms of technology under today's turbulent economic conditions.

Not surprisingly, the active members of the capitalist class are also concerned about the possible competitive advantages as well as the potentially disruptive impact of all this new technology. Both the World Trade Organization (WTO) and the World Economic Forum (WEF) have published recent reports covering the 'Fourth Industrial Revolution'. As might be expected, as caretakers and practitioners of capitalism, they are somewhat more circumspect in their predictions of job loss. While rehearsing the usual arguments about how such 'creative destruction' brings new jobs, occupations and even industries, the WTO's 2017 report cites two McKinsey Global Institute studies which claim that although 60 per cent of US occupations could involve some automation, only '5 percent of occupations could be entirely automated using current technologies'. Its own estimate is that about 9 per cent of jobs in the United States and 21 OECD countries are 'susceptible to full automation'. The WTO report notes that costs are a factor in the introduction of new technology, but goes no further in assessing the likelihood that such investments will be made.[8]

The WEF's 2016 report *The Future of Jobs* estimated that between 2015 and 2020 there could be a net loss of 5.1 million jobs to automation in the 15 countries, including the USA, that their survey of senior executives covers. As they point out, however, there are 1.86 billion workers in those countries, so this projection seems even more modest than the WTO/McKinsey estimates. When the WEF survey asked executives what they thought the main 'drivers' of change were, only 9 per cent answered 'Advanced robotics and autonomous transport', while even fewer named 'Artificial intelligence and machine learning' or '3D printing'. In comparison, 44 per cent, the highest percentage, answered 'Changing work environment and flexible working arrangements'. Could they have meant some version of lean production methods and related new management practices? The only economic barrier to new technology mentioned in the survey was 'Pressure from shareholders, short-term profitability'.[9]

THE FORWARD MARCH OF THE ROBOTS STUMBLES

One of the few attempts to quantify the actual implementation and impact of robots on US industry is the 2017 National Bureau of Economic Research study, *Robots and Jobs: Evidence from US Labor Markets*, by Daron Acemoglu and Pascual Restrepo. This received a lot of media attention, which usually took its findings to indicate catastrophic job losses in the not too distant future. Using a rather complex simulation of 'labour markets' and data from the International Federation of Robotics (IFR) for 19 industries (15 manufacturing, four service), Acemoglu and Restrepo conclude that from 1990 to 2007, just before the Great Recession took hold, the introduction of robots in the United States cost between 360,000 and 670,000 jobs or about 21,000 to 40,000 jobs a year on average. They also predicted a tripling or even quadrupling of the number of robots between 2015 and 2025 that would destroy jobs at about the same rate per robot (5.25 workers per 1 robot).[10] This presumably could mean a loss of as many as 2.7 million jobs over ten years or about 270,000 a year if robots increased by four times. That is a lot, but is not the 'end of work' in a workforce that is now composed of over 153 million men and women and that has grown by 14 million since 2010 despite a sluggish recovery and a large reserve army of labour.[11]

The Economic Policy Institute (EPI) criticised Acemoglu and Restrepo's simulation model as 'highly stylised' and based on 'stringent and likely unrealistic assumptions', and concluded: 'we find nothing in their report that establishes that automation broadly defined (including robots and non-robot automation such as information technology) explains recent trends'. In any case, the EPI argued, 40,000 jobs a year is hardly a massive loss if employment is growing in other areas, as it generally was, albeit in low-wage occupations and slowly since 2008.[12] Since robots are heavily concentrated in manufacturing, Acemoglu and Restrepo's figures are too small to explain the loss of 2.5 million production and nonsupervisory jobs.

Other growth projections are even more modest. The IFR's projections for 2015 to 2020 show only a doubling of annual robot shipments for the USA from 27,504 to 55,000, while the Boston Consulting Group estimates US robot spending to increase by one-and-a-fifth-times to $24 billion from 2015 to 2025. However, their estimate for 2015 of $11 billion in robot sales equalled less than 3 per cent of GDP expenditures on 'Machinery' that year.[13]

In global terms, the United States is actually behind most of the rest of the industrialised world. The IRF's report 'World Robotics 2017' shows that while global shipments of industrial robots have grown significantly, those from 'The Americas' have never amounted to more than 18 per cent of the world total, and by 2016 were down to 14 per cent of which 20 per cent came from Canada, Mexico, Brazil and the rest of Latin America.[14]

Further evidence for the relatively slow growth in robots lies in their uneven application across industries. According to a Brookings study, as of 2015 half of the nation's 233,305 industrial robots were in auto with a huge concentration in the Midwest and upper South, the site of most car and truck-supplier and final-assembly plants. Of those 116,653 robots, 30,000 or over a quarter belonged to General Motors alone.[15] Despite rapid growth in robots in a few US industries, the *only* industry with extensive use of robots globally as well as in the United States is automobile manufacture – and that more than a half-century after their first introduction. In 2014, the US auto industry deployed 117 robots per 1,000 workers. No other industry came as close as 10 per cent of that level, and most had less than one robot per 1,000 workers in spite of significant increases in some industries.[16]

Even in automobile manufacture, where robots have been used since the 1960s and have proliferated more than in any other industry, total employment in auto and auto parts in January 2017 was 945,000, compared to the all-time high of 1,004,900 in 1978, or 94 per cent of the industry's highest employment level.[17] This is possible because today's auto workforce produces many more cars and light trucks than that of the 1970s. To be sure, this workforce is now spread over a different group of companies, located in different geographic areas, heavily de-unionised, and subjected to two-tier wage patterns, gutted benefits and intensified labour even where there is a union. What all this indicates is that job losses and gains do not correspond directly to the increased use of robots. Competition and the ups and downs of the car and truck market continue to be major factors in employment levels along with various methods of work intensification. More broadly, the level of output and sales, i.e. the realisation of surplus value, remains a factor in employment levels in almost any industry.

That is not to say that automation and robots do not displace workers. Yet the loss of 2.5 million jobs went along with recurrent economic crises, changes in plant structure and layout, lean production, alternative shift patterns and other forms of work reorganisation and intensification.

BEHIND THE LOSS OF MANUFACTURING JOBS

Martin Ford sees the massive loss of manufacturing jobs that is the major contributor to the rising reserve army almost totally as the result of new technology.[18] Robots are one factor in the loss of manufacturing jobs, but they are not even the main one given their limited use so far in most manufacturing industries, as shown in Acemoglu and Restrepo's and the IFR's figures. Determining with any precision just how much job loss is due to technology and how much to changes in, and the reorganisation of, work in the past 30 or so years is probably impossible. As we will see below, however, the level of investment in both information processing and industrial equipment across the US economy has declined as a proportion of new private investment, while the growth in the ratio of capital stock to GDP has slowed down to a crawl. At the same time, the spread of lean production methods, work reorganisation, and more recently the monitoring and measuring of work by electronic and biometric technology, has increased. So, although technology plays a role, the rate of investment in robotics and automation has decelerated, while that of economic turbulence and work intensification by other means, that is, essentially class war waged by capital, has increased.

The major sources of job loss in manufacturing came not from robots or imports, but from the volatile course of the economy as huge numbers of manufacturing jobs were destroyed in the recessions of 1980–2, 1990–1, 2000–1 and 2008–10, and from large productivity gains between recessions due mainly to the implementation of capital's major tools of class conflict *de jure*: lean production methods beginning in the 1980s; work reorganisation; the introduction of 'alternative work schedules'; the reduction of break time; and the accelerated monitoring, measuring and standardisation of work via computerisation and new surveillance technology.[19]

The intensification of work through the reduction of rest-time per minute has been accomplished through lean production methods by *Kaizen* (continuous improvement) teams, computerised job measurement systems like Six Sigma that rebalance jobs to the lowest employment-to-output level, and more recently by electronic and biometric methods of work measurement and monitoring. The classic case was the GM-Toyota NUMMI plant in California where, beginning in 1986, the number of seconds of actual work per minute rose from 45 to 57 seconds. While most factories are not likely to meet the 57-second standard, an increase of a few seconds per minute in a plant with a few thousand workers can create hundreds of extra hours of work at no cost to the company and without any change in technology.[20]

The introduction of 'alternative work schedules' beginning in the 1990s allowed manufacturing firms to take advantage of shift lengths that maximised the curve of productivity – generally ten hours as opposed to eight.[21] Another job-busting non-tech strategy is the simple reduction of break time. One study of workers 'performing routine tasks in middling occupations' found that, on average, break time in the United States had been reduced from 13 per cent of the working day in 1985 to 8 per cent by 2003.[22] This continued in auto in 2016 as the United Automobile Workers granted Ford a reduction in break time of one minute per hour worked.[23] With 53,000 production workers this amounts to just over 7,000 extra hours of work per eight-hour day at no extra cost to Ford and a potential loss of nearly 1,000 jobs.

To be sure, technology, particularly software, plays a role in lean production methods. But its role is not primarily the direct replacement of workers, *à la* robots or computer numerical controlled machines, but of forcing the workers themselves to reduce the workforce through increased productivity. This difference is important. What, then, of the progress of robots in industry?

SMART COMPUTERS, CLUMSY ROBOTS

Any self-confident techno-booster will argue that the use of robots is accelerating and that the future promises an escalation the likes of which we have never seen. Look at all those gains in artificial intelligence (AI)! What about Moore's Law of exponential growth in computer capacity, as the number of transistors per chip doubles every two years? The problem here is that most industrial robots do not require the most advanced versions of AI or super-high levels of computer capacity. They are, as even Martin Ford puts it, 'blind actors in a tightly choreographed performance'[24] – the choreography residing in the program or algorithm. Thanks to 100 years of Taylorism and three decades of lean production methods, most industrial-production jobs are basic and low or middling skill in nature. On the one hand, that makes these jobs a potential target for robotisation. At the same time, however, it means that the advances in industrial robot performance have been minimal – from three positions to six or seven since the 1960s – that is, over more than half a century, for standard industrial robots such as are used in auto. Furthermore, they still lack dexterity and mobility.

In addition, as Ford points out, 'industrial robots require complex and expensive programming', so their deployment is costly.[25] While computers may be able to unravel the human genome, win at *Jeopardy*, and more recently at the ancient Chinese game of *Go*, industrial robots are mostly deployed to perform simple tasks. Moore's Law does not apply here. In fact, as we will see below, Moore's Law has, as Robert J. Gordon puts it, 'gone off the rails'.[26] Thus, one reason for the relatively minor role of robots in job loss is that their development has not been the smooth process many imagine.

Part of the reason for this is that they are subject to 'Moravec's paradox'. As robotics expert Hans Moravec put it, 'It is comparatively easy to make computers exhibit adult-level performance on intelligence tests or playing games, and difficult or impossible to give them the skills of a one-year-old when it comes to perception and mobility.'[27] In other words, it is difficult to translate all the great leaps in artificial intelligence and computer capacity into the physical and mechanical functioning of robots, without which they are of limited use in industry. So, while computers are outsmarting people in some endeavours, robots remain clumsy or limited operatives in factories, warehouses and elsewhere.

With their faith in the inevitable improvement of all things digital, Brynjolfsson and McAfee predicted with complete confidence in their 2014 book, *The Second Machine Age*, that the Pentagon-sponsored Defense Advanced Research Projects Agency (DARPA)'s Robotic Challenge, launched in 2014, would see much of the problem of mobility overcome. In fact, when the contest took place in 2015, as *The Economist* reported of the robots' mobility, 'They fell on their faces. They fell on their backs. They toppled like toddlers, they folded like cheap suits, they went down like a tonne of bricks.'[28] Such physical limitations, of course, make them shaky investments. This, however, is only part of the reason for their slow adaptation to the work of producing and moving material things.

To be sure, there are robots with more advanced AI able to solve problems and learn. Some, like Rethink's Baxter, can be fitted with sensors to detect the presence of humans in order to work alongside them.[29] There are also advances in the use of robotics in medicine, biotechnology and some other areas. Our concern here, however, is with the impact of automation on those workers who produce the bulk of the nation's goods and services. Most industrial robots that are actually used in manufacturing and auto in particular perform basic operations such as painting, welding and simple assembly. A new generation of 'collaborative robots' or 'co-bots' provides extra muscle for assembly-line workers, acting as an extension of the worker. In 2016 these accounted for only 3 per cent of global industrial-robot sales, but are expected to increase to perhaps a third.[30] No doubt these will increase productivity, but they do not directly replace the worker.

The ultimate reason the progress in the application of industrial robots has been so slow lies not in technology *per se*, but in political economy. No technology will be invested in unless it can be expected to increase profitability, and if sufficient profits are available – and these are the problems of this era.*

THE POLITICAL ECONOMY OF AUTOMATION

The underlying methodological problem with the work of techno-futurists such as Ford and Brynjolfsson and McAfee, as well as that of their major critic Robert J. Gordon, is that they are technological determinists. Neither the problems of profitability nor of class conflict enter their analyses. For them history moves forward as a result of technological innovations by bold entrepreneurs. They argue that there has been no human progress from the time of Rome to the invention of the steam engine. Brynjolfsson and McAfee actually produce a figure showing that the curve of human social progress is led by technological change, and in particular the invention and application of the steam engine by James Watt between 1765 and 1776. They state forthrightly that the Industrial Revolution was 'the first time our progress was driven primarily by technological innovation – and it was the most profound time of transformation our world has ever seen'.[31] There is no recognition here that there was something besides entrepreneurial genius behind this technological innovation and its application along with many other innovations in what became the Industrial Revolution – namely the prior development of capitalism with its competitive drive for 'improvements' in production and profitability.

As Ellen Meiksins Wood summarised the distinct nature of capitalism as it arose first in agrarian England prior to the Industrial Revolution, 'This system was unique in its dependence on intensive

---

* Editor's note: At this point, the original article features two sections on automation in the logistics sector and experiments with driverless vehicles.

as distinct from extensive expansion, on the extraction of surplus value created in production as distinct from profit in the sphere of circulation, on economic growth based on increasing productivity and competition within a single market – in other words on capitalism.' What drove this need to intensify the extraction of surplus value 'was not the emergence of steam or the factory system but rather the need inherent in capitalist property relations to increase productivity and profit ... the factory system was result more than cause.'[32]

At the same time, these techno-futurists tend to rely on mainstream neoclassical economic assumptions. One assumption is that machines, just like humans, can produce value as well as physical products or services (use values) of various sorts. The counter assumption here will be that while machines can produce *use values*, only human labour can produce value; in other words, the classical Marxist view of the social relations of production and value creation at the heart of capitalist dynamics and limitations.

Following neoclassical assumptions, for most techno-futurists, whether academic or popular, markets and knowledge are assumed (perhaps unconsciously) to be 'perfect', and the spread of new technology, therefore, rapid and even within and between industries as leading firms adopt the new methods. As Howard Botwinick argues, however, Marx's view of the impact of actual capitalist competition is one of uneven development due to the prior existence of accumulated fixed capital and differential profit rates among competing firms. Not all firms can afford to jettison their old machinery and purchase new technology simultaneously. In addition, there tends to be a leapfrogging effect as late-comers adopt a more advanced version of the new technology, leaving the initial innovators behind. As Botwinick writes, '*Rather than creating identical firms, competition therefore creates a continual redifferentiation of the conditions of production*' (emphasis in original).[33]

We can see the unevenness of the spread of robots across industries in the figures Acemoglu and Restrepo reproduce from the IFR, showing that only auto has adopted robots extensively. But even within auto the spread of robots was neither even nor rapid. While GM introduced its first robots in 1961, Ford waited until the 1970s. Many 'service' occupations, by contrast, have yet to feel the force of automation, while even those that have, such as warehousing and hospitals, continue to create jobs even in the face of automation. Outside of auto, and, to a lesser extent, computer and electronics manufacturers, most companies are still waiting despite all the hype.

From the vantage-point of political economy, there are both fundamental and contingent reasons, including timing, why the progress of implementing automation has been relatively slow and why it is likely to remain so. One contingent reason for the slow pace of capital investment in the latest technology is found in the very success employers have had in imposing relatively high levels of productivity in manufacturing and some related industries, and flat or declining real wages in general through lean production and the more open forms of assault on labour over the past three decades or more. In manufacturing in particular, the combined impact of recurrent crises and work intensification eliminated millions of production jobs even while output doubled between the early 1980s and today, with significant ups and downs to be sure. This combination has, in effect, done what robots were supposed to do, but at much lower costs to capital.

At the same time, more and more of the new jobs in growing sectors of the economy, such as many services and warehousing, are low-paid and largely without benefits. In some cases, this is accompanied by rising productivity. While real wages in warehousing, for example, were almost flat, productivity in general (not refrigerated) warehousing rose by an average of 5 per cent a year from 1987 to 2009.[34] With productivity high in relation to wages in key industries, and low-wage jobs proliferating, the incentive for large-scale investment in costly and potentially risky technology has been reduced, while that in low-wage industries has increased.

As Marx noted in his discussion 'Machinery in Large-Scale Industry', 'In the older countries, machinery itself, when employed in some branches of industry, creates such a superfluity of labour ("redundancy of labour" is how Ricardo puts it) in other branches that the fall of wages below the value of labour-power impedes the use of machinery in those branches and, from the standpoint of the capitalist, makes the use of machinery superfluous.'[35] In other words, as manufacturing sheds workers, many have been forced to move to low-wage jobs, thus putting further downward pressure on wages.

That the wages of many of these workers are below the value of their labour power is indicated by the fact that 30 per cent of the workforce relies to some extent on one or another form of public assistance.[36] This, in turn, removes the incentive to automate these low-wage jobs.

The rise of new jobs in areas such a social reproduction, healthcare, maintenance, waste management, cleaning, material handling, etc., is not a function of Schumpeterian 'creative destruction' or a spin-off of technology, as mainstream economists and the apologists at the WTO or WEF argue, but of the now-affordable investment in these necessary functions mostly performed in the private sector at pitiful wages. Thus, one of the mechanisms behind this shift in employment to these lower-paid 'service' jobs is this sizable reserve army of labour which both supresses wages and provides desperate workers. As Marx put it: 'But if a surplus population of workers is a necessary product of accumulation or of the development of wealth on a capitalist basis, this surplus population also becomes, conversely, the lever of capitalist accumulation, indeed it becomes a condition for the existence of the capitalist mode of production.'[37] Without a 'surplus population', the expansion of capital into new areas is impossible. The turnover in the reserve army is a consequence not only of technology, but of the various aspects of lean production in reducing the manufacturing workforce even though this sector produces more than ever, on the one hand, and is an enabler of growth in low-wage employment, on the other.

More fundamental to the uneven progress of automation, however, is the rate of profit that is the driving motor of capitalism. Capitalist competition, both domestic and international, drives firms to invest in machinery or new technology to lower labour costs and increase profits. But there is a problem, a contradiction. As the share of fixed capital increases, the *rate* of profit tends to decline, even if the mass of profits increases to some extent as they have. Martin Ford, no Marxist, wrote in an earlier work, *The Lights in the Tunnel*: 'the more machines begin to run themselves, the value that the average worker adds begins to decline.'[38] Since in Marxist political economy it is human labour power that creates the value that eventually translates into money and profit, that means a falling rate of profit. Profits, in turn, determine the level of investment. As the Marxist economist Michael Roberts puts it: 'The movement of profits leads the movement of investments, not vice versa.'[39]

Furthermore, as Anwar Shaikh points out in terms of capital's willingness to move from one industry or firm to another, 'it is the rate of return on the new investment, not the average rate of profit on all vintages, which is relevant to the mobility of capital.'[40] This is important, as much of the innovation in technology comes from relatively new start-up firms. The survival rate of such high-tech firms barely exceeds a third. This applies to robotics firms as well. As the magazine *Canadian Business* warns investors, 'robotics is a long-term play'. Some, it points out, lose money. As one investment counsellor told the magazine, 'You don't know when there's going to be a payoff.'[41] This is not music to the ears of most of today's short-term-oriented investors who are the potential providers of new investment.

The argument here is not that capitalism as a system is incapable of strong technological advance. Indeed, its competitive dynamic tells us that over the long haul it should be accumulating capital and innovating through such investment. Here is where timing comes in. The rate of profit has been increasingly turbulent in western capitalism at least since the late 1960s. This led to the slump of 1974–5 and the 'stagflation crisis' that characterised most of that decade. Profit rates rose in the 1980s and 1990s when capital investment in relation to total labour costs (the organic composition of capital) was relatively low and productivity rising, but never achieved anywhere near the high levels of the post-Second World War boom era. They then collapsed with each recession and became somewhat weaker after 2000.[42] Investment decisions for the past forty years or so have been made in the context of increasing crises, volatile ups and downs, relatively slower growth, and turbulent profit rates. Thus, Rifkin's predictions, and even those of the earlier *Triple Revolution*, faltered on the unfolding volatility of capitalism that had its origins in the late 1960s decline in profit rates – itself a consequence of the capital spending spree of the 1950s and 1960s.

As a result, all the neoliberal redistribution of income and wealth upward for the last thirty years or more has not encouraged large-scale investment in expensive industrial technology. Rather, to a greater degree than in earlier times, much of this money, when not just sitting in some offshore tax haven, has gone into government bonds, mergers, stocks, derivatives, or at best more conventional plant and equipment. While the 'financialisation' of capital can be exaggerated, one indicator of the movement from new investment in real capital assets (and the short-term mindset of today's capitalists) has been the shift of the share of profits towards dividends rather than internal investment; i.e. the redistribution of profits upward. Whereas, in the 1960s, during the postwar boom, an average of two-thirds of after-tax profits were internally retained and invested, with the rest going to dividends, by the twenty-first century retained profits had fallen to 40 per cent on average, while the proportion of dividends had soared.[43] Insofar as capital funds its investments from retained profits, which at the aggregate level is generally the case,[44] this is another indication of the slower growth of investment in labour-saving or -enhancing machinery and technology.

The derailing of Moore's Law mentioned above is, itself, a result of economic rather than technological forces. Gordon cites Hal Varian, a founder of Intel and now chief economist at Google, to the effect that research on increasing computer capacity in PCs and laptops ceased 'because no one needs a superfast chip on their desktop'. The problem, he said, was one of 'demand'. So, research shifted elsewhere and transistor density no longer doubled every two years.[45]

HIGH TECH IN SLOW MOTION – THE TREND

The slowing-down of investment in high-tech equipment is not just a theoretical proposition. According to the political economist Anwar Shaikh, 'the appropriate measure of technical change is the ratio of current GDP to current-cost capital stock'.[46] This, of course, is the *economic* measure of change, not a measure of the efficiency of the technology, but as such it gives us a guide to capital's investment behaviour. What this shows is that, while there has been growth in this ratio over the 35-year period from 1980 to 2015, the rate of growth has been slowing down significantly decade-by-decade, nearly grinding to a halt between 2010 and 2015 despite some growth in the economy. During the 1980s this ratio grew by an average of 1.8 per cent a year, itself not all that strong. But in the 1990s the annual rate of change slowed by half to 0.9 per cent, then dropped to 0.3 per cent from 2000 to 2009. From 2010 to 2015, during the period of recovery, the rate of growth in the ratio of technical change all but vanished at 0.08 per cent a year.

Looking further into the course of capital investments, we can see that investment in new 'information processing' and 'industrial equipment', as defined by the Bureau of Economic Analysis (BEA), has not taken the course techno-futurists' predictions would suggest. Investment in both information processing and industrial equipment has fallen as a proportion of total equipment investment since the early 1990s, while that in transportation equipment has risen – no doubt as a result of the expanding logistics sector. Growth in investment in information-processing equipment was surprisingly slow, at an annual average of 2.4 per cent over the 23-year period between 1992 and 2015. That in industrial equipment was faster at about 5.8 per cent a year, but very little of this is digitally driven, robotic, or high tech in nature, according to descriptions in the BEA's Handbook *Concepts and Methods* and as we saw above in the case of 'Machinery'. The biggest gain came in transportation equipment which grew at 11 per cent a year.[47] Roberts also notes that growth in investment specifically in new technology has decreased in recent years. Economic Policy Institute figures show the same trend.[48]

Another common measure of the growth of technology and its application is that of the increase in occupational employment associated with computerisation: the BLS category of Computer and Mathematical Occupations. This remains an above-average growth group, but this measure, too, has slowed to a crawl, from 12 per cent a year from 1983 to 2000 to 3 per cent from 2000 to 2014. The BLS projections on future occupational growth show a further decline in the annual rate of growth for computer and mathematical workers to just over 1 per cent from 2014 to 2024.[49] Thus, by almost any measure, the advance of new technology in *economic* terms does not substantiate the techno-futurists' predictions.

Given all the gains in technology these futurists describe, the mystery of this poor and declining performance lies in the volatility of the US and world-capitalist economies since the 1970s and the continuing problem of profitability. Profitability was not strong enough and could not be sustained long enough under these circumstances to justify large and continuous investments in new technology of any kind. The problem was compounded by the rapid rise in corporate debt over these years. As a result, as Roberts argues, 'this increase in debt means that companies must raise profitability or be forced to reduce investment in productive capacity to service rising debt'.[50] It appears they have done the latter. Future investment in the US and worldwide auto industry, the major user of robots, is further limited by the persistence of global overcapacity in car and light-truck production.[51] Yet another indication that large-scale investment is not likely in manufacturing in the near future is the relatively low level of capacity utilisation, which has fallen from above 80 per cent in the 1990s to an average around the mid-70 per cent rate since, compared to the mid-to-high 80 per cent level of the 1960s.[52] Short of an economic miracle, the pace of automation and the march of the robots in much of industry is likely to be bumpy and slow.

CONCLUSION

While the past is not always a reliable guide to the future, for there to be a substantial increase in investment in automation there would have to be a prolonged period of stable economic growth and rising profit rates. That has not been the case and is not likely to improve as the very slow and drawn-out recovery of the US economy since 2009 shows. A prolonged period of stable growth would most likely require a catastrophic depression on the scale of the 1930s to clear the way for a new period of substantial growth through the massive destruction of older, less efficient assets. In all likelihood, it would also bring rising worker discontent and, at least, the possibility of an alternative. Should the alternative be postponed yet again, and a sustained period of rapid growth bring on the rapid elimination of living labour from production via automation, advanced robotics, etc., the system would certainly face yet another crisis of profitability.

For the techno-futurists, however, the massive productivity gains inherent in the rise of automation in its various forms would be the salvation of the system, the road to higher productivity and profits, though also the destroyer of employment. But technology, for all the AI gains or improvements in robots, does not introduce itself to the factory or warehouse. It has to be introduced through actual investment that promises substantial increases in profit rates to the capitalists who advanced the money. The hope that that will materialise on a scale big enough to bring about the robot revolution in the foreseeable future seems like the biggest piece of futurism of them all.

8

Productive Power in Concrete Terms

Lightweight collaborative robots and their difficult beginnings

Sabine Pfeiffer

To make it clear from the start, I will do my best to resist the temptation of proclaiming a new variety of capitalism. The question of what is really new about capitalism in the digital age is not answered by a premature proclamation of a novel ***-capitalism on the basis of (often poorly understood) new technological phenomena. The analysis of concrete historical developments instead requires a glance at concrete manifestations in both labour *and* technology. And that is precisely what I shall attempt to do here, albeit while consciously confining myself to lightweight robots as one of the many technological facets of what has been termed Industry 4.0 ever since 2011.

On the one hand, lightweight robots are generally quite technologically advanced and ready to use in practice these days; at first glance they resemble their old heavy relatives – large-scale industrial robots: much like them they are without humanoid features and mostly equipped with only one arm and several degrees of freedom (DOF). But they are much lighter and smaller. Lightweight robotics therefore offers, not least due to a far lower cost factor, new possibilities in both technical and economic terms.

Referred to in marketing terms as 'Cobots' (collaborative robots), lightweight robots, *on the other hand*, have so much technological innovation to offer that they promise a new quality of interaction between humans and technology. Unlike their cumbersome predecessors, they are equipped with highly sensitive, adaptive sensors and thus allow for deployment outside the safety fence area, which is mandatory for industrial robots. The much-cited 'robot co-worker' steps 'out of the cage' (or cell), and humans and robots – as goes the technological and marketing promise – not only *coexist*, but either share the same workspace alternately or sequentially (*synchronisation*), use this space together and simultaneously without directly processing the same component (*cooperation*), or indeed work on the same component at the same time (*collaboration*).[1]

That is to say, lightweight robots *on the one hand* allow for the expansion of the classic rationalisation approach (replacement of variable with constant capital) into industries and areas in which investment in large-scale industrial robots is uneconomical, such as low-tech serial production. When Marx notes that '[m]achine production drives the social division of labour immeasurably further than manufacture does', the lightweight robot in this sense allows for the increase in productive power of the 'industry it seizes upon'.[2] *On the other hand*, the lightweight robot promises, moreover, something Marx did not foresee in this way, namely the recovery, or new invention, so to speak, of the manufacture for capitalist use; the lightweight robot could in fact 'increase the productive power [...] to a much greater degree'[3] in those areas where customised products are manufactured in the smallest quantities and in such an immense variety that the 'special skill of each machine operator' – in contrast to the 'machine operator, who has now been deprived of all significance' in large-scale industry – is expendable only to a limited degree.[4]

Considering its largely mature technology (in contrast to, say, AI) and this dual promise of productivity increase, lightweight robotics really ought to have set out on a conquest across industries by now. And the product range is quite diverse, too: around 25 manufacturers offer lightweight robots that are ready for mass production, easily controllable and relatively cheap.[5] What is more, around 86 per cent of companies surveyed by the German-language website www.produktion.de in 2014 stated that they intended to invest in lightweight robotics.[6] This suggests that a boost in measures towards efficiency increase and rationalisation should be empirically ascertainable. However, that is not the case. The heading of the following (and central) section of this chapter perfectly summarises the current dilemma of lightweight robotics. We shall explore the causes in two steps: to start off, we consider the effects and interrelations of the distinct operational use regimes governing lightweight robotics. Subsequently, we analyse in more detail the specific option of collaboration associated with this approach to robotics. In doing so, we will show empirically and discuss theoretically the current development of adequate use regimes for lightweight robots. To conclude, we seek to illustrate that what is qualitatively new is not only expressed empirically and in very specific forms, but that what can be observed (and the corresponding requirements) also harbours new contradictions which a capitalist economic mode aiming at abstractification (in an economic sense) is increasingly struggling to solve.

MORE TO IT THAN MEETS THE EYE: ON THE DIFFICULT BEGINNINGS OF LIGHTWEIGHT ROBOTS

The term 'robots' is increasingly used to describe highly diverse technologies – including those which do not process materials. In the following, lightweight robotics is understood as outlined above, that is, as resembling traditional robotics in the sense that the robot handles the movement of physical objects, with its productive use in a business context taking centre stage. So, we are dealing with a known subject matter – i.e. tested use regimes – with regard to the objective, the basic underlying technology and its areas of application. At the same time, lightweight robots represent a very recent novelty. In contrast to their heavy predecessors, they are marked by 'harmlessness ensured through design or safety regulations', intended to allow for their operation without separating safety guards and, precisely as a result thereof, for 'scalable automation' and a substantial contribution to economic viability – especially given that they could also be used in many other industrial and non-industrial areas without safety fences.[7]

The low investment costs allow for the introduction of familiar patterns of automation in areas which hitherto did not lend themselves to cost-effective automation – for example, (mostly) manual assembly involving small batch sizes with multi-variant packaging, or manufactural production in various industries and closer to end-customer markets. Lightweight robots have not only been technologically refined and applicable for some time, but can today be obtained at a price of less than 10,000 euros. Correspondingly, everything seems to suggest a wholesale proliferation, including the accompanying effects regarding work and employment. However, the numbers in this respect are scarce and, besides that, contradictory.[8] Studies on employment effects remain at the macro level.[9] The few exceptions include a study based on the European Manufacturing Survey (EMS),[10] in which manufacturing firms were canvassed, as well as a study based on the occupational career data of workers in manufacturing.[11] Both studies link up data of their own with data available from the International Federation of Robotics (IFR) on sales figures for robotics.[12] Although the latter has more recently introduced a distinction between industrial and service robots,[13] the most current dataset available still indicates no figures pertaining to lightweight robotics specifically. Each of these studies attests Germany's top score in the global ranking of robot density (number of robots per 10,000 workers). Concerning the effects, however, there is little agreement: while some confirm an increase in productivity without any negative impact on employment,[14] others suggest robotics deployment has a negative effect on wages,[15] while still others hold robots responsible for a dramatic loss of jobs in the manufacturing industry.[16] All the cited studies refer, not least due to the periods they cover, to the use of classical industrial robots up until the present. It thus remains an open question as to whether the findings can be transferred to the future as well as to lightweight robotics and its application, including in other areas. Historically speaking, it was the industrial robots whose widespread deployment made conveyor-belt manufacturing more productive than ever before.[17] None of the cited studies leave any doubt about this; yet the distinct and partly contradictory results nonetheless show that the effects of technology are not one-dimensional but depend on multiple concrete historical conditions – conditions which find expression in *specific organisational forms of constant capital and in differing forms of use of variable capital* in the respective enterprise. In the next section, we take a look at the current state of research on the application of robotics and the exact mode of implementation concerning work organisation and qualification.

NEW CHALLENGES FOR OPERATIONAL USE REGIMES

From a technical point of view, 'robot-based automation', together with other technologies associated with Industry 4.0, is invoked as a new automation paradigm, putting the question about the relationship between humans and machines in an entirely new light. 'Will one half of the workforce "programme" the robots [...] while the other half [...] takes orders from them?'[18] Although such a scenario is not really in sight yet,[19] it certainly would entail considerable effects for qualification. One of the few studies on qualification in the context of lightweight robotics considers both an upgrading as well as a loss of expertise at the level of skilled workers a possibility, depending on the deployment scenario.[20]

The use of robotics in non-industrial areas – a clear advantage of the lightweight robot from the perspective of capital – could lead to very different qualification effects from those in the industrial sector with its concrete, historically developed automation stages, use regimes and skill profiles; for example, the deployment of robotics in surgery results in the emergence of a hyper-specialisation among only a very small group of surgeons.[21] It appears, then, that any qualification effects resulting from lightweight robotics depend on the specific existing operational use regime at a given workplace.

The manufacturers of lightweight robots rely on user companies integrating them into their immediate production processes, which only occurs given the prospect of productivity effects. However, integration means finding specific solutions, solutions which require a certain (and, most of the time, new) interplay between variable and constant capital. The robot as a means of production cannot only be defined via the human–technology relationship: the relations of production must always be considered as well. Only when all this interlocks can a new use regime be established. Indeed, variable and constant capital represent analytical concepts, but they also always require a concrete historical expression. This was already the case with the first generation of large-scale industrial robots. In the wake of their introduction in the 1980s, a threefold work-organisational structure of variable capital emerged which has largely persisted to this day:

The division of labor between workers assigned to robots is orga-nized on three hierarchical levels: 1) programming (jobs for engineers and technicians); 2) setting, maintenance, routine cor-rection of programs (jobs for the maintenance department); and 3) feeding and minding of robots (jobs for production workers). The job structure reflects the traditional division of labor. Painting and Welding, which used to be skilled jobs, are now performed by industrial robots. Programmers and maintenance workers are the winners in the rationalization process; production workers are the losers. There is no mobility chain leading from level 3 to level 2.[22]

Then, as now, this non-mobility should have no factual basis, given that workers in production and maintenance in the German car industry for the most part are skilled manual workers (often with advanced training qualifications) and can therefore more easily advance to one of the levels listed based on their professional and experience-based knowledge.[23] With regard to industrial robots, Windolf confirmed as early as the 1980s that the separation of skills and tasks depends exclusively on the respective form of work organisation and that the technologies that were new at the time were compatible not only with a rigid and hierarchical division of labour, but with other forms of allocating responsibilities in production too.[24]

At first glance, it appears as if the question of qualification and work organisation could be socially organised completely independently of the respective technology in use, and is only restricted, if at all, by the relations of power and domination inside a given workplace. CNC programmers, for example, were initially recruited from a company's own ranks instead of the labour market, once they were in increas-ingly high demand from the 1980s onwards. They were for the most part skilled professionals who had completed advanced training to obtain a master craftsman's certificate or become a technician, but had thus far not been employed in their relevant capacities. Apart from that, the fact that opportunities for promotion and advanced training in a capitalist enterprise are also always both an expression and a means of relations of power and domination applies on the *shop floor* as well. So far, so good – but the matter remains insufficiently clear for a more comprehensive analysis and too unspecific with regard to robotics. After all, the question often omitted is whether certain tech-nological settings simultaneously suggest certain forms of division of labour. Unfortunately, one result of the lasting controversy surround-ing technology's (non-)determination of the social dimension[25] is that the concrete technological settings (that is, the concrete mani-festation of constant capital) only rarely find their way into critical analysis. And that is the case even though there are those limitations and facilitations prompted by technology, factual requirements and almost inevitable path dependencies, which constitute an important (albeit not the only) explanatory dimension regarding concrete pro-duction processes. Indeed, they are almost always inextricably linked to the economic conditions of their deployment, but that does not exonerate us from taking a closer look. Let us imagine this with regard to the example of the classic industrial robot. Given that the latter has to operate within a safety cage, there is only a limited number of examples of its operational deployment and design of variable capital that are similar to the use of other machines: the industrial robot, mostly used for joining/assembly and handling tasks, can thus be treated, in technical terms, just like the cutting machining centre or the remodelling press. In the metalworking manufacturing industry, the execution of the actual work steps therefore, since the 1980s:

a) occurs automatically in a closed safety corridor without, at least at this point, any immediate action by the worker;
b) requires sophisticated programming, which can usually take place in a spatially and temporally decoupled manner;
c) occurs, as per investment volume, in a large-scale machine park geared to high-volume output;
d) requires the capacity to change over to other variants while simultaneously ensuring a high number of variants;
e) necessitates, for technical-functional reasons, precise repeat-ability and
f) for economic reasons, a minimisation of the scrap rate;
g) occurs in a complex production environment with multidimen-sional influence quantities and dynamic tribological behaviour and must therefore constantly be protected from failure;

h) can be realised without interruption in the long term only if prescient and quick-response maintenance (mechanical, electrical,
electronic, pneumatic, etc.) of the most diverse sub-compo-
nents is ensured; etc.

This list could be further extended and specified in more detail, but
what it illustrates, above all, is that the structure of work organisation
and qualification[26] observed during the 1980s can be understood
neither outside the context of a capitalist-constituted factory, comprising all the elements of the 'faster-higher-further' principle, nor
without any consideration of the given technical-functional conditions. This kind of manufacturing can be realised in the most
productive way, and with the utmost minimum share of variable
capital, on the basis of (just a few) relevant and broadly skilled labour
forces (the three-year professional-technical training serving as the
institutional basis) and well-established forms of division of labour
with regard to control, maintenance and programming (which,
depending on the specific context, may require less or more additional operative or professional training and skill).

COLLABORATION AS COMPLETE RENEWAL?

These operational use regimes of variable and constant capital established for economic and technical-functional reasons may be typical
of large-scale industry, but they are anything but exclusive to large
industrial robots. If we go by the marketing messages of the manufacturers, however, the above-mentioned generic characteristics can
now be overcome. The lightweight robot:

a) can leave the safety zone and work together with humans in the
same workspace, executing the same work steps and processing
the same component simultaneously;
b) requires no sophisticated programming and can therefore be
operated by non-skilled staff as well;
c) requires only minor investment.

The lightweight robot should thus have set out on its – empirically ascertainable – conquest by now, seeing as countless areas that have thus far not lent themselves to automation could now be profitably automated. Added to this – and this is precisely why I concentrate on this technological facet of 'Industry 4.0' here – is the fact that we are dealing, despite all novelty, with a sophisticated and viable technology which has completed its testing stage and can be bought 'off the rack'. And yet, this conquest has so far failed to materialise; this is obvious from a glance at these three dimensions alone: *collaboration, programming* and *investment*:

– *Collaboration beyond the safety zone.* The model that can be ascertained empirically to prevail for the time being is that of *coexistence,*[27] in which humans and the cage-free robot work *next to one another* yet do not share the same workspace. The variants of human–robot *cooperation* presented above, which intend for a shared workspace, can rarely be found in practice. And this is all the more true for the most elaborate form of division of labour between robots and humans: *collaboration*. But this would be the actual revolutionary novelty, because the processing step here is executed on the same component simultaneously by the human worker and the robot. By comparison: the major productivity advancement in the shift from the conventional to the programmable processing machine (regardless of whether via punch card or CNC, or whether programmed in the workshop or pre-programmed during work preparation) consisted precisely of the temporal and spatial separation of man and machine. The conventional machine tool still required a rather active operation and direct control by humans, therefore creating strong reliance on the latter. Only after the separation of machine and human action through the program sequence did a new rationalisation phase set in; only then could several machines be controlled by a single person and only because of this could variable capital be replaced on a large scale. Moreover, it was only then that the above-described triad of operation, programming and maintenance was established. Although it may have been the vision of *collaboration* associated with lightweight robots that inspired the marketing neologism 'Cobot' (merging the terms 'collaboration' and 'robots'), this is precisely what is absent in practice. This is exemplified by the head of development at a lightweight robot manufacturer, who asked during a group discussion: 'Now, everyone here is an expert. What I'd really like to know is if anyone can think of a situation in which a human and a robot really work together simultaneously on the same component? We have poured millions into the development of our [robot name], but these cases of application do not exist. Nobody needs it, am I right?' The sales manager at another manufacturer summarised his experience in sales: 'We should never have used the term Cobot, because you raise completely false expectations among management. They think they buy it, place it in the production facility, and then cooperation simply takes off. But far from it. Next thing they are desperately looking for suitable applications.'[28]

– *Easy programming.* A distinction is made between classic programming and programming 'through demonstration' in which the robot is 'taught directly or indirectly through intuitive input methods'.[29] On the one hand, it is usually the easy operation of the new robots that is advertised, as it no longer requires any programming skills but is limited to mere guidance of and 'demonstration' for the robot (the so-called teach-in).[30] On the other hand, it is often doubted as to whether this can be set at the level of skilled work, although it certainly requires substantial advanced training. We find an astonishing contradiction here: if programming is so simple that it is not even referred to as such anymore (that is, no longer in terms of geometrical and processing commands in a mostly manufacturer-specific script language), then it should not constitute a problem for modern metalworking and electrical professions. After all, CNC programming of processing machinery – thus far considered to be somewhat complex – has been firmly included in the training curriculum since the metalworking professions were first reformed in the 1980s. What is far more important than the robot's programming in terms of position-defining commands is what the robot is supposed to do. This applies to the big industrial robot as much as to its lightweight brother. Just as the programming of an industrial robot for spot-welding along the geometry of a vehicle body cannot be successful without the skilled and experience-based knowledge about inert gas welding or the materials of the parts to be welded, the lightweight robot also requires more general and, depending on the place of deployment, skilled knowledge than simply that of its correct positioning (for example, regarding the sense and nonsense of certain assembly or packaging requirements and step sequences). This is where the real – but also, at the level of skilled work, non-critical – challenge lies, including for lightweight robotics: there is no problem when it is used in areas involving the metalworking and electrical professions, but when the new robots are deployed outside these industries, various problems become apparent.

– *Investment.* The indicated intentions behind the investment in lightweight robots include primarily an increase in cost effectiveness, alongside, of course, an improvement of ergonomics and the testing of innovative technologies. However, the payback periods have proven in practice to be far longer than is the case with classic automation.[31] Brynjolfsson et al. consider this to be typical of so-called *general-purpose technologies* (GPTs), i.e. technologies such as AI or robotics, deployable for the most diverse applications.[32] In their view, earnings and productivity resulting from the introduction of these technologies are lower than expected during the first years, with a considerable increase setting in only at a later point – because a large part of initial investments are needed not for the actual acquisition of the means of production, but for the required 'intangibles' (meaning the costs for the redesign of business processes associated with these technologies, the co-investment in new products and business models, and investment in 'human capital', all of which is difficult to quantify economically). That is to say, what is needed is a large quantity of variable capital in order to redeem the *general-purpose* promise and turn it into profitable, constant capital. When speaking to experts from the industry, two patterns pertaining to the issue of investment become apparent. On the one hand, the buying intention is often voiced in the sense of a '*me too*' decision, as the expert at one of the manufacturers reported: 'Our [robot name] is, of course, often purchased by top management or the managing director. He might have seen it at a business fair and his golf buddy also already has it, and then he wants to have one as well. At times, it really is a question of status, while the question of whether it makes sense economically turns out to be secondary.' An engineer recounted: 'Well, and then the thing was there, and the aim was to do something presentable with it at all costs, if possible, something for the improvement of ergonomics, to boost acceptance and so forth. The final result of it all was something that could have been achieved at a far lower cost and much earlier with conventional handling automation.' A study by the Fraunhofer Institute of Labour Economy and Organisation (IAO), which surveyed 25 cases of application, found that the costs for deployment without a safety fence were higher than originally expected in all cases.[33]

In sum, the simpler and more intuitive programming of lightweight robots, as well as the collaboration options and low investment costs, provide options for saving on variable capital which could previously hardly be realised to this extent. The failure of this realisation thus far could be interpreted as a transitional phenomenon or a symptom of mismanagement. And both may indeed be true, but this alone does not explain the gap between the productivity promise and its non-redemption. The failure of the novelty thus far, *firstly*, is quite obviously not due to the actual means of production and their material specificity as artefacts. Nor is it caused, *secondly*, by the lacking or incompatible skills of workers. To conclude this chapter, we will seek a more elaborate explanation.

THE FAILURE OF THE NEW USE REGIMES ON THE SHOP FLOOR

Another explanation could be that the capital unit applying the product has been fooled by the manufacturers' promise of productivity increases and therefore (and because of the frenzied digitalisation discourse) did not calculate the factual and economic viability of the lightweight robot in sufficient detail beforehand. In fact, Marx already described machinery as a 'superior competitor', a 'power inimical to [the wage earner], and capital proclaims this fact loudly [...] as well as making use of it'; one could write an entire 'history of the inventions made [...] for the sole purpose of providing capital with weapons against working-class revolt'.[34] Capital is surprisingly successful at *proclaiming* the new technologies via the discourse of digitalisation and Industry 4.0,[35] while the press uncritically adopts the manufacturers' marketing lines.[36] But capital is far less successful at *handling* said technologies. The fact that this is the case even with lightweight robotics – although there are far fewer technological obstacles here than with regard to other Industry 4.0 technologies – demands further analysis. The marketed *killer application* concerning lightweight robotics is the capacity for collaboration, for the direct cooperation between humans and robots. Marx sees the use of cooperation as one essential element of capitalist production: 'Not only do we have here an increase in the productive power of the individual, by means of co-operation, but the creation of a new productive power, which is intrinsically a collective one.'[37] Marx distinguishes between two types of cooperation, which peculiarly remind us of the distinct forms of cooperation between humans and robots described above, but, at the same time, precisely do not describe the interaction between an individual human being and an individual artefact: in *simple cooperation*, two equals are grouped after or next to one another,[38] while in *combined cooperation* in a more complicated labour process, by contrast, 'the sheer number of the co-operators permits the apportionment of various operations to different hands, and consequently their simultaneous performance. The time necessary for the completion of the whole work is thereby shortened'; the result is a 'restriction of space and extension of effectiveness'.[39]

Apart from these generic, abstract remarks, Marx also makes it clear that the increased productivity of such a *combined working day* can have very different underlying causes, be it the exponential mechanical enhancement of labour power, or the possibility of setting 'at the critical moment [...] large masses of labour to work', exciting 'rivalry between individuals and [raising] their animal spirits', or be it the ability to '[impress] on the similar operations carried on by a number of men the stamp of continuity and many-sidedness', or be it to economise the means of production through their 'use in common' and, in doing so, to lend 'to individual labour the character of average social labour' – all these possibilities, according to Marx, arise 'from co-operation itself'.[40]

This is precisely where an immanent obstacle emerges for the lightweight robot: only at first glance and when clinging to the term 'collaboration' could it be interpreted as a new stage of, say, an *expanded cooperation based on the division of labour*. In that case, however, it should be possible for it to be more easily integrated into the labour process. After all, the lightweight robot encounters a certain state of the 'development of machinery' which, according to Marx, arises 'only when large-scale industry has already attained a high level of development and all the sciences have been forced into the service of capital, and when, on the other hand, the machinery already in existence itself affords great resources'.[41] This takes us to the very essence of the matter and thus to my first thesis: *The cooperation that has developed in capitalism thus far, in all its different varieties – in its most developed production forms of current large-scale industry – has reached the limits of its economisation.*[42] This was demonstrated, in terms of work organisation, by the limits of erstwhile Taylorism and the various responses by Toyotism (from lean production via holistic production systems to agile production). And it is also apparent, regarding the means of production, in the sluggish introduction of the lightweight robot.

My *second thesis* is therefore that the lightweight robot, in its collaborative form of use, does not constitute an economic step forward for the highly automated and highly subdivided forms of cooperation of today's large-scale industry in the developed capitalist countries, as this form of cooperation based on the division of labour, historically built up over long cycles, is ultimately unable to integrate any manufactural individual cooperation (even when it takes place between man and machine).

The lightweight robot, by contrast, would – and this is the *third thesis* – fit perfectly into the setting of individualised and customised, as well as decentralised, on-demand production. The latter is often posited as the future counter-model to mass production: it is implied that currently, in the car industry, only one type of car can be manufactured in serial production, whereas an increase in customised products is allegedly only possible based on Industry 4.0 in the future. This juxtaposition, then, ignores the developments over the last decades towards modularised and customer-specific serial production. Correspondingly, a single manufacturer today provides a selection of around 1,032 vehicle outfitting and equipment variants;[43] and, even today, each individually ordered vehicle is identifiable and specifically manufactured. This goes to show that on-demand production would absolutely be possible today, at least in technical terms, but it would mark a break with the dominant economic logic. More specifically: it would have a negative impact on performance indicators, i.e. the financial ratio pertaining to plant productivity. If an insufficient number of specific customer orders are placed, special models are later produced in larger batches and elaborately marketed in order to keep the means of production running. Either way, whether in today's production form of *mass customisation* or any other individualised or personalised form, on-demand production would be technically feasible and ecologically highly recommendable without question – but it is viable only in certain niches, as it contradicts the principles of a capitalist economy doomed to grow (and engender overproduction). Production would only occur once the concrete use value for an individual product is specified. The situation is quite similar with regard to the possibilities associated with lightweight robots, which could improve ergonomics and facilitate the realisation of age-appropriate and, more importantly, clock-independent production. Yet what is important here, too, is that often enough there are already other technical possibilities to achieve this – if only the quality of work were to take top priority in decisions concerning investment and the deployment of technology. However, most of the time it is only a deduced factor, or an item negotiated in conflicts around the arrangement of work, not the principal determinant. Qualitative aspects related to the environment and living labour could be improved today or tomorrow – and could have been in the past – but there is no automatism here, for any qualitative concerns contradict the dominant economic logic and are usually only implemented when they can be realised in a cost-neutral way. Indeed, it cannot be ruled out that the potential of collaborative lightweight robots for an expanded form of cooperation may be used in an economically viable way even within the capitalist logic. However, that would require – and this is the *fourth thesis* – that capital identify the concrete potential provided by the interplay between a specific constant capital and existing constant and variable capital. The lightweight robot does not develop its potential endogenously, but only in an innovative and often entirely newly configured interplay with existing technology and processes – frequently even linked to design changes at the product level. Finding solutions for this requires a well-attuned team of specific living labour (say, of design engineers in research and development together with automation specialists in engineering, and experienced skilled workers in production and maintenance). In those industries in which this concrete historical formation of living labour exists as a result of a 150-year-long history of development, this requirement, given the low investment volume associated with lightweight robots, is often not even considered in strategic terms and its specific impact is underestimated. In other possible areas of deployment, such as logistics or trade, precisely these manifestations of living labour are lacking. In both cases – and this is true in one way or another for many of the new technologies associated with Industry 4.0 – the management oriented towards the exchange value side underestimates the significance of living labour for innovation. One solution to this dilemma – and one that is inherent in the capitalist logic and thus not impossible – would be the establishment of a business model which addresses precisely this dilemma. Already, some small consulting firms and start-ups are offering to serve as 'integrators' for lightweight robots along these lines. In other words: capital can utilise the use-value side of its variable and constant capital and, on this basis, repeatedly and incrementally optimise the exchange-value side. But it has great difficulty in understanding the use-value aspects of both resources sufficiently to develop a strategic and innovative use that would go beyond the existing logic. For this to happen, invention has to become 'a business, and the application of science to immediate production itself becomes a factor determining and soliciting science'.[44] That is to say: the lightweight robot as individual constant capital is useless; what is needed first is a qualitatively new form of (and, for a transitional period, quantitatively more) use of human labour power in order to create the environment for its surplus-value creating deployment (at that point, on an altered technical organisational basis).

Ultimately, the statement from the Machine Fragment ought to be taken seriously, according to which, along with the development of large-scale industry, 'immediate labour as such ceases to be the basis of production. That happens because, on the one hand, immediate labour is transformed into a predominantly overseeing and regulating activity.'[45] According to Marx, then, it is not the appropriation of alien labour that ends, but only its form of direct productive activity. This phrase could be complemented, with regard to highly automated and networked production, to include my *fifth thesis*: *While the quantitative significance of variable capital decreases, its qualitative significance for the implementation and guarantee of the lasting productivity of the process as a whole increases.* And the significance of human labour increases not only for ensuring existing production, but also for the constant restructuring (in terms of planning, networking, reorganisation) of the process as a whole. This may even lead to a heightened quantitative demand for human labour power in the correspondingly required special qualifications, at least for a transitional period – a transition which would unlikely be a quasi-automatic shift from capitalism to some kind of post-capitalism, but rather from the existing use regime of constant and variable capital to a new one *within* capitalism.

Friedrich Krotz conceives of robots dialectically as a 'technically produced species in an ambivalent relationship with the human species', for they are 'on the one hand, subordinate actors and, on the other hand, simultaneously actors who compete with humans, insofar as they follow orders and fulfil tasks while at the same time issuing instructions and demanding the completion of tasks'.[46] This is not a new development either. It is not the artefact – for Krotz, *the* (i.e. all?) robot(s), or the lightweight robot in this chapter – that is interesting from a critical Marxist perspective, but rather the question as to whether it can be linked to a new leap in productive forces. The latter, however, involves much more than what occurs in immediate production. If the actors who are dominant in that context do not sufficiently understand the specific potential of technology and human labour capacity, if new use regimes between variable and constant capital fail to materialise there, that would mark a new threshold. The potential for a leap in the development of the productive forces towards a more ecological, decentralised on-demand production remains stuck in an irresolvable contradiction vis-à-vis the resource-depleting and resource-wasting logic of an extended large-scale industry in an exchange-value-oriented economy. It will not be the *robot overlords* who drink Champagne in Davos in the future.[47] Moreover, in the words of David Harvey, given the technological change, the question remains (and produces increasingly dramatic and long-term impacting answers): 'who gains from the *creation* and who bears the brunt of the *destruction*?'[48]

9

Drones, Robots, Synthetic Foods
Digitalisation in agriculture

Franza Drechsel and Kristina Dietz

'The Brain' controls everything: how much fertiliser or water is needed by which lettuce head and when; at what time and into which container it should be re-potted; where each robot is currently located and where it is needed more urgently; as well as when the lettuce is to be packaged and how long it is edible for. 'The Brain' – a nickname given to the computer programme that oversees it all – is in use at an indoor farm in California run by agritech start-up Iron Ox. It renders human labour almost redundant, ensures economical use of water, energy and nutrients, guarantees efficient production in a small area and ensures a fresh daily supply of healthy heads of lettuce.[1]

Iron Ox's 'Brain' ties in with a narrative of digitalisation in agriculture that is currently becoming dominant in discussions about the future of food production. Three central elements form its core: digital technologies increase efficiency and productivity on fields and in stables; they guarantee resource-efficient, sustainable and climate-neutral production; and they contribute to prosperity in rural zones. In sum, the implication is that the digitalisation of agriculture can simultaneously tackle the global food crisis, the ecological crisis in the agricultural sector, and the social crisis in marginalised rural areas. In this sense, agriculture hardly differs from industry and trade. Digitalisation promises revolutionary productivity increases in all areas, new valorisation opportunities and more prosperity as the result of necessary but 'manageable' adjustments in the world of work. In terms of real facts, however, little is actually known beyond these promises. In which areas is the digital revolution in agriculture to take place, and where is it already occurring? Which effects do digital technologies have on the relations of production in agriculture and on the relationship between human society and the natural world? Where do the contradictions of digital agriculture lie, and where are the starting points for political intervention?

These are the questions we intend to address in the following pages, both from a global perspective and under consideration of structural inequalities. Our aim is to identify current tendencies in the process of digitalisation, illustrate them based on a number of selected examples and assess their potential effects. We argue that the introduction of digital technologies will not fundamentally change the dominant modes and relations of production in agriculture. Instead, what can be expected is an intensification of those structural changes which have characterised agriculture since the neoliberalisation of the sector: concentration and centralisation, social differentiation and increasing global inequalities. Moreover, the ecological contradictions of conventional agriculture are just as inherent in digital agriculture.

To start off, we present our theoretical framework, which is based on historical-materialist approaches to the analysis of capitalist developments in agriculture and political ecology. Subsequently, we examine the crucial areas in which the digitalisation of agriculture is taking place and describe, based on specific examples, the current state of developments. This is followed by an analysis of the expected consequences for relations of production and society–nature relations. In the concluding summary, we discuss the contradictions of agricultural digitalisation and identify starting points for their politicisation.

THE AGRARIAN QUESTION AND THE POLITICAL ECOLOGY OF AGRICULTURE

In order to analyse the impact of digital technologies on the productive forces and relations of production in agriculture, the first question to be addressed is that of the general development of the capitalist relations of production in agriculture. In political economy, this is referred to as the 'agrarian question'. It encapsulates discussions about how the transition to capitalism takes place in agriculture and how important agriculture is for capital accumulation. While capitalism had successfully pervaded almost every area of agriculture in western Europe by the twentieth century, the question remains today as to how this process occurs in rural societies marked by small-scale farming, i.e. relations of production often understood as pre-capitalist relics.[2]

As a general rule, the development of capitalist relations of production in the agrarian sector can be gauged by three characteristics: the degree of incorporation into national and global markets, the emergence of wage-labour relations in agricultural production, and capitalist relations of ownership of the means of production (land, seeds, etc.). Judging by these characteristics, global agriculture is currently marked by diverging production forms which differ in terms of labour productivity and relations of production.[3]

In the Global North, that is in western Europe, the United States, Canada and Japan, agriculture is organised almost entirely along capitalist lines; this is expressed, among other things, by the market-adequate ownership structures. Only enterprises that can assert themselves vis-à-vis others on the market succeed in ensuring access to and ownership – and, if need be, expansion – of the land necessary for agricultural production, whereas all others disappear. The decrease in absolute numbers of productive farms and agricultural holdings over the course of the twentieth century in Europe – in West Germany referred to by the term '*Höfesterben*' (which translates as 'death of (small) farms') – as well as the rise in average land ownership per farm (land concentration) support this argument.[4] Cultivation takes place predominantly in an automated, capital-intensive form and requires only little human labour power. Similarly, in Latin America, Africa and Asia, an agricultural sector has been established over the past decades that also fits this description. Specialising in the export of soybean, meat, crops, palm oil, citrus fruits, etc., this sector contributes – due not least to cheap production conditions (particularly regarding wage costs and climatic conditions) – to the supply of 'cheap' and non-seasonal foods and animal feed as well as biofuels to world markets. This export-oriented agriculture is both capital- and land-intensive and is continuously expanding. The social consequences include a rise in unequal land ownership, the displacement and dispossession of small-scale farmers and fewer work opportunities in rural areas. Despite these tendencies, smallholding agriculture – a labour-intensive and often hardly mechanised form of agricultural production – constitutes the central source of subsistence for the majority of the rural population in the Global South. The bulk of foodstuffs worldwide continues to be produced by small-scale farmers in accordance with market conditions and requirements. Continuing commercialisation and the expansion of agro-industrial production complexes aside, small-scale agriculture has consolidated in recent decades. We argue that the 'agrarian question' and associated structural differences must serve as the starting point for an analysis of the effects of digitalisation in agriculture.

For the analysis of the ecological contradictions pertaining to the digitalisation of agriculture, we draw on insights from political ecology.[5] From this perspective, ecological crises in agriculture are not the result of mismanagement, efficiency deficits or a lack of modern technology. Ecological crises are instead considered inherent in the capitalist mode of production and linked to the social relations of power which support them (regarding class, gender and race). Hence, the ecological crisis becomes a question of distribution.

Similar to eco-Marxist considerations concerning the relationship between nature and capital, political ecology assumes that nature possesses certain material properties, that is to say, a specific materiality. The process of capitalist reproduction relies on this materiality. The natural world cannot be infinitely appropriated, technologically subjected or manipulated at will. When this is attempted regardless, the material properties, such as soil fertility or the capacity of plants to absorb CO_2, manifest themselves as ecological crises. Elmar Altvater demonstrated the link between ecological crisis and capitalist reproduction in the late 1980s.[6] His point of departure was the Marxist notion that capitalist production is both a labour and valorisation process, and that both processes are set in tense relation to one another. The purpose of capitalist production consists not in the production of use values, but in the production and realisation of surplus value. Consequently, the capitalist mode of production is in a highly contradictory relationship with the specific properties of nature. This is apparent particularly in capitalist agriculture: no other previous mode of production matches the extent to which it transforms nature (soils, etc.) and the degree to which it develops the productive forces. In material terms, it is utterly dependent on nature and harnesses its special properties (soil fertility, photosynthesis, metabolisms) in order to create new needs and develop new products and technologies to satisfy them. At the same time, it entails an abstraction from these dependencies, that is, it is indifferent vis-à-vis the spatiotemporal and biophysical characteristics of nature.[7]

THE DOMAINS OF DIGITAL AGRICULTURE: HARDWARE, 'SOFTWARE', FINTECH

Current developments indicate three central areas of digital transformation in agriculture: hardware, 'software' and financial technology.

Hardware

The term *hardware* in digital agriculture refers to machines, drones and robots. Machines possess autonomous propulsion technology but are operated by humans despite partly automated processes. Drones are remote-controlled aircraft (or watercraft) without passengers. If they are able to move autonomously, they are classified as robots. The latter are characterised by the fact that they are computer-controlled, or programmed, i.e. that they act without any direct human operation. Some are equipped with Artificial Intelligence (AI) and thus capable of learning.

The deployment of machines in agriculture is, of course, nothing new. Wherever machines are in use, they are usually controlled by humans. In the future, this is to change. World market-leading agricultural machinery manufacturers John Deere (USA), CNH (UK), AGCO (USA) and Kubota (Japan) have already developed autonomous, driverless tractors.[8] They will plough by themselves, decide independently which seed is to be sown when, which fertiliser and pesticide a plant is to be treated with, how much irrigation it needs, and when it is to be harvested. This requires a corresponding infrastructure (large cultivation areas, roads, workshops, petrol stations) as well as suitable crops that are compatible with automated sowing, planting and harvesting; for example, wheat, corn and soy. The harvesting of coffee, bananas or cocoa, then, will likely continue to be performed by hand.

In industrialised agriculture drones are deployed in and on water and in the air. They monitor farmed plants for pest or fungus infestation, produce aerial photos for mapping purposes or conduct plant pollination as roboticised bees. In Japan, one third of rice cultivation is monitored by aerial drones, while cattle farmers in Australia are experimenting with drones to herd their livestock. In Malaysia and Indonesia, drones are used for the surveillance of workers on oil palm plantations. The use of aquatic drones appears particularly promising in deep-sea fishing, where they drive fish into the nets autonomously, or repair and monitor mobile fish cages.[9] Robots are already in use at other stages in the supply chain. They substitute for human labour in produce cultivation (see the example of Iron Ox), assist in the periodic repositioning of beer barrels, package and label vegetable produce, mix cocktails or fry burgers.[10]

The essential aspect of said hardware is that it is equipped with GPS systems and sensor technologies through which it not only receives programmed instructions but also translates all work processes and other relevant information into data. Data on soil conditions and photosynthesis, climate and weather conditions, and on workers' travel and break times are linked up with satellite information, combined to create key indicators and stored on data platforms. They are available to both the agricultural producers and the equipment manufacturers. To the former, they allow for a timely and targeted intervention – say, in the case of infestation, drought or nutrient deficits – and the surveillance of work. The latter receive constant feedback on the performance of their systems and learn how they can optimise them.

'Software'

In contrast to the hardware, consisting of machines, drones and robots, the new digital genetic engineering technologies and synthetic biology (*SynBio*) constitute the so-called software of digital agriculture. While the production of genetically modified seeds in the past required the complicated insertion – with a high error rate – of the genetic sequence of one plant into the genome of another, today genomes can be split into sequences, cut up and recomposed in a targeted manner in what is called computer-based *genome editing.*[11] This way, new plant varieties, which are more resistant against pests, aridity or heat, produce more fruit, contain more oil or develop specific flavours, are created at the click of a mouse. *Genome editing* allows not only for the breeding of plants: disease-resistant pigs or cattle that develop more muscle mass can also be genetically designed. In July 2018, the European Court of Justice decided that these new procedures should be grouped together with conventional methods of genetic engineering. Genetically modified meat or fish products are therefore not yet approved in the EU, but in Canada and the United States the sale of genetically modified salmon is already permitted.[12]

SynBio techniques make it possible to artificially produce food, tissue, scents and flavourings using yeast and algae.[13] This in turn allows for a reduction of both climate-related risks to production and the dependency on labour-intensive production processes, as, for example, in the production of vanilla. The extraction of natural vanilla is based on a labour-intensive process of growing and fermenting the pods of the vanilla plant or wood pulp. In comparison, artificial vanilla flavouring that is almost identical to the original can be produced in a lab using yeast DNA and costing very little.[14] Synthetic food production, however, is not limited to flavourings. The American agribusiness Cargill is investing in the development and marketing of meat cell cultures for burgers. The 'Impossible Burger', which is produced using genetically modified yeast, is already available in US restaurants.[15]

FinTech: transactions via blockchains

A third area of digitalisation that is significant for the entire supply chain is that of financial technologies (*FinTech*), such as cryptocurrencies or blockchains. Blockchains are technical procedures for the swift, network-based handling of trade and financial transactions. They consist of chronologically organised chains of data units, the so-called 'blocks'. Blockchains can be used in multiple ways in agriculture: contracts, seed databases or land registries can all be managed digitally via blockchains. Companies along the agricultural supply chain can use blockchains in order to accelerate the production, processing and transport of certain foods through direct, digital access to consumer data. For example, if a supermarket is running low on soy yoghurt, it can input this information into a blockchain, which then leads, without any further communication, to the soy producer increasing production. The blockchain will ensure that the transport vehicles are available at the right moment to take the soy to the already informed processing plant. As soon as the yoghurt is produced, the trucks are once again on standby to take the product to the respective supermarket. At no point is there any need for direct contact, as quantities, prices and deadlines are all digitally communicated via the blockchain. Blockchains are supposed to lower transaction costs and reduce delivery times and food waste. Such procedures are also interesting for small-scale producers. Using blockchains, subsidies can be directly transferred and products marketed without intermediaries, as long as there is an internet connection and an adequate technical device available.[16]

THE EFFECTS OF DIGITALISATION

The impact of digitalisation on the relations of production in agriculture and the relationship between human society and the natural world can thus far only be discerned to a certain extent. There is some indication of a continuation of the neoliberal structural changes that began in the 1970s on the back of green technology, except that the control of data as a power resource is gaining in importance. As a result, work processes change and concentration processes increase without the ecological contradictions being resolved.

Work and employment relations

One aim of political funding for the digitalisation of agriculture is to create new sources of income and increase prosperity in rural contexts. Indeed, according to the common assumption, automation will likely eliminate jobs, but simultaneously create new, high-skill jobs, too. According to the Food and Agriculture Organization of the United Nations (FAO), half the world's population lives in rural regions and the majority is employed in agriculture,[17] with income diversification increasingly becoming the norm. The rural working class is composed of people who combine different forms of labour in order to secure their livelihood: mostly informal and seasonal labour in agriculture, self-employment in a family-run agricultural business, informal work in the service sector, etc. Apart from the material basis as such, the reproduction options for this group are fragmented by differences along the lines of gender, ethnicity, religion, caste, etc. Opportunities on the already precarious rural labour market are not distributed equally, and increasing digitalisation will not change this either.[18]

One of the central developments in capitalist-organised agriculture, apart from the separation of farmers from the means of production (land, seed, etc.), is the mechanisation and automation of the labour process, i.e. the replacement of human labour by machines. In the past, this was one of the main reasons for the increase in labour productivity in agriculture. Seeing as labour is already highly automated in the Global North, digitalisation will do little to change existing relations here. The situation in the Global South, however, is different. Here, structural change in rural labour markets as a result of further mechanisation is likely. This is evidenced, for example, by the gradual mechanisation of harvesting in the Brazilian sugarcane sector since 2007.[19] The deployment of sugarcane harvesters rendered the work of those who used to secure their income through sugarcane cutting redundant. This particularly affects low-skilled agricultural workers. At the same time, new (albeit few) jobs have been created for drivers, mechanics, etc., which, however, are only rarely performed by those who previously worked as manual labourers in sugarcane harvesting.

Moreover, work processes as such are being altered through digitalisation: those who control the machines are in turn monitored and controlled by them. Drones monitor workers on oil palm plantations; harvesting machines in the sugarcane sector record how much each worker has harvested over which period of time (and how many workers there were), and when (and how often) they took a break or were slower than others. Digitalisation serves, above all, the surveillance, standardisation and acceleration of work, resulting in a reduction of the autonomous action scope of workers worldwide.[20]

Similarly, digitalisation also affects the labour of self-employed small-scale farmers, especially when labour-intensive small-scale production becomes redundant as a result of genetic modification and synthetic production methods. During the 1990s and 2000s, genetic research on rice triggered major protests: Thai jasmine rice accounted for a large share of fragrant rice imported to the United States. Patented genetic modification was to make it possible for this type of rice to be cultivated in the United States. These plans have not been implemented thus far, but could potentially cause 5 million small-scale farmers in Thailand to lose their livelihood if rice cultivation is no longer economically viable.[21]

Concentration processes and dependencies

Another promise of digitalisation includes greater transparency, decentralisation and decreasing costs through efficiency improvements. It is alleged to create a competitive environment that is also open to start-ups and small enterprises. And yet, it is evident that the main beneficiaries from both digital technologies in terms of hardware and the methods of genetic modification and patenting are above all financially strong enterprises and corporations. This is due, on the one hand, to the capital intensity of the technologies and, on the other, to the growing competition for cultivation and consumer data. Agricultural machines with digital technology are expensive and their use is only profitable over a sufficiently large area. Consequently, they are acquired mainly by enterprises and corporations with access to capital and land. Indeed, there are all kinds of assurances that digitalisation will make genetic engineering procedures cheaper and thereby offer small start-ups the possibility to invest in them as well. However, start-ups are frequently bought out by large corporations.[22] Hence, under existing conditions, this apparent competition only leads to further monopolisation and thus the consolidation of existing relations of production.[23]

Furthermore, the competition for access to and control of data increases not only the rivalry among companies within a single sector, but across sectors as well. In the agricultural sector, it is above all cultivation and consumer data that take centre stage in this regard. Internet corporations like Google or Amazon are particularly interested in this Big Data. Such data is gathered mainly by agricultural machines. This, in turn, makes the sector appealing for producers of pesticides and fertilisers, who are able to adjust their products based on the cultivation data. Already today, 80 per cent of worldwide trade in crops is dominated by three corporations; 65 per cent of trade in corn seed is in the hands of only two. Pat Mooney predicts that the three nodes along the agricultural supply chain (inputs, agricultural machinery and food processing) will be controlled by only one or two companies in the future.[24] Specifically, this could mean that the company producing agricultural machine X will decide which of its own seeds will be sown when and which of its own fertilisers and pesticides will be used and at what time. The machine is simply incompatible with the products of other companies, securing the market position of the company that manufactured it. The farmers, then, would be increasingly unable to make their own decisions, as they are forced to use the products from the same company as a complete package.

Blockchains promise decentralised and transparent, tamper-proof dealings in networks because, at least theoretically, all computers in a network – i.e. all those involved: farmers and agriculturalists, agribusinesses, banks, supermarket chains, etc. – can form blocks. This promise, however, is based on the assumption of equally powerful actors within a network. Yet the power across the network is distributed highly unequally: the more computing power, the more influence an actor can exert. Blockchains in agriculture are nothing but the digital assertion of the law of '(computing) might makes right'.[25]

The ecological contradictions of digitalisation: capital and technology versus nature

Finally, digitalisation raises the hopes of increasing efficiency on the fields and thereby guaranteeing a more resource-friendly, sustainable and climate-neutral production. If, in the future, measuring probes report nutrient levels in the soil, this will allow for a more demand-based use of fertiliser. Regular information on fungus or pest infestation levels provided by drones can facilitate the more targeted and selective use of pesticides and herbicides, replacing the blanket spraying that is common today. All this may give us hope that soils will be less over-fertilised and fewer insects will die from pesticides or herbicides. A second argument is that digital technologies will raise yields and productivity, as a natural world that is monitored 'around the clock' can be exploited more efficiently in pursuit of profit maximisation. What both arguments ignore, however, are the social relations and ecological contradictions associated with an agriculture geared towards surplus-value production and the domination of nature.

After all, in capitalism, even a system of digitalised agriculture must grow. The expansion of machine-readable production processes in monocultures displaces not only locally adjusted modes of production focused on biodiversity, but also causes rebound effects.[26] Driven by the compulsion to continue growing, more and more farmland is needed so that it can be worked by the digitally enhanced machines. The development of this land is only possible through the displacement of other forms of use, the transformation of green spaces and wetlands, and deforestation. Given the coupling of hardware and 'software', i.e. machines and genetically modified seeds, fertilisers and pesticides, the increase in cultivated farmland also increases the overall input of nutrients and pesticides, despite any potential reduction thereof per individual land unit.

Up until the 1960s and '70s, capitalist agriculture was marked by enormous productivity increases. The reasons for this were the reduction of production costs through mechanisation and the use of synthetic fertiliser and pesticides. Since the 1980s, crop yields have begun declining in proportion to the use of fertiliser, and the same is true for the ratio between harvest yields and chemicals input. Increasingly heavier tractors and harvesting machines, moreover, increase the compaction of the soil, resulting in lower soil fertility.[27] This shows that even technologically advanced agricultural production relies on nature's capacity for reproduction. Ignoring this fact and instead assuming that a technologically enhanced domination of nature will solve the ecological crisis is precisely what will lead to its intensification.

CONCLUSIONS

In this chapter, we have considered the trajectory of digitalisation in agriculture and the question of what effects on production and society–nature relationships can be expected. Digital technologies will not fundamentally change the dominant relations of production in agriculture. Instead, we should expect an aggravation of existing structural inequalities and ecological contradictions. This is where the starting points for political intervention lie.

Technological changes in hardware, 'software' and finance make technologies and mass data available to agribusinesses, which will change existing capitalist-industrial agriculture. The industry will get by with (even) less human labour power and will further regulate labour and labour processes through close surveillance. This creates uncertainty among the remaining labour forces. Digitalisation will see the obstacles for industrial action grow in size rather than shrink.

Digitalisation promises an enhanced domination of nature with the aim of increasing productivity and processing the ecological consequences of an exploitative agriculture. This may be possible in a spatially confined context, for only some people and for a limited period of time, but the impact will be the suppression and externalisation of ecological consequences.[28] In a world of digital agriculture, the future will see fewer of those who are part of the rural working class – including small-scale farmers – able to find work in a rural context, while more will increasingly be affected by the ecological consequences of climate change, groundwater pollution, species extinction, etc. That said, small-scale agriculture will not disappear from the rural space, but will most likely face more difficult reproduction conditions. Instead of contributing to a general rise in prosperity, then, digitalisation will amplify inequalities in the rural world. A differentiated analysis indicates that digitalisation actually serves the continuation of a redistribution from the bottom to the top. Without a radical transformation of existing structural conditions – that is, property and ownership relations – only the propertied classes and a few skilled workers will benefit. Ultimately, even a dig-italised capitalist agriculture, as a valorisation process, undermines, in the medium term, precisely those social-ecological preconditions on which it relies as a labour process. This contradiction can only be resolved socially, not technologically.

SynBio techniques are supposed to revolutionise the essence of food. Synthetically produced meat or drought-resistant plant seeds produced by digital databases, however, not only raise old questions about the ethical treatment of and interference with life as such. They also provide a host of opportunities for new patents and thus the control of knowledge, resulting in additional new dependencies. Added to this, the industrial cultivation of genetically modified plants entails a reduction in biodiversity, and less diversity means that mistakes have far greater repercussions. The resulting lack of biodiversity undermines local adjustment to climate change.

Progressing digitalisation fosters the competition between companies in various sectors for access to and control over data. Instead of a democratisation and decentralisation of production through new platform and blockchain technologies, the outcome is the formation of monopolies and a concentration of power. Corporate mergers such as that of Bayer and Monsanto are just one example of the currently ongoing merger mania in the agricultural sector; even internet giants such as Google and Amazon hope to profit from the control of data and are buying up start-ups or smaller companies. Increasingly fewer companies thus control the production of an ever-growing amount of food in more and more segments of the agricultural supply chain. That way, they control what we eat and how that food is produced.

As a result, these corporations also have the most power over cultivation and consumer data. Given their objective of increasing their own profit, here are the most important starting points for political intervention: a first important step would be to stop concentration processes and regulate the ongoing cross-sector mergers. More fundamentally, the task is to socialise access to and control over data. What is needed are collective decisions about which data is collected and by whom, how it is evaluated and what it is used for. Openly disclosed algorithms, moreover, help people make sense of machine information and, in case of doubt, make informed decisions of their own. There are already numerous examples today that show how small-scale farmers or cooperatives can increase their income or receive subsidies by drawing on network-based communication, production and trade.

III

Digital Work and Networked Production

10

Networked Technology and Production Networks

Digitalisation and the reorganisation of global value chains

Florian Butollo

An analysis of the permanent revolutionising of productive forces building on Marx' writings must today take into account the fact that production networks are fragmented. Rationalisation is not occurring at the individual company level alone, say, through the deployment of machines in order to increase productivity. Rather, it is focused on achieving an optimal interlocking of functionally and spatially separated production processes in the sense of 'systemic rationalisation'.[1] Leading brand-name enterprises not only exploit global inequalities by offshoring production to low-wage countries; they also take advantage of a hierarchical integration of supply chains: broadly speaking, the produced surplus value is realised according to the power resources of the involved businesses, especially their capacity to control innovation processes and the sale of end products.[2]

The bundle of applications subsumed under the term 'digitalisation', particularly digital process management via the Internet of Things (IoT) and novel processes of automated data analysis, is eminently impacting the relationships between economic actors, that is, the structure and the geography of global value creation. In the following, I examine this link between networked technologies and production networks. Surprisingly, this is hardly ever the case in the media and academic discourses on the digitalisation of industries, which rarely address the transnational interlinkage of globalised production and the inequalities inscribed therein. Industry 4.0 is a decidedly national project, consciously building on the 'German virtues' of diversified high-quality production. More recently, this has been carried to extremes with the label 'AI made in Germany', the quintessence of the competitive German Artificial Intelligence (AI) strategy. This national focus constitutes an anachronism in an era of global production networks and an internationally operating and cooperating research community (especially in the area of AI). It corresponds to the rationale of preserving or expanding national competitiveness through technology leadership, while neglecting a systematic discussion about the impact of the current phase of digitalisation on global production networks. Although it is postulated that Industry 4.0[3] indeed impacts the 'entire value chain',[4] networked production seems to take place only on the solid shop floor of the individual enterprise, namely in the form of concrete artefacts such as tablets or Smart Glasses.

In the following, some theoretical considerations will be presented with reference to a number of empirical cases, exploring the impact of said bundle of new technologies on the geography and structure of value creation. The discussion shows that the expectation of a *reshoring* of automated industrial manufacturing to so-called high-wage countries is rather one-sided, as it ignores the fact that the combination of e-commerce platforms and a data-based optimisation of logistics networks entails precisely the opposite effect, namely the geographic fragmentation of manufacturing processes. As is demonstrated in the second section of this chapter, structural changes can rather be expected as a result of the establishment of the *industrial internet* (IIoT) platforms,[5] which introduce and consolidate elements of platform capitalism[6] in the industrial domain. One possible outcome of this is the increased significance of user data in digital-hybrid manufacturing processes, expressed by the race to centralise and operationalise data.

THERE'S NO GOING BACK FOR GLOBALISED MANUFACTURING

The Adidas Speedfactory in Ansbach, Bavaria, is a factory producing sports footwear.[7] It is also producing a narrative, which is expressed in the company's advertising imagery, boasting scenes of fully automated shoe production shrouded in momentous-seeming clouds of steam. The Speedfactory's message is that sports shoes are once again being produced in Germany: a model for the future. This counter-narrative to the company's actual practice – the factory in Ansbach produces around 500,000 pairs of trainers per year, while those in Asia account for roughly 400 million pairs – is gladly adopted by the press and politicians alike for its welcome message: German-based production can once again be profitable! The fear of job cuts as a result of offshoring is a thing of the past![8]

This myth rests on two claims: *firstly*, that the labour cost differential between so-called high-wage and developing countries is becoming increasingly irrelevant because automation has advanced to a point where wage costs no longer constitute a pertinent factor. *Secondly*, that production in direct proximity to end customers in volatile and increasingly differentiated markets is advantageous. It can thus be concluded, so the argument goes, that the regional integration of production and target markets is once again profitable – and the days of global sourcing are numbered.

However, the effects of automation are being misinterpreted. Firstly, the *reshoring* argument underestimates the persisting obstacles to automation, which continue to render full automation of production unrealistic for the foreseeable future.[9] Indeed, an increase in the organic composition of capital, i.e. a predominance of the expenses for investment goods in relation to the entire wage bill, does diminish the relevance of the labour cost differential, but significant cost differentials with regard to the availability of land and the up- and downstream production activities remain nonetheless. Furthermore, production cost reduction through automation does not lead to the results assumed by proponents of the reshoring thesis. On the contrary, given the cost reduction of automation equipment through advancements in the processing capacity of semiconductors, investment in automation is becoming profitable even in those locations in which the production regime was hitherto marked by the seemingly infinite availability of cheap labour. China is currently undergoing such a rapid process of 'catch-up automation',[10] while leading car manufacturers in Eastern Europe today operate at the same level of automation as plants in Germany – although wage costs are still markedly below the German standard.[11] The result of this blend of high tech and low wages is an increased productivity of production units in emerging countries – and thus a continuous pressure to relocate from so-called high-wage countries to areas with a cheaper cost structure. There is certainly no mass exodus of major shoe or textile producers from China towards Europe or the United States.

The argument emphasising the advantages of regionally integrated production resulting from the proximity to end customers is equally one-sided. The closeness to customer markets has always been an essential motive for the globalisation of production, and, given the growth of consumer markets in major emerging economies, is gaining additional importance. After all, Volkswagen's investment in nine new plants in China does not reflect a strategy of producing cars for the European market, but is intended to serve the Chinese market and thus reduce transport costs, counter uncertainties regarding protectionist measures and allow for a more flexible response in product development and product mix to specific preferences in the respective markets. Investment strategies along the lines of the '*produce where you sell*'[12] paradigm in this sense offer competitive advantages vis-à-vis pure importers who not only have greater transport costs, but are usually less able to accommodate the target markets' demand profiles.

That said, for a number of reasons these advantages must not be understood as a universal law that forecloses options for global sourcing. The first question is, quite generally, to what degree does the differentiation of markets really require a company's quick responsiveness and make the geographic proximity to end consumers an absolute necessity. This is being suggested in the context of the Industry 4.0 concept that declares 'batch size 1' – that is, customised production according to customer preferences – the universal principle of a new 'stage' of industrial production. According to this interpretation, companies need to *react* as customers increasingly demand customised products that exactly fit their individual needs. Yet, approaches like the widely publicised Speedfactory reveal the aspiration of enterprises to *create* precisely such demand among consumers. In this sense, hidden behind the promise of growth associated with Industry 4.0, we find an attempt by industry to pursue new sales strategies – the success of which is rather questionable given stagnant consumer demand and increasing social inequality.

But even assuming – beyond the exaggerations of the 'batch size 1' paradigm – increasingly differentiated and short-term oriented markets, their servicing does not necessarily require production in direct customer proximity. One reason for this is that many complex products, such as cars or IT hardware, can be assembled from standardised components that are configured according to customers' preferences. These components are sourced from a network of suppliers who need not necessarily be located near the end customer and whose products are not customised but standardised. For example, who needs a customised wiper motor or cylinder head in their car – parts that no one ever sees? While the advantages of a local clustering of a supply chain in one area are certainly given in the car industry, the IT industry remains the prime example of global production and *global sourcing*. In both industries, at least for the time being, the combination of automation and the potential advantages of market proximity is hardly leading to any significant changes in the spatial manufacturing structure.

This consistency is also related to an important counter-tendency to the regional integration of markets and manufacturing: the e-commerce/logistics nexus. The example of Amazon illustrates this: the company can deliver products to customers so quickly because it is able, based on consumer data, to anticipate future orders. Correspondingly, goods are stocked in sufficient volumes at local warehouses from where they can be delivered at short notice. The 'annihilation of space by time',[13] which Marx describes as a tendency intrinsic to capitalism in the *Grundrisse*, is the object of rationalisation strategies in the logistics sector, strategies which are, in turn, additionally perpetuated as a result of new possibilities for data transparency in the context of the IoT, options that are mostly realised through data centralisation via online platforms. The case of Amazon underscores the idea that *global sourcing* and the objective of quick responsiveness to differentiated consumer demand do not contradict one another, but can be mediated via the e-commerce/logistics nexus.

Although there are considerable differences between online retailers serving private customers and the *supply-chain management* of major companies, some elements of the described logics also apply to the supply chain. Since the early 2000s, contract manufacturers in the electronics industry such as Foxconn and Flextronics, who produce consumer electronics products for major brand-name companies in the IT industry, have set up hubs for the configuration of products in proximity to target markets, while actual manufacturing takes place in Asia. The secret to their success lies not only in the combination of high tech and low wages, but also in their sophisticated logistics networks which minimise storage costs thanks to data monitoring and increasingly sophisticated predictive analysis. Generally, the logistics sector serves as an experimental ground for new forms of automation and process innovation it is hoped will further reduce transport costs.

Depending on the respective product and manufacturing logic, instances of the geographic integration of consumer markets and manufacturing capacities contrast with instances of renewed geographic fragmentation. A de-globalisation tendency intrinsic to digitalised capitalism, which is insinuated in the context of the reshoring debate, cannot be confirmed.

DATA, THE *INDUSTRIAL INTERNET* AND PLATFORMS

One noticeable effect on competitive relationships in digitalised capitalism seems to emanate from the development of innovation and business models based on the generation, processing and evaluation of data. The appropriation of private user data as a new type of raw material[14] constitutes the foundation of the rise of leading tech companies such as Google and Facebook and their Chinese counterparts Alibaba and Tencent. The organisational form of the platform is appropriate for these business models because it combines practical use value for users and the function of generating and centralising data about their user behaviour. The purpose of the latter is ultimately the sale of user data to third parties, in the sense that they, as major advertising agencies, provide their customers with the means to develop personalised ads.

160

What is interesting with regard to the impact the current techno-logical advances are having on the structures of global value creation is the extent to which certain elements of this operational approach are also influencing the industrial domain – and this is precisely the intersection at which a race for new business models and applications has ensued, captured in the buzzwords *industrial internet* and *IoT platforms*. As was the case in past phases of socio-technical change, or technical-organisational innovation, it constitutes an open-ended competitive process that results in the redistribution of value between old and new actors.

The platform principle is not necessarily new in the industrial sector. Company software such as SAP or Oracle has become almost indispensable since the early 2000s and testifies to the consider-able significance data-based processes have acquired in recent years. Similarly, Siemens has long been selling management software for industrial enterprises comparable to operating systems for the indus-trial sector. Here, too, there is the danger of mystification, an element that has come to characterise the digitalisation debate more generally: the novelty of developments is exaggerated because continuities are being overlooked. On the other hand, the level of data integration is significantly higher due to the increased capacity of processors (and sensors), the availability of huge datasets, and efforts to standardise the interfaces between various layers of enterprise data. Prospec-tively, the Internet of Things will allow for the comprehensive digital monitoring of material processes in order to optimise them. Such applications and the associated platforms are currently being devel-oped for industrial use, a process in which both classic industrial enterprises (Siemens, Bosch, Trumpf) and data specialists (SAP and, in China, Alibaba in particular) are competing for market shares.

The field is experiencing considerable competitive dynamics with new market entries, significant failures and the partial success of a diverse set of players because the evaluation of application data potentially represents a considerable source of product and process innovation. The more data are available on consumer preferences, user habits, purchasing behaviour, but also capacity utilisation and procedures in manufacturing, the better these points of intersec-tion can be optimised. The all-encompassing collection of data thus becomes a factor in innovation-driven competitive relationships. These data constitute the essential raw material for the development of so-called Artificial Intelligence applications, as new approaches to *machine learning* are based above all on the analysis of Big Data. In the following, some applications of such platforms and their potential impact on the structure of value creation are discussed.

IOT platforms for process optimisation

The platforms of leading industrial equipment manufacturers, such as Siemens, Bosch and Trumpf, aim especially at the monitoring and evaluation of manufacturing data which can be used for the opti- misation of individual processes. One specific example is so-called *predictive maintenance*, which, based on a broad set of process data, allows the maintenance and repair works required in indus- trial facilities to be predicted. This helps reduce the likelihood of process interruptions and streamline the work process of mainte- nance workers. While, in the past, the latter only came into action in case of a malfunction, now maintenance and repair works can be planned regularly and with foresight. This area may entail a polarisa- tion between higher- and lower-skilled tasks: operative maintenance could be reduced to a routine component exchange, whereas data analysis by IT specialists involves additional skill requirements.

The field of maintenance, however, is only one example of process optimisation on the basis of Big Data. The monitoring of data on material properties, manufacturing problems or production flows carries the scientification of production, as mentioned by Marx in the *Grundrisse*,[15] to new extremes. Workers encounter the produc- tion process as an objective entity to which they have to adjust, and this entity is increasingly intertwined with sales figures in 'real-time' and the data-based predictions about further market development.

Given that this entire organism is supposed to respond to markets in a variable and flexible manner at all times, the skill requirements for workers, who are to keep up with this permanent change, rise continuously. Simple deskilling is thus unlikely, and, in the work- place context, a subtle pressure to undergo advanced training seems more likely: only those who constantly optimise themselves and keep up with the most recent technological trends will find permanent employment among the well-paid core workforce. At the same time, however, the supply of skilled professionals in Germany is decreasing. Companies react to this with the deployment of digital assistance systems designed to allow less skilled workers to meet the requirements of the productive organism. These technologies can be interpreted as an attempt to accommodate the increase in flexibility requirements without comprehensively upskilling the entire workforce. The permanent need to train and retrain the workforce on the one hand and deskilling through assistance systems on the other constitute conflicting tendencies: skilled labour in the core industrial sectors is being upgraded, but in other sectors – say, in the warehouses of major logistics firms in industry or at suppliers of standardised goods – the employment of a large, low-skilled workforce is increasingly common.

The 'smart factory as a service'

The data-based optimisation of the production process as a whole allows the process itself to be turned into a commodity. This approach is pursued through business models which provide production capacities to other companies – which may pertain to the entire manufacturing process of a product or individual production steps. The commodification of the process as a whole takes place, for example, via the model of the '*smart factory as a service*', which robot manufacturer Kuka, in cooperation with Porsche subsidiary MHP and the reinsurance company Munich Re Group, is seeking to establish. This consortium promises its customers the prospect of taking charge of the entire manufacturing process while guaranteeing compliance with requirements regarding quality, flexibility and diversity. This business model thus replicates the logic of contract manufacturing, symbolised by the division of labour between Apple and Foxconn in the electronics industry, but extends it to areas of diversified high-quality production such as the car industry. Such models are based on the conviction that the value creation of the future will rest above all on the mastering of innovation and marketing, whereas process optimisation and manufacturing in the narrower sense can be outsourced to specialised contract manufacturers. According to this vision, the model is now viable in more complex areas of manufacturing because permanent process optimisation and adjustment can today be ensured via IoT platforms. Should deviations from the promised target occur regardless, any losses are recouped by the Munich Re Group.

In the electronics industry, this separation of brand-name companies and contract manufacturers has led to a drastic polarisation of the supply chain between highly profitable tech companies on one side and contract manufacturers on the other. The business models of the latter are based on the 'optimisation' of global manufacturing processes, taking advantage of the labour cost differential and ethnic and gender inequalities.[16] It is far from certain that business models such as the 'smart factory as a service' – should they prove successful in the first place – would have the same effects. This is all the more true considering the major differences in the nature of manufacturing and the respective skill requirements. Such approaches, however, do raise the question of which companies can actually achieve market leadership in the future. Ambitious pursuits like the widely discussed announcement by Google that it will build its own cars, based on its competence in the area of driverless vehicles, then, would become more realistic if there are manufacturing specialists in place who offer their services. A further redistribution of the realised surplus value from manufacturing to areas of product innovation and distribution also appears likely.

Product-related platforms as an expansion of e-commerce

And yet, there is also that counteracting tendency to such a separation between manufacturing and distribution through a blending of models known from e-commerce and manufacturing. This may be driven by producers, i.e. by traditional industrial companies, or by e-commerce enterprises that increasingly move into manufacturing.

The stylised image of the Industry 4.0 factory corresponds to the first variant: customers can configure their products via the online platform, and products are subsequently produced according to their preferences. Such a model presupposes above all, on the part of man-ufacturing, sophisticated lean production models that ensure the coordination of market requirements and manufacturing processes via the fine-tuned control of operations. Effectively, this is not an Industrial Revolution, but a consecutive refinement of the produc-tion models of the 1990s and 2000s, whose strategic goal has always been the reconciliation of the conflicting objectives of high efficiency through *economies of scale*, and the dynamic adjustment to market demand through flexible (but costly) adjustments of the manufac-turing process.[17] In the car industry, business models that flexibly adjust production without major losses in efficiency have already been established, and other industries, such as the Chinese house-hold appliances industry, are also experimenting with such business models.

These variants of manufacturing according to the principle of 'batch size 1', however, contrast with network-based approaches that do not rest on the high-tech enhanced individual plant, but on the flexibility of the network. With its platform *Taogongchang*, Alibaba is pursuing an approach in which the principles of e-commerce are being transferred to manufacturing. The outcome is a giant net-worked factory composed of tens of thousands of micro-producers. Customers go online to select appropriate suppliers with whom they can place their specialised orders, which can be supplied even in very small quantities. Alibaba is thus returning to its original core com-petence, namely the brokering of orders between buyers and a vast network of Chinese producers. These functions, however, are com-plemented by Big Data analyses that facilitate anticipatory capacity planning. The consumer data of the present allows the needs of the future to be assessed, which helps companies plan their product range and capacity utilisation.

This production and distribution model manages without high-tech capabilities on the part of producers. In what is termed 'Taobao villages', hundreds of small-scale producers with modest technolog-ical equipment process the online customers' orders. This allows Alibaba to 'update' small-scale Chinese manufacturing in line with the 'batch size 1' principle, thereby conserving it. It is a mistake to assume that production in the digital age will mainly follow the path of high-tech manufacturing along the lines of Industry 4.0. Rather, the Chinese path illustrates the bandwidth of online-to-offline business models which, from a manufacturing point of view, are by all means compatible with low-tech production and cheap labour.

DATA-DRIVEN RATIONALISATION
IN THE TWENTY-FIRST CENTURY

The diverse approaches to the reorganisation of value creation via digital technologies suggest that, for one, the notions of a new stage of industrial production, as propagated in the context of the debate around 'Industry 4.0', are one-sided. The objective of an extremely versatile individual factory, capable of a flexible and quick response to individual customer preferences, consciously builds on the strengths of diversified high-quality production in Germany. However, it neglects the competing approaches of a digital production driven by e-commerce or networks, perhaps not least because Germany has thus far been lacking adequate players to pursue such pathways. Consequently, the discussion in the context of Industry 4.0 programmes about the restructuring of value chains in Germany is often reduced to the individual company-level role of the Smart Factory, while the far more important question of the redistribution and reallocation of the realised surplus value in production networks and their indirect consequences for workers is left unconsidered.

A realistic assessment of current developments is not easy, as it is impossible to determine which approaches will prevail in the ongoing competitive search process. Moreover, the pursued solutions vary depending on the respective sector, product and state of technology. One common denominator that has crystallised, then, is the integration of customer data and manufacturing processes, on the one hand, and the gathering and optimisation of production-related data on the other. The organisational principle of the platform seems to promise solutions for both requirements, which is why the race for the establishment of industrial internet platforms has ensued. For the time being, it remains difficult to say whether this will entail a similar concentration process as in the area of online shopping or social media platforms. One indication to the contrary is that data generation requires a far greater effort at the level of creating infra-structure (installation of sensors, etc.) and that the applications are more specific, that is to say, they leave room for various providers with differentiated fields of operation.

Nevertheless, industrial internet platforms will probably assume a more dominant role in value chains because the data they centralise play an important role in the control of production processes. Leading companies in both industry and data analysis are currently competing for a dominant position and at times forge strategic alliances.

With regard to the structures and geography of value creation, the question that matters most is whether immaterial processes of product development and marketing will be further decoupled from manufacturing in the narrower sense, which in turn will absorb a smaller share of surplus-value realisation. This tendency was virulent over the past years, for example, in the IT and garment industries, while it was not as prevalent in the automotive industry. The significance of this question is ultimately whether manufacturing will be affected by a similar kind of devaluation as was the case in IT hardware production, and whether it will lead to a similar devaluation of labour.

Concerning the geography of production networks, the trend towards a stronger integration of customer data and manufacturing processes may by all means facilitate tendencies towards a stronger regional integration, as production will most likely respond far more strongly to the preferences of local customers than in the past. Considering the reasons stated in the second section of this chapter, however, a reshoring of manufacturing appears unlikely. What seems to be more probable, then, is a kind of *near-shoring*, i.e. moving production for European markets to Eastern Europe, or production for the United States to Mexico. That said, the effect of the counteracting tendency of anticipatory and increasingly efficient logistics networks is that a stronger regional integration need by no means necessarily contradict a continuation of *global sourcing*.

When construing the new technologies as a (big) step towards perfecting flexible global manufacturing processes, as attempted in this chapter, the theoretically intriguing question arises as to whether misallocations and thus overproduction crises can be avoided by an increase in the adaptability of capital in the future. Responsive production in accordance with the notion of 'batch size 1' may even be interpreted as the realisation of a cybernetically supported, needs-oriented form of planning which is able to avoid the rigidity of bureaucratic economic planning.

As Simon Schaupp and Georg Jochum elaborate in this volume, this is certainly possible – at least in the sense of a theoretically conceivable potential. Yet it is improbable that this potential will be realised as long as production and distribution processes are organised in a competitive manner and exposed to the dynamic of increasing financialisation. In contrast to the hope for a more balanced and sustainable economic development, evidence of renewed speculative exaggerations, overinvestment (as is currently the case, e.g. in robotics) and a race among the geo-strategic blocs is growing. One clear indicator of this is that these days the discourse concerning technological developments only seems possible in hype cycles.

11

Computerisation: Software and the Democratisation of Work as Productive Power

Nadine Müller

The productivity-enhancing effect of industrial cooperation and the division of labour, which includes the separation of intellectual and manual labour and the contradistinction between management and task execution, is being lost in the process of computerisation. Yet current conditions are preventing a new form of cooperation from developing and thus the *productivity* of computerisation from being unleashed; instead, compromises in work organisation are being implemented that are marked by contradictions and have a negative impact on the *quality of working conditions*. Labour is becoming precarious and being intensified, while the possibilities for workers' self-organisation and democratic participation are only very limited.[1]

FROM INDUSTRIAL CAPITALISM TO COMPUTERISATION

When considering the genesis of industrial capitalism, Marx describes the significance of cooperation and the division of labour for productive power. While feudalism was marked by a low level of division of labour and the main form of property was landed property,[2] *capitalist* private property entails the emergence of more sophisticated forms of the division of labour and cooperation. Only the concentration of the means of labour, the machines in the factory in the form of individual capitals, made a certain mode of cooperation and division of labour possible on which the development of the social productivity of labour rests. He explicates this productive function of capital in the following passage:

> We showed in Part IV [on the production of relative surplus value] how the development of the social productivity of labour presupposes co-operation on a large scale; how the division and combination of labour can only be organized on that basis, and the means of production *economized by concentration on a vast scale; how instruments of labour which, by their very nature, can only be used in common, such as systems of machinery,* can be called into existence; how gigantic natural forces can be pressed into the service of production; and how the production process can be transformed into a process of the technological application of scientific knowledge. When the prevailing system is the production of commodities, i.e. where the means of production are the property of private persons and the artisan therefore either produces commodities in isolation and independently of other people, or sells his labour-power as a commodity because he lacks the means to produce independently, *the above-mentioned presupposition, namely co-operation on a large scale, can be realized only through the increase of individual capitals, only in proportion as the social means of production and subsistence are transformed into the private property of capitalists.*[3]

At the same time, private ownership of the means of production is the precondition for exploitation, that is, the appropriation of alien surplus labour,[4] and entails the separation of management from actual task execution. This double-sidedness of economisation on the one hand, and exploitation on the other, characterises capitalist productivity: the manufacturing of goods is productive in capitalism when it achieves a profit. Hence, it is not necessarily more productive, or more profitable, when the labour time necessary for goods production is shortened; in fact, the opposite can be the case. 'Here, as everywhere else, we must distinguish between the increased productivity which is due to the development of the social process of production, and that which is due to the exploitation by the capitalists of that development.'[5]

On the one hand, then, the capitalist production of goods implies the aspect of exploitation, or rather the increase in the rate of exploitation as the cause of increased profits or productivity. On the other hand, there is the aspect of general-social productivity: the shortening of labour time necessary for production through technological progress, mainly by the improvement of machine systems in industry.[6]

It is evident that whenever it costs as much labour to produce a machine as is saved by the employment of that machine, all that has taken place is a displacement of labour. Consequently, the total labour required to produce a commodity has not been lessened, in other words, the productivity of labour has not been increased. However, the difference between the labour a machine costs and the labour it saves, in other words the degree of productivity the machine possesses, does not depend on the difference between its own value and the value of the tool it replaces. [...] The productivity of the machine is therefore measured by the human labour-power it replaces.[7]

In contrast to this industrial-capitalist cooperation and productivity, the process of computerisation leads to a fundamental transformation of the central means of labour, namely technology, and to the development of a corresponding organisation of work, particularly in the sense of division of labour and cooperation, which pertain to the aspect of 'general-social productivity'. Productivity is principally determined by the means of production (object of labour and means of labour), especially by the given *technical state of the means of labour*, as well as by labour power and, in the context thereof, particularly by the *state of the division of labour and cooperation*. In this chapter, I intend to demonstrate how the productivity-enhancing effect of industrial cooperation and labour division – the separation of intellectual and manual labour – is increasingly being lost. Proceeding from that insight, it shall be discussed how neoliberal relations will sustain the separation of management and task-performing functions nonetheless, and what consequences this may have for the labour market and the quality of working conditions.

Given that a new, complex form of cooperation cannot fully develop, the process of computerisation leads to productivity deficits.

COMPUTERISATION AS A SHIFT IN DOMINANCE

Computerisation is marked by a transformation of the dominant *means of production* and the *organisation of work* (particularly the shape of the division of labour, cooperation and ownership). In the process of computerisation, a shift in dominance[8] is taking place from physical labour with machines – as the central means of labour, or work tools, in industry – to creative, intellectual tasks assisted above all by software.

Software as the dominant means of production

From the mid-1970s onwards, microelectronics – the application and development of which rely on software – led to the automation particularly of a large number of mainly physical routine tasks in industrialised nations. While the monitoring and control of machine production required only few workers, the number of *employees* rose – above all in the *programming* of numerically controlled (NC) machines, in *research and development* and in the area of scheduling.[9] In the 1980s, Burghardt noted that mechanics were increasingly being replaced by software, while the bulk of costs shifted from manufacturing to development.[10] The focus of development efforts moved from hardware to software.[11] New software concepts allowed for 'personal computing'.[12] That was one reason why software expanded beyond manufacturing and into other increasingly important services and areas of production. In the 1990s, Hirsch-Kreinsen and Seitz noted that the key role mechanical engineering played in industrial development had now shifted to information and communication technology (ICT).[13]

After the 2008 economic crisis, the ICT industry managed to considerably increase its gross value production to a total of approximately €89 billion by 2013 in Germany. Its contribution to commercial value creation thus stood at 4.7 per cent and was on a par with car manufacturing, ranking even higher than mechanical engineering. At 91 per cent, ICT service providers accounted for the bulk of the entire ICT industry's gross value creation in 2013.[14] According to a forecast by the business federation of the German digital economy (Bitkom), the software business in particular is in the ascendant, as it has been over previous years, rising by 5.5 per cent to €20.2 billion.

The development of technology is also marked by the increasing relevance of software, as (both automatic and semi-automatic) robots are also controlled via computer programs: 'In 2018, almost one in six enterprises (16%) with 10 or more persons employed in the manufacturing sector in Germany uses industrial or service robots. [...] Industrial robots are used, for example, for welding, laser cutting and special paintwork. Service robots are used for controlling, transport or cleaning.'[15] The manufacturing sector still employs around 17 per cent of German wage earners, while the service sector today accounts for about three quarters of all jobs.[16] In 2018, Germany had a total labour force of around 44.7 million people.[17] In the same year, some 7.7 million people were employed in the manufacturing industry, whereas 33.4 million worked in services.[18]

In the service sector, some 83 per cent of surveyed workers stated that their work was being affected by digitalisation; 63 per cent of respondents even claimed the impact was significant or very significant. 'Digitalisation has been introduced most comprehensively in legal and tax consultancy (97.7%), IT services (96.1%) and insurances (95%). By contrast, the degree of digitalisation is currently the lowest in the areas of facility management, landscaping and gardening (41.7%), and second lowest in social services (67.3%).'[19] Only 16 per cent of respondents work with computer-controlled machines or robots in their jobs, with those working in the health sector ranking highest at 29 per cent. In the service sector, electronic communication devices are the most widespread at 72 per cent, followed by electronic device-assisted work (55%) and software-controlled work processes such as route and schedule planning (50%).[20]

Work organisation: the requirements of computerisation

As software is emerging as the new dominant means of production, the organisation of work, especially the division of labour and cooperation, are being transformed. This is the second crucial aspect of computerisation. As illustrated above, its duality must be taken into consideration when it comes to productivity. Consequently, the changes in the organisation of work are analysed at two distinct levels here: firstly, the *requirements for work* are considered, which, according to the Project Automation and Qualification (PAQ), represents an analytical approach. They include that 'which would ideally have to occur for the new technology to be used to its full potential'.[21] Only at the second level of analysis is the *practical fulfilment* of these requirements in the process of computerisation considered. This method of 'contradiction analysis' focuses on problems of work in their most advanced state, not least in order to explore the potential scope for emancipation contained in these problems (or rather in the solution thereof).[22] Here the requirements of computerised work are summarised in four essential dimensions: (a) skills, (b) planning, (c) division of labour and (d) cooperation.

(a) As a result of the rationalisation of the bulk of routine tasks and the higher skill level of workers on average – i.e. software skills are on the rise as a share of overall skills – *creative work* assumes central importance. Creative work is becoming more prevalent in the process of computerisation because innovative tasks are growing in significance compared to routine tasks – the latter of which can be more easily replaced by software. According to Baukrowitz and Boes, there is in fact a parallelisation of innovation and work process.[23] A survey conducted by PricewaterhouseCoopers (PwC) found that 83 per cent of surveyed companies considered innovation to be important or indispensable when seeking to assert themselves in the global competition.[24] In a survey conducted by the German service union ver.di, more than three quarters of responding works council, staff council and supervisory committee members agreed with the statement that digitalisation increases the need for innovation – i.e. introducing ever-more innovations in ever-shorter time spans.[25]

The rise in the proportion of creative, innovative activities carried out as part of computerised work means that the latter increasingly involves shaping the world of work and life in a technical as well as political, social, organisational and cultural sense: decisions are made about how sociality is to be formalised in computer programs.[26] The creative labour process, in turn, cannot fully be structured 'from above' by software or planning. Decisions must also be made about social relations which *cannot be formalised*. Correspondingly, the skills of workers increasingly comprise not only technical skills but also social and economic knowledge, including so-called soft skills, such as the ability to work in a team.

In the service sector, about three quarters of all jobs are marked above all by 'interactive work', with requirements ranging from cooperation and emotional work to 'subjectivising work activities'.[27] That is to say that those employed in the services industry work with individuals and therefore not all aspects of their work processes are predictable. That is why they have to cope with uncertainties and imponderables by proceeding in an explorative, dialogue-based manner, e.g. using all their senses, forming empathetic relationships, etc. This indeterminate dimension of service work requires creativity, which is why it has been examined – with the aim of professionalisation – along the same lines as 'artistic activities'.[28]

The *independence* of workers increases along with their new skills, which in turn leads to a heightened self-initiative on their part. One example of this is self-organised evaluations of projects after completion. The emergence of creative skills in the process of computerisation represents the first argument for the necessity of an increased participation of workers in decision-making processes and a greater degree of self-organisation.

(b) Due to its increasingly creative character, computerised work cannot be fully subdivided and planned like manual operations on a machine. Work in (software) development and in most services[29] is, to a large extent, unpredictable, not least because of new developments and difficulties concerning specific work processes. In software development, in particular, technical and customer requirements change constantly and designated plans are often outdated within very short time periods. That is why management frequently resorts to planning horizons and estimation procedures. Estimates of staff costs are included in planning; developers increasingly conduct estimations and planning of their own. Only intensive cooperation between all those involved in a software development project allows for flexible responses to unpredictable factors and the constant incorporation of process improvements. This is one reason why workers are increasingly not waiting on instruction from management but taking the initiative and exploring other, better practices and agile methods which are gaining in popularity and emphasise individual abilities and the self-organisation of teams.[30] The process of computerisation makes *cooperative planning* necessary. This is another indicator of a growing need for workers' self-organisation.

(c) Alongside the proliferation of computerisation, the *specialisation of skills* emerges as a new dominant form of the division of labour, differing significantly from the subdivision of labour tasks common in industry. This specialisation of increasingly innovative, creative and complex work is occurring both inside and outside of the newly formed professional field of computer science and IT, in software development and beyond. What is required are skills in development – including different programming methods and coding languages – and in software application, often referred to as IT or media skills. Moreover, additional special knowledge is required, for not all tasks can be performed via software, and often enough it is only the respective contextual knowledge that allows for an adequate development and application of programs. Brynjolfsson and McAfee predict a rise in demand for highly skilled workers and a simultaneous decline in simple tasks:

> As we'll demonstrate, there's never been a better time to be a worker with special skills or the right education, because these people can use technology to create and capture value. However, there's never been a worse time to be a worker with only 'ordinary' skills and abilities to offer, because computers, robots, and other digital technologies are acquiring these skills and abilities at an extraordinary rate.[31]

The proliferation of this form of specialisation and the increasing responsibility that it entails is leading to a general *individualisation* of workers, which will make the individual more indispensable in the future: empirical studies show that, for example, the work of a developer cannot be entirely standardised by a predefined process, which in turn means that they cannot be replaced at will.[32] Said specialisation is characterised by increasingly long theoretical and practical training periods as well as work experience, which is seen as an essential element of personal development. The knowledge (including implicit knowledge) accumulated in the process cannot be transferred from one person to another wholesale. Furthermore, the application of specialist knowledge during work tasks which constantly undergo changes in the process of computerisation requires workers to actively engage continuously with the respective subject matter. 'Permanent learning' and advanced training thus become ever more important. This specialisation and individualisation, then, additionally substantiate the need for an increase in workers' self-organisation.

(d) The specialisation of skills is a unique form of new cooperation, one which sees a transition from a 'simple' set up to a more 'complex' one. The complexity initially feeds on the already mentioned characteristics, namely creativity, cooperative planning and individualised specialisation, as well as the spatial expansion of production: its global decentralisation. Cooperation is increasingly occurring in a cross-company and transnational manner, especially in software production.

In addition, cooperation is no longer only directed at the metabolism with nature as in industrial production, but also at complex economic and social processes, as exemplified by SAP's business software. Moreover, cooperation in the labour process is structured around the distinct interests of the involved parties (customers, owners, managers, workers, etc.).[33] The handling of potential conflicts of interest is thus part of the performed work and further complicates cooperation.

Hierarchical management becomes inefficient because the planning, evaluation and integration of tasks performed by workers is more flexible and operationally effective. Complex cooperation can in this sense be better accomplished through workers' self-organisation. Due to the new dominant division of labour which is based on the specialisation of knowledge – in contrast to the industrial form, namely the subdivision of tasks into manual sub-operations – the separation of management and task execution becomes a problem, making the democratisation[34] of the division of labour imperative: 'We may anticipate the development of a non-antagonistic, cooperative individuality as productive power.'[35]

THE NEOLIBERAL MANAGEMENT OF COMPUTERISATION

Instead of consistently implementing the requirements of computerised work outlined here, companies are increasingly moving to intensify the output of workers via profitability management in the sense of 'strategic marketisation'.[36] This leads to overtime, unpaid extra work and employers' attacks on the eight-hour working day and legally specified rest periods. Attempts to compress and thereby maximise output through specified (and often too tight) turnaround times, moreover, can lead to stipulations not being complied with or, in the worst case, projects being cancelled altogether. Protagonists of agile programming methods therefore advocate the practice of *sustainable pace*. Due to having to constantly work overtime, developers are almost unable to consistently produce clear and lucid code. They become unproductive and make more programming mistakes.[37] It is not only in the field of software development that productivity declines as a result of longer working hours.[38] Strategies such as profitability targets and reducing staff costs therefore raise productivity in the 'general-social' sense only to a limited extent and in an unsustainable way. Furthermore, extensive working hours and constant work intensification lead to poor quality outputs, resulting not least in a rise in psychological stress.

The quality of work in the service sector

A confirmation of the aforementioned was provided in the form of a representative survey conducted by the German Trade Union Federation (DGB) in the context of the 2016 'Good Work' index focusing on digitalisation: almost half of those working to a (very) large extent with digital devices in the service sector stated that their workload had increased as a result. The additional strain is related mostly to an increase in the work volume (56 per cent) and a rise in multi-tasking (57 per cent). Some 59 per cent indicated that they have to work under time pressure often or very often. Another 47 per cent of respondents reported an increase in surveillance and control of their work. In general, the findings suggest that psychological strain is on the rise as a result of digitalisation, whereas physical strain is decreasing. By contrast, the scope for individual decision-making has increased only to a limited extent on average (some 25 per cent indicate an increase). Wherever working conditions are poor overall, the scope for action narrows, while it grows disproportionately for those executive staff and workers performing (highly) complex tasks.[39]

A continued ambivalence of productivity and the productivity paradox

On the one hand, it is obvious that computerisation raises productivity:[40] according to a study conducted by the German Economic Institute (IW),[41] between 2001 and 2014 some 300,000 jobs in industry disappeared, while 1.3 million jobs were created in the healthcare and social sectors, owing not least to the demographic change. Concerning the projected required labour volume in the main professional fields, the Institute for Employment Research (IAB) points out in its forecast that most working hours will be accounted for by office-based and commercial service occupations (7.9 billion working hours) by 2030. These professions will, at that point, no longer be directly followed, however, by manufacturing, processing and maintenance occupations (7.5 billion hours), but by healthcare, social and personal hygiene and the cosmetic professions (7.8 billion hours).[42] Osborne and Frey conclude that digital automation will put 47 per cent of American jobs at risk over the coming years, while Brzeski and Burk calculate an even higher figure for Germany: according to their numbers, some 59 per cent of jobs in their current form, i.e. both employment liable to social security payments and marginal employment, are threatened by automation. The authors assume that the underlying cause of this difference is the fact that industry plays a more significant role in Germany.[43] What is certain is that the process of computerisation is leading to rationalisation and the job losses that such a move entails, and this trend is set to continue.

On the other hand, it is difficult to precisely determine the productivity of computerised labour. There is much reason to believe that a measure different to that used for industrial production is needed, as they differ fundamentally. For example, in the early 2000s, the total productivity of software production was still considered to be relatively insignificant.[44] Various authors have confirmed a 'productivity paradox' in their studies on 'information technology'.[45]

Unfulfilled requirements of computerisation: productivity deficits

Frequent delays and budget overruns in software development projects, which are common in many companies, suggest computerised work has a fundamental productivity problem. Time delays occur particularly in the analysis stage of the development process. This is the stage in which product requirements are established, demanding intensive cooperation between developers and users. Given the fiercely competitive attitude developers have towards each other (and even customers), however, this frequently does not take place. It turns out that the mediation of knowledge exchange via superiors takes up too much time and leads to a lack of flexibility in problem-solving. Management staff no longer have the detailed planning expertise, leading to flawed and delayed decisions. Crisis management and permanent reorganisation, which as such already generate productivity problems, are the result.

As shown with regard to four essential requirements (creativity, cooperative planning, specialisation of skills and complex cooperation), the need for increasing self-organisation and thus approaches towards 'cooperative individuality' is emerging as a counter-tendency to the hierarchical separation of directing functions (management) and task execution (workers). The division of labour typical in industrial capitalism, in the form of a subdivision of work and the separation between manual and intellectual labour, *has become unproductive in the process of computerisation.*

The contradiction between persistent hierarchies in current political-economic relations and cooperative individuality is resolved in practice mainly through so-called matrix project organisation,[46] as well as through indirect control and an increasing yet inadequate implementation of agile methods, i.e. as a combination of the management–worker separation and a limited, relative self-organisation of workers. The remaining hierarchy is still sufficient to cause numerous problems: apart from other severe problems such as a rise in psychological strain, there are excessive job cuts and an inefficient division of labour that goes beyond the specialisation of workers, resulting in a waste of skills.

The transformation of capital

If, in the past, the productive function of private capital in industry was to enable 'simple cooperation' in the factory, it has come under pressure in the process of computerisation: cooperation is no longer mainly focused on the factory, but relies – in its complex form – on a global, cross-company exchange of knowledge. Private capital is thus transforming in three ways.

Firstly, it is becoming transnational and forming global production networks. In order to increase profits, the global decentralisation of production plays an essential role in the process of computerisation. It started off with flexible automation during the 1970s and, with the rise of the internet, from the 1990s onwards allowed for a transnational coordination of work processes. The result was an aggravation of the (by then almost global) competition on the labour market.[47] Lower wage costs in countries that had until that point experienced very little industrialisation were not the only reason to relocate production processes: the undermining of trade union rights and protests are equally important to capital. The neoliberal policies of transnational corporations pushed back nation-state-based welfare services in pursuit of higher profits.[48] Jobs were not only automated, but in part relocated. Yet the competition between and within companies, whose production sites are usually conceptualised as profit and cost centres, also complicates the knowledge exchange and prevents synergy effects – especially in development.

Secondly, the area of so-called intellectual property is expanding and becoming a fiercely embattled terrain,[49] particularly in the context of software patents and licences. Over the past decades, an increasing number of patents have been issued; however, the positive impact they have had on innovation is rather contested. Many inventions remain business secrets. According to Gröndahl, the fiercest disputes concerning software patents in recent years have been about those whose licensing has been legally formalised in the United States since the 1980s;[50] in Europe, 'programs for data processing equipment' are officially excluded from patenting – although it is common practice to award software patents nonetheless. At this point, a decisive aspect of the transformation of private ownership manifests itself: different new licence models allow for formerly free software[51] to be transformed into proprietary software, or a combination of both. Based on these licence models, the economic advantages of free software at least become partially exploitable. These advantages result from a new model of software development and coding in which 'thousands of people all over the world' work together in a *self-organised* manner.[52] But because of their privatisation and the associated restriction of use, these licences at the same time obstruct or limit efficient cooperation, as a result of which the transformation of capital remains crisis-prone and embattled.

Thirdly, another strategy pursued by companies in order to harness the advantages of cooperation via the internet is crowdwork: additional labour is acquired (in most cases) selectively from single self-employed workers. The 'placement service' is conducted by online platforms.[53] Here, again, the aim is to expand cooperation beyond the individual company, so that globally distributed knowledge becomes available as quickly as possible. Yet this is not only about the self-initiative of software designers and other individual workers: it is a business model. 'Labour costs' play an important role and are (for now at least) reduced by, among other things, this global competition. The savings, especially in Germany, pertain to social security payments and other operational or contract-related costs, as single self-employed workers usually receive no holiday or sick pay, and no advanced training. They are responsible for their own occupational health and safety. No Labour Protection Act or workplaces ordinance – whose addressee is usually the employer – applies here. Such poor protection not only constitutes a personal risk for the affected workers, but in fact challenges – the more widespread it becomes – the funding of the social security system as a whole. Furthermore, additional risks emerge for companies, too, for example as a result of the lack of loyalty on the part of contracting agents or the loss of expertise.[54]

DEMOCRATISATION AS AN ALTERNATIVE: LABOUR POLITICS FROM BELOW

The process of computerisation is engulfing all economic areas and industries, albeit with differing degrees of intensity. Computerisation is currently at a stage where its potential – including for an increase in social productivity – has become apparent yet cannot be fully developed. What has asserted itself so far is rather a mix of compromises and makeshift solutions at the level of work organisation, based in part on models from industry, profitability management, and thus on job cuts, longer working hours and work intensification. Correspondingly, working conditions have deteriorated for a large section of the labour force.

The starting point for improving the quality of work, but also for developing cooperative individuality and social productivity as a whole, has to be the contradictory nature of developments in the process of computerisation. One crucial contradiction of the neoliberal management of computerisation that is provoking conflict is that between a persisting hierarchy on one side and workers' self-organisation both inside and outside of the workplace on the other. Given the need for the active integration of specialised skills, this self-organisation objectifies social ties within the computerised labour process. Workers thereby develop the potential for cooperative individuality.

One central task of workers' representatives would thus be to promote the self-organisation of the workforce in accordance with their desire for greater direct participation in decision-making. According to Trautwein-Kalms, trade unions stand a better chance of recruiting new members when the 'development of individuality is supported by union work,'[55] i.e. when the unions offer more opportunities for participation and *democracy*.[56] The trade union initiative for 'Good Work' as a 'labour politics from below'[57] may well serve as a starting point for such efforts. It has thus far been able not only to achieve initial success in terms of alleviating the *precarisation* of employment relations associated with neoliberal privatisation policy,[58] but has also identified the problem of employees' *overwork* and contributed to some initial solutions such as collective bargaining agreements preventing work overload and stipulating adequate staffing, or regulating mobile work, health and safety management and (matters related to) digitalisation. In this sense – and especially with a view to the developments taking place in Artificial Intelligence – the trade unions are pushing for an expansion of co-determination.[59]

12

Designing Work for Agility and Affect's Measure

Phoebe V. Moore

Today, sensory and tracking technologies are being introduced into workplaces for self-managed wellness as well as productivity tracking, in ways Fredrick W. Taylor could only have dreamed of. This process merges wellness with productivity to measure and modulate the affective labour of resilience that is necessary to survive the turbulence of the widespread incorporation of the work design model called 'agile', in which workers are expected to take symbolic direction from machines.

In this chapter, the agile work design method is assessed critically from a Marxist feminist perspective, adapting a labour process theoretical commitment to studies of workplace control through technological advancements, but looking at how, for example, affective labour[1] is measured rather than the age-old methods of identifying and absenting specific and accepted productive actions. The agile method, with the use of tracking technologies, prioritises profit for business, not through, as the capitalist labour process usually dictates, refusing to recognise all extended socially necessary labour time, but by the extraction of surplus value through actually *revealing* aspects of usually invisibilised labour time, through the use of increasingly invasive technologies such as wearables or tracking devices with which previously unrevealed aspects of work can be measured.

First, the chapter outlines the origins and development of the agile method. Like other work design models originating with scientific management, the workplace model of agile is designed to make sure work gets done effectively in line with industry and management expectations. However, where it differs from preceding models, is that agile comes with a range of new features that are focused on the ever-accelerating pace of market change, the inevitable rapidity of machine intervention, and the range of new technologies available now to develop industries *and* quantify work. The chapter then examines the implications of agile for workers' subjectivities and what is required to become a quantified agile worker. Finally, I present and discuss our findings regarding the *Quantified Workplace* project we were able to study.

AGILE

Agile production in manufacturing was introduced in 1991 by 150+ industry executives composing the Twenty-First Century Manufacturing Enterprise Strategy group, who envisaged the immediate future of manufacturing in the USA, and from which the Agile Manufacturing Enterprise Forum (AMEF) was born.[2] Agile responds to 'complexity brought about by constant change' and is an 'overall strategy focussed on thriving in an unpredictable environment'. Agile, as these authors discuss it, is proactive in the client/producer relationship rather than isolated to a hierarchy that reflects Fordist assembly line production. While the origins of agile are in manufacturing, the rebirth of this set of principles occurred in 2001, when a group of 17 software developers who were fed up with bureaucracy and obstacles to technological development formulated their ideas for how an ideal production team should operate, summarised in what they called the Agile Manifesto.[3]

The manifesto reflected other IT workers' sentiment as they felt the waterfall system, used in factories, was ineffectual for software development. The waterfall method relies on a traditional sequential development of production processes, where a linear method prevails. Agile introduces a distinctive alternative to waterfall approaches, which should 'help teams respond to unpredictability through incremental, iterative work cadences and empirical feedback'.[4] Agile requires a frequent, simplified, self-organised team-based software development and delivery model for work and production. Agility relies on the 'ability to both create and respond to *change* in order to *profit* in a *turbulent* business environment'.[5] Agility in both the manufacturing context and in software development assumes that disruption and uncertainty are normal, that technology will inevitably transform, and that workers simply must keep up with a range of self-preparation and preservation techniques to deal with constant instability, including self-tracking for wellness and productivity. An agile work design method puts new pressures on workers by a) altering the relationship between humans and machines, where we are expected to 'keep up'; b) expecting workers to find ways to self-manage such turbulence; and c) creating new employable competences for teamwork and supposed horizontalism that require a specific subjectivity.

Agility requires a group work design model because 'individual roles are interdependent and there is a need for collective working'; 'sociotechnical systems principles were early influences on group work design'.[6] Parker, who has published extensively on job and work design, states that attention has been given to group autonomy in recent work design research. Studies in organisational psychology show that group autonomy leads to job satisfaction and organisational commitment. The 'inputs' for an 'input-process-output' model are group-led work design, group composition and contextual influences; 'processes' involve intermediary group states and group norms that become attributes; and 'outputs' are what Parker calls 'team-member *affective* reactions'. Affect, in organisational psychology, refers to positive shared emotions, which is quite different from the way it is used by Spinoza and in Marxist feminist and post-autonomist approaches.

Often, in any case, group work is said to have an effect on psychological empowerment, but group work does not always lead to positive outputs. Workers appear to impose values on themselves rigidly, and initially excited and energetic participants find they start to feel burdened. At times, people may feel too much group work can turn into an 'insidious form of control'[7] reminiscent of a panopticon.

After the Agile Manifesto was written in 2001, companies in many industries began to recognise the value of operational agility where workers and management have the 'ability over time to respond quickly and effectively to rapid change and high uncertainty'.[8] Agile is a 'co-evolution of workplace and work'; an adaptation of *kaizen*, or 'continuous improvement';[9] 'neither top-down nor bottom-up: it is outside-in'.[10] So, agile is a form of total quality management *and* a high-performance work system, oriented around an approach whereby companies invest in human resource quality as a primary means to be and remain competitive.[11] High-performance practices involve the introduction of employee involvement programmes. The company whose special workplace organisation is outlined below communicated a vision of the ideal agile workplace and set up systems to make this happen, fully involving workers by setting them up as subjects in an office experiment, reflecting total quality and high-performance systems.

Agile emphasises the reduction of waste, similar to Taylorism and lean production. Yet while Taylorist 'scientific management' redesigned work processes through unilateral management decisions (supposedly to the benefit of all), the agile concept expects workers themselves to actively participate in decision-making and shaping their workplace. However, as Lazzarato critically points out, the techniques of participative management seen in related systems are a 'technology of power, a technology for creating and controlling the "subjective processes"'.[12]

THE QUANTIFIED, AGILE WORKER

Having discussed the tenets of agility, let us now take a look at how workers might self-manage the process through developing specific subjectivities and skills as part of a contribution in affective labour, which is inherent to its operation and success. We may establish that agile workplaces require agile workers.

Agile assumes that changes to the workplace are inevitable, because technology inevitably changes. This work design model was, as noted above, conceived in its current form by software engineers and programmers who aimed to reduce the delay in getting software projects onto the market by cutting red tape and organisational obstacles. Thus, the urgency for technologies to be 'set free', launched, invented and, in a way, discovered, trumps all other concerns. Therefore, agile apprehends a certain relationship between the human and the machine. The machine will advance, whether or not humanity does, so we must position ourselves to allow this.

Of course, there is a long history of arguments about the relation between the human and the machine, and Marx had much to say about this, as in the much-cited Fragment on Machines, where the human functions in the service of the machine. Agile goes even further in the sense that the supremacy of machines becomes so inculcated into the everyday that workers struggle to know whether they are in competition or in cooperation with them. Workers are expected to self-manage the impact of the constant change of technology through emotional management and affective control and the cultivation of new subjectivities which are amenable to group work and constant personal transformation. Managing change thus becomes an 'all-of-life' responsibility, where wellbeing is the worker's remit. Needless to say, corporate wellness programmes are made available to support workers' resilience in the face of constant, inevitable change, rather than to *prevent* change or instability. The latter initiative seems to have left the building.

In principle, the agile method eliminates the traditional manager and levels the playing field of management, requiring co-workers to consistently respond to clients and ensure the right technologies, products and services are delivered. Agile, of course, requires agile workers: agile in the sense that people are prepared for constant change and to make personal subjective changes, but also always on the move and mobile. These trends fit well with the quantified work trend,[13] where workers are also expected to be perpetually available as well as trackable. Because of the shifts in work design that blur the lines between management and worker, work, identity and life become entangled, and it is increasingly difficult to log out, switch off, tune out.[14] Agile workers 'struggle to be left alone rather than to be included, a type of refusal that would have looked strange to their Fordist predecessors'.[15] Affective labour under agile conditions increases because of the insecurity this work design model engenders, and tracking it may help management discover the extent to which workers are likely to disengage or collapse – a kind of people analytics.

Phoebe V. Moore

TRACKING AFFECTIVE LABOUR

Affective labour is social reproductive labour, where usually unseen and unrecognised work allows for the continuation of capitalist labour relations and the reproduction of capitalist subjectivities, and where workers must be resilient to survive conditions of inevitable change. Affective labour refers to 'forms of labour that produce and circulate states of being, feelings of well-being, desire, ease and passion,'[16] which occur at a pre-visceral stage of experience. While affective labour (AL) is usually expected of women, it 'does not refer to gender specific forms of work although [it is] at times defined as "women's work". AL refers to the interactive character of work, to its capacity to promote flows of communication, thus it is polyvalent with regard to the activities associated with it.'[17] Affective labour reaches below, behind and above the corporeal. Measuring it is a form of management control by means of the 'modulation of affect,'[18] by recording bodily and affective capabilities, as in the study outlined below, and by providing self-tracking devices, thus predicting worker collapse. Forms of affective labour become a 'moral' obligation imposed by corporate power, where subjectivities are required to be resilient to instability and where subjects take responsibility for personal wellness rather than associate stress and illness with poor working conditions.

The process whereby affective labour is measured and quantified – which is what, as I argue below, happened in the Quantified Workplace experiment – involves attempting to capture 'invisible labour', which in feminist literature refers to work that goes unrecognised and overlooked.[19] Through agile systems, then, capital attempts to turn the use value in affective labour into an exchange, turning the concrete into divisibilities and abstractions, thus commodifying affect and potentially circumventing resistance. Affective labour, however, is not invisibilised without intention. Invisibility has the potential for revelation, but regulations for its viewing are already authored within specific parameters, dictating what is permissible, what is 'seen' and thus what is measured, which is a basic premise for the theory of working time.[20]

The following section outlines fieldwork results from the author's study of one quantified corporate wellness initiative which the

190

company entitled the Quantified Workplace. Project participants were, of course, not *explicitly* asked by management to self-track 'affective labour' in the experiment, but our findings show that via tracking and measurements for 'stress', 'subjective productivity' and 'wellbeing', alongside physical movement, heart rate and sleep tracking, this is what occurred. Framing affective labour as facilitative of, and required for, change management at a personal level – and given that the project took place in the midst of a corporate transformation involving both a merger and a management shift to an agile system – the project reveals that new forms of affective work measurement become, potentially, an arena for management control.

THE QUANTIFIED WORKPLACE

The Quantified Workplace project was run by one company over a period of 12 months from 2015–16 in the Netherlands. Management distributed Fitbit Charge HR Activity Trackers devices to 30 employees and installed Rescuetime tracking software on their work computers.[21] The company provided individualised dashboards as well as a shared dashboard where all data from these tracking activities was stored and made visible to all other participants. Participants also received workday lifelog emails asking them to rate their *stress*, *subjective productivity* and *wellbeing* on a Likert scale from 1 to 5 for each item.

The project occurred during a period of change management, involving a move towards a new workplace design agile model and a merger in which a multinational real estate company absorbed a smaller company of mostly work design consultants. The smaller company suggested and led the Quantified Workplace project. The project manager indicated that his intentions were to help workers adapt to an agile and mobile working environment and to see to what extent employees' self-awareness, stress, wellbeing and 'wellbilling' (which he described as the amount of revenue an employee generates for the company) would be impacted during the period of transition. The company was interested in comparing subjectively and objectively measured productivity, as linked to health and activity tracking and 'billability'.

The research findings revealed that workers were expected to self-manage any emotional or physical impacts of the change, and self-reports via the daily lifelog emails represented a year's worth of data on this process. Workers reported increased workloads and increased expectations for travel resulting from the corporate merger. While our study did not link specific change expectations to specific forms of affective labour, there was a notable rise in employees' self-awareness, self-management and personal investment in wellness and physical and emotional preparations for work, as became clear from the results of data gathering exercises by the company itself and from our own surveys and interviews. Management wanted to know about this, which became clear from the required workday lifelog emails about stress, subjective productivity and wellbeing. This self-reporting data provided management with ways to cross-check productivity scores across individuals' perceptions and what we indicate as involving affective labour, while also increasing workloads and agile responsibilities for mobility and teamwork.

Interviewees readily shared their own experiences of the impact of workplace changes, noting a heightened awareness of waning privacy, given the new tracking practices being rolled out; stress resulting from increased workloads and expectations for travel and mobility of work; feelings surrounding individual autonomy; as well as an increased sensitivity to physical and psychological wellbeing. Findings based on surveys and interviews showed that the highest increases in participants' expressions surrounding the rise in affective labour related to feelings of increased autonomy, a concern for privacy and a sense of the need for support and coaching.[22]

The data we obtained on people's views on privacy are related to affective labour because, for example, the awareness of a desire for privacy is generated from a pre-visceral sense that becomes labour when it becomes a defence mechanism against changing management practices such as a corporate merger and the introduction of an agile management system. Workers' responses in interviews showed some individual increases in awareness of activities that fall outside traditional work parameters which we classify as falling into the categories of affective labour:

'I see when I'm frustrated my heartbeat is higher.'

'[Participation in Quantified Workplace makes me] more conscious of activity, heartrates and wellbeing.'

'I learned about my feeling of productivity, so productivity has nothing to do with invoices we can send to our clients and before I was thinking, okay, productivity is like just hours I'm working for my clients, but sometimes I feel very productive, just the internal things, so therefore it helps, the way I think about productivity.'

'I'm more aware of the productivity, I think that's it. It's not that I directly improve my productivity, but I'm more aware of at what moments I'm productive, yeah, but that's the next step, to base some actions on that.'

'I'm sure it makes you aware of things you do.'

One participant indicated that he became more aware of his body as a result of participating in the project:

'I think awareness is even more key than total change of behaviour, but that you are more aware of your body and what's the problems for it and that you address that and start to organise your agenda around it.'

There was a high rate of exit from participation, at 75 per cent by the end of the project. There was also a high rate of increase in people indicating they had stopped using the technologies continuously, at 73 per cent. Research results demonstrate resistance, both passive (based on interviews) and active (based on active withdrawal). While it was not possible to interview those participants who had dropped out of the project by the time the second set of interviews were held, the survey and some interviews demonstrated difficulties in using the technology as well as high levels of uncertainty about the validity and usefulness of the project, which may have applied to others who stopped participating in the project:

'A big question for me and for a few others as well, is uh, how reliable the FitBit is.'

'This thing [FitBit] might be more intelligent than just recording my data.'

One respondent in the second round of interviews indicated frustration:

'I don't get any answers, I just fill in my things, but I don't get an answer if it's good or not, I just want to know if I was good and just start working.'

For those who stayed with the project, responses to the question 'How have your thoughts about the Quantified Workplace project changed?' in the second stage of interviews showed further resistance, including such statements as:

'I still have doubts about the project. And I don't wear the Fitbit very often. And when I wear it, it is for myself and to see how active I am.'

'It confirmed my thoughts, which I had in the beginning. It is better to change your behaviour based on your feelings rather than a device.'

'After monitoring my workplace behaviour over a couple of months I found out that it didn't change a lot.'

'I didn't learn very much from it.'

It became clear that the Quantified Workplace project was implemented to help employees self-manage the impact of corporate changes and to produce data about what I have identified as affective labour, which are areas of work that have historically been ignored by management. Data-driven technology acquired information about workers' experiences of workplace changes. Given that quantification allows for seemingly 'objective reason and disinterested rationality',[23] the very real possibility is that this kind of practice masks the intensification of performance management. New tracking technologies and their applications neutralise actions taken on the basis of accumulated Big Data and facilitate the new arena of human resource management called people analytics.

CONCLUSION

New uses of technologies in the quantified workplace are part of an emerging form of an updated Taylorism, that is, processes of subordination in which the quantification of new areas of work through tracking technologies may help corporations keep up with cut-throat competition. In the long term, this approach may subsume life to capital to an unsustainable degree, destroying any possibility for qualitative experiences outside of capitalism, which both provide the basis for capitalist relations (as use value, labour power, desire), and are likely to trigger continued resistance and worker struggle. At a minimum, we can establish a declining wellbeing of workers and an associated regime of total mobilisation and surveillance as tracking technologies create anxiety, burnout and overwork. Neoliberalism continues to attribute such problems to workers' failures to adapt, personal psychological shortcomings or educational deficits. They are, however, systematic effects of a particular labour process.

Capital is tempted to invest in new self-tracking technologies not because it may improve the public good, regardless of the rhetoric of wellness that informs current wellbeing initiatives for workers, but because it can increase its profit ratios. But quantification of affective labour as part of the agile work design model assumes that all performers start at an equal level of competence to play such a game of survival and to thrive. Existing skills, working time capacity and/or unequal access to social capital are ignored. These assumptions can easily result in discriminatory judgements and appraisals or induce extra stress and lead to work intensification and speed-up.

Indeed, management did not reveal their subsequent use of data from the Quantified Workplace project to the author (nor, it seems, to the participants), but the possibilities are clear. The EU's General Data Protection Regulation (GDPR), rolled out in May 2018, will deal with some of the risks that new forms of data gathering in workplaces introduce, through requiring transparency and consent as well as human intervention into any decision-making using automated and algorithmic data collection.[24]

Power relations in capitalist reproduction reflect Marx's points of critique, and machines are now more than ever before the symbols for 'the ordering of life itself',[25] accelerating the labour process and dragging workers with them. Workers' responses, including in the explicit disengagement with the case study outlined above, demonstrate an awareness of the tensions surrounding new control mechanisms, underscore ongoing struggles in the contemporary labour process where agile is a key meme, and substantiate the urgency of reviewing all-of-life management strategies such as agile.

The corporate project reported here demonstrates that agile systems rely on workers' affective labour to self-manage external transformation, thereby running the risk of creating agile subjects under a perpetual state of alienation. After all, as the Agile Manifesto makes clear, computers and machines inevitably change and develop in accelerated ways, meaning workers must constantly train and adapt anew. While the power relations between humans and machines are taken into consideration, agile as a system does not fully crystallise what is at stake for workers: the (im)possibility of a life outside of capitalism and beyond externalised parameters for data acquisition about working lives; encroaching alienation and subsumption as the surpluses of affective labour are perpetually abstracted and calculated to identify the possibility of worker collapse; and the acceleration of the calculation of everyday lives within neoliberal capitalism, where people are increasingly told to 'measure your way out of misery'.[26] We are reminded that 'today's management thinking takes workers' subjectivity into consideration only in order to codify it in line with the requirements of production'.[27] Indeed, the significant worker resistance to the Quantified Workplace project indicates that new digitalised management practices are not a fait accompli. Future research must focus on how alienated workers respond to such methods of measurement in workplaces, and identify the emerging psychosocial and even physical risks that workers face in quantified, agile workplaces.

IV

Platform Capitalism under Scrutiny

13

Old Power in Digital Garb?

The labour process on crowdworking platforms

Christine Gerber

The push towards greater advances in technological innovation and the introduction of new machines have always fuelled fears of deskilling and a loss of both autonomy and jobs. Yet if we look back at the history of automation, we see that it also allows for the creation of new tasks, as is currently impressively evidenced by platform-based online work, so-called *crowdwork*.[1] This can be defined as the 'paid provision of labour delivered digitally by geographically dispersed and formally self-employed/freelance workers, outsourced via an internet platform and managed entirely online throughout its execution'.[2] Platforms like Upwork, 99designs or Clickworker organise a great number of tasks, ranging from simple audio transcription and image categorisation to sophisticated product development and solutions to scientific problems. Some of these tasks are separated from the workplace-based labour process, while others are entirely new or were never organised in such a way to begin with. On the whole, they comprise tasks that are performed by humans using a computer, but which computers cannot perform by themselves. The technological basis of this is provided by new information and communication technologies (ICT), in particular algorithms that collect and analyse data and control processes and that are easily available through cloud computing. They allow forms of networking and coordination that integrate labour processes independent of location in a seemingly novel and seamless manner and decentralise production. Through digital mediation, platforms not only expand access but indeed dissolve the boundaries that limit access to labour power and allow ostensibly infinite productivity potential to be tapped.

Yet valorising labour power at a profit presents specific challenges to capital. Just like traditional enterprises, platforms must first transform the labour power of the crowd into actually exerted and surplus-value-creating labour. According to Marx, this takes place in what is called the labour process, which management seeks to control.[3] However, platforms lack the traditional workplace structures for doing so; instead, their management is confronted with an anonymous, mobile and globally dispersed workforce.

In the literature, two distinct notions exist as to how crowdwork platforms organise labour processes in order to solve the transformation problem. On the one hand, there is the thesis of the industrialisation of intellectual labour (that is, indirect, information-processing tasks) via new digital technologies and the platform as the machine system of 'digital capitalism'. In Germany, it is in particular Andreas Boes and his colleagues who argue that because of the informatisation of the production space, 'intellectual tasks' can no longer be organised 'based primarily on individual dexterity, but via a division of labour in an "objective process" as with machine systems in "heavy industry" or with the assembly line in Fordism'.[4] Some authors therefore also refer to crowdwork as 'digital Taylorism',[5] with the focus on platforms like Amazon Mechanical Turk that organise standardised microtasks at low piece rates. According to this view, the actual novelty is the peculiar individualisation and invisibility of human labour as a result of the socio-technical design: as part of the software architecture, it assumes the appearance of a code which is available on demand and thus subjected to the platform's rhythm.[6] The digital work environment, the argument continues, also allows for seemingly all-encompassing control. This description resembles twenty-first-century Taylorist assembly line work: with the aim of maximising the relative surplus value, platforms systematically intervene in the subdivision and performance of labour. Labour is thereby subsumed in real terms, too, and subjected to the rhythm of the platform as the equivalent to the machine system.[7]

Another interpretation conceives of platforms as intermediary, hyperpotent infrastructures in which transaction partners (i.e. buyers and freelancers) can find and interact with one another, while a large proportion of the operational costs (e.g. for fixed capital, qualification and control) is entirely outsourced.[8] The crowd, comprising ostensibly self-employed workers, produces immaterial goods independent of their location and in a largely autonomous manner. For the most part, they themselves own the means of production. Following this reading, platforms cannot assert full control over the process of value creation for they are unable to centrally dictate the labour process or the pace of work. In this sense, platforms replace traditional organisational control with market control. By owning the infrastructure, however, platforms can subsume the communicative labour and social knowledge resources that converge here and extract them in the form of valuable data.[9] Hence, such an interpretation, which ties in with the ideas of post-operationalism,[10] regards the subsumption of labour on platforms to be only *formal*, implying an expanded scope of action for those offering their labour: in addition to a higher degree of self-determination and autonomy for workers, their market power also increases, as the conception and execution of work, and thus production-related knowledge as a whole, is placed back in their hands. The implications of these two interpretations contradict one another: should the platform be regarded as a virtual variant of the traditional workplace form, or does it represent something entirely new? Can labour be subsumed under capital, even in real terms, via the platform, or is the autonomy of labour expanded?

Proceeding from these questions, this chapter examines, *firstly*, how platforms organise the labour and production process against the backdrop of the specific problems of control and management. This serves, *secondly*, the purpose of finding an answer to a more general question: to what extent is a new, stable type of dispersed production and capitalist labour emerging? The findings indicate that platforms by all means function as an alternative workplace: they organise a labour process independent of location and thus management functions as a commodity for individual capitals. In this, they are guided – depending on the complexity of tasks – by known forms of work organisation, namely Taylorism and agile methods, which are then applied to the production of digital commodities. Although labour regimes emerge that are certainly more complex and flexible than is often assumed, it seems safe to believe that this work model represents a long-term rationalisation strategy only in certain niche

areas due to the short-term and anonymous nature of labour relations. The particular relevance of the work model appears to lie in
the exploration of new, technology-based management systems for
the transformation of labour power. It is above all the advanced and
peculiar technological appearance in which workers are confronted
with domination that dissipates and individualises the workplace
conflict between labour and capital.[11]

CHALLENGES FOR THE PLATFORM-BASED LABOUR PROCESS

One central topic for the sociology of work is the question of which
forms of work organisation and workplace control management are
developing as capital's workplace representation in order to transform labour power into surplus-value-creating labour. The labour
process debate initially developed its theories on the basis of the
guiding image of *Taylorism* which dominated the industrial rationalisation paradigm throughout the twentieth century.[12] In the Taylorist
model, management secured its control over the labour process via
the separation of execution and planning of manufacturing steps in
accordance with the Babbage principle. As a result, processes were
created in which unskilled labour forces manufactured complex
products in many individual steps and could be directly controlled.
Their work-related knowledge was objectified via the codification of
work steps into machines; work was standardised and deskilled.

The rising technological composition and complexity of production, shorter innovation cycles, a higher degree of market competition,
and the increasing significance of indirect production areas within
industrial enterprises (such as administration, IT, research and development) engendered new guiding principles of work organisation.
On the one hand, management teams discovered their staff's creative
capacities and experience-based knowledge as a resource for rationalisation and harnessed it through decentralised coordination and
teamwork. On the other hand, the possibility of regulating performance solely through direct control was reduced. Management
teams thus increasingly relied on indirect control in order to establish a certain degree of 'consent' and 'responsible autonomy'.[13] The

new guiding principles were based on this logic of a systemic ratio-nalisation via the decentral interlinkage of the individual work steps: lean production in industrial production and *agile management* in indirect production areas.[14]

At first glance, platform-based online work appears to constitute an entirely new rationalisation paradigm for capital. Production is decentralised and overheads are largely externalised. Labour power can seemingly be accessed in a matter of seconds, at any given time of day and for any type of location-independent task. Consequently, new productivity potentials can be tapped and a global reserve army becomes available. The crowd is individualised and scattered, het-erogeneous, and often only temporarily active, making collective solidarity rather difficult, let alone organisation. Moreover, the time- or result-based competitive nature of platforms places workers in direct competition with one another.

And yet even platform management teams are confronted with the transformation problem of labour. Added to this is the fact that they lack the traditional mechanisms of workplace-based labour man-agement and control: instead of a shared workplace, working hours, colleagues and permanent tasks, they are confronted with anonymity, mobility and volatility. Radical marketisation presents platforms with specific management and control problems. On the one hand, crowd-workers can withdraw their labour power at the click of a mouse and move to other platforms; many crowdworkers are in fact registered on several platforms. For platforms relying on network effects and monopolisation, this represents a crucial risk factor and can push them out of the market in a very short matter of time.[15] The par-ticularly high mobility could thus constitute a potential negotiating power for digital producers.[16] At the same time, challenges emerge with regard to quality control and performance regulation, for labour forces cannot be trained, work knowledge cannot be stored, and subjective work potentials cannot be planned when an order is potentially processed by, at times, thousands of anonymous crowd-workers simultaneously, who work flexibly around the globe.

The crowd has a large degree of autonomy in the labour process due to the lack of direct access to the actual physical workers. The unknown and independent crowd mostly own their means of production, as the production of digital goods takes place on their own personal end devices and initially represents a black box for the platforms. The objectification of work and securing of domination within the labour process in this sense poses a special challenge, for the labour process can only be managed via the general, digital infrastructure. Vaguely worded instructions, technical problems, a lack of direct communication, and inadequate or falsified qualifications can cause all kinds of difficulties to arise during the realisation of projects. Digital infrastructures, moreover, are not ironclad and the system can be gamed, both individually and collectively. For example, several people can work from one and the same account, give false information in their profile or deliver flawed work on purpose due to a lack of incentives or loyalty to the organisation.

In the following, the ways in which platforms deal with such problems are examined.

LABOUR PROCESSES ON CROWDWORK PLATFORMS

The literature lists three central functions of platforms.[17] Firstly, platforms translate customer orders into structured *workflows*: they modulate the order into clearly defined and delimited units of labour, defining the mode of competition, quality control and payment. Secondly, they coordinate *task allocation* via algorithms, based on the constantly collected information that is centralised on the platform. Contrary to the crowdwork promise, access to work is by no means open to all. Thirdly, they establish *sanctioning and incentive mechanisms* in order to indirectly mobilise activity and regulate performance, with digital reputations and game elements playing an important role.

There are, however, differences in the particular arrangement of the labour process according to the complexity of tasks. This chapter distinguishes between microtasks and macrotasks.[18]

Microtasks

Many platforms (such as Clickworker or Figure Eight) specialise in the organisation of simple routine or auxiliary tasks (image categorisation, audio transcription) or tasks that do not require any special or professional knowledge (surveys, app testing, short text production). The nature of these tasks allows for them to be broken down into short, extremely standardised and clearly defined task units that can be processed in a few seconds or minutes. Each *microtask* is designed so that a crowdworker can complete it independently of others, at any given time or place, and without needing to be familiar with either the customer or the end product. For the crowd, work becomes visible on their job dashboards only in the form of sub-tasks, and it can mostly only be processed there as well.

If, for example, a company wants to digitalise thousands of photographs, the platforms break the task down in a way that one task unit is the tagging of pictures according to a certain category (e.g. colour). Content, such as product listings for a homepage, is translated by the platform into a large number of short text tasks with clear instructions, a defined word count and key words. As one crowdworker explains: 'You get a certain number of words and are allowed to use only the information that is given to you. Sometimes these very closely defined specifications do restrict your work.'

This *taskification* is reminiscent of the Taylorist rationalisation paradigm: the separation of the immediate labour process from the individual skills of the worker; the separation of planning and task execution; central instruction in the sense of *one-best-way* work procedures; and comprehensive optimisation and control of the individual work step. The breaking down is done either directly by a platform staff member (*full service*) or indirectly via the provision of standardised order screens (*self service*).

As a result of this specific task design, the required knowledge is formalised and codified, and thereby centralised and expropriated. This way, the need for implicit, experience- or team-based work-related knowledge is intended to be minimised as far as possible and labour reduced to its quantitative value creation.

There are indeed distinct skill levels on microtask platforms as well: for example, tasks involving the writing of texts often require a qualification test or a minimum ranking. Yet the tests are mostly as standardised as the tasks themselves. Likewise, the digital reputation often evaluates *microworkers* predominantly on the basis of objective performance criteria (past work evaluations, level of activity, membership period on the platform). The skill levels mainly serve as general control thresholds in order to exclude poorly performing online workers from certain, more sophisticated tasks. Individual selection based on qualifications or (specific, case-to-case) applications does not take place.

In principle, all registered crowdworkers are supposed to be able to complete the microtasks without communicating with each other or being familiar with the customer or the overall product. Decentralised communication, teamwork or coordination between producers of the individual production steps, as in lean production, are unnecessary and mostly not even provided for by the digital infrastructure. This mode of labour division, which is inscribed in the technological design of the platform, allows digital goods to be produced in a serial and geographically dispersed manner and with an anonymous and ever-changing workforce. At the same time, the scope of application of this work and production model is severely limited as a result.

That said, even microtasks require a minimum amount of communication. Most platforms allow for exchange in separate forums outside the actual labour process. They primarily serve to promote the self-help and self-regulation of the crowd, allowing freelancers to solve work-related or technical problems, similar to the break room at a workplace, for they are often matched by only a small number of actual platform staff. At the same time, these communication spaces give the platform a human face, which can help raise the crowd's company loyalty and motivation.

The breaking down and standardisation of work into microtasks, furthermore, allow for a margin of error and direct control of work steps, both of which are required due to the high probability of error inherent to crowdwork. The final result of the sub-tasks can be determined to a certain degree beforehand and checked for correctness, for example, in terms of whether the T-shirt in a picture really is yellow, an audio sequence was transcribed correctly or the spelling and required key words for a short product description are accurate. It is often assumed that controlling is mainly carried out by algorithms. And for very simple tasks like photo categorisation, such automated control solutions do exist (for example, pre-programmed test tasks).

Most tasks, however, continue to be controlled by humans. This is an indicator of the limitations of algorithms. Human labour fills the gaps of automation even in the management systems of platforms.

Controlling, in turn, is mostly outsourced as a paid task to crowd-workers who have qualified for that task through high rankings or special tests. Yet no long-term work profiles or responsibilities follow from this, as they would in a workplace-embedded occupation: the controlling crowdworkers are usually just as anonymous and alternate just as constantly as the entire crowd. Many crowdworkers criticise the unpredictability resulting from this. Given that not every microtask can be checked by a human, complementary algorithms are used, such as for the regulation of access to tasks or for the establishment of control intervals; both depend, among other things, on the reputation score.

The crowd's autonomy that results from management's lack of direct control over and access to the individual physical workers nonetheless continues to make platforms prone to error. The crowd is stripped of this autonomy to some extent by the platform, as the platforms' digital infrastructure is the actual work tool. With some exceptions, most tasks are technically designed to be completed directly within the platform interface. However, one central aspect of workplace-based labour management and real subsumption cannot be transferred to the virtual workplace: the exact work cycle. In industrial work processes, the subdivision of work steps is coupled to the production pace, and management is able to directly control the work cycle via the machine system. Yet crowdworkers can freely decide when they wish to work and which tasks they want to perform; in addition, it is up to them how long they take for a specific task, as long as they meet the specified deadline for the order. The work cycle cannot be directly integrated into the digital infrastructure, but only indirectly stipulated, namely via the piece rate, time-based competition and the digital reputation.

Microtasks are usually remunerated with a piece rate that can range from less than one euro/dollar up to a two-digit figure. It mostly corresponds to a minimum hourly wage that is broken down to the estimated processing time and in line with the (minimum) pay rate crowdworkers have accepted in the past. Crowdworkers must therefore complete tasks with a certain degree of time pressure, for if they take longer, the wage they receive is effectively lower. Indeed, this is a common point of complaint among crowdworkers. Furthermore, time frames are indirectly influenced by time-based competition, as tasks are allocated to those who accept and process them first. In order to conclude a task more quickly, i.e. to increase the work cycle rate, the piece rate is increased: the higher financial incentive increases competition for the task. Finally, it is also quite conspicuous that activity represents a central variable in the digital reputation of many micro-platforms: frequently, only the ratings from the last month are taken into consideration; if a worker is inactive for several days, their ranking drops, and on some platforms this happens even when a worker does not actively reject an order. All this is designed to mobilise permanent activity and performance.

By and large, the labour process on micro-platforms is heavily fragmented and standardised in order to valorise the labour power of a large mass of anonymous, constantly changing crowdworkers at a profit. The final product emerges as a result of the platform dis- and re-integrating the sub-units, thereby managing the labour process in a centralised manner. It therefore seems perfectly admissible to speak of an objectification and real subsumption of labour under capital.

Macrotasks

What has gained far less attention is the great number of platforms (such as Jovoto or Upwork) which organise tasks with a high degree of required creativity or professional knowledge. Customers place an order with a platform for, e.g., the preparation of designs and product ideas, the development of software programmes or to find solutions to scientific problems. Although the tasks specify concrete targets, the end product cannot be entirely determined and standardised beforehand given the complexity of the production process and the required expertise: in most cases, there is no definitive right or wrong outcome. Therefore, the labour process cannot be directed in a centralised manner nor be broken down into sub-tasks. Instead, *macrotasks* are organised as projects that last several days or weeks. Remuneration is significantly higher here (three- to five-figure sums) than on microtask platforms, but also more uncertain as the matter at hand is not the quantitative processing of tasks, but the acquisition of the best entry submitted.

Marketplace platforms like Upwork resolve the resulting uncertainty by limiting themselves to the placement function, creating (almost) pure marketplaces. Using complex tracking and ranking algorithms, they *match* a selection of potentially suitable freelancers with customers. The latter, however, place their orders online themselves, select and communicate directly with freelancers, and negotiate project schedules and remuneration bilaterally. The labour and production process is not tied to the platform but can also be transferred to other channels.

This is contrasted by contest-based platforms such as Jovoto or CrowdMed, where customer orders are organised as contests lasting several days or weeks with somewhat standardised briefings and schedules. The *launch* of a project is followed by the *submission phase* in which the crowd compile their own submissions and upload them to the platform. This in turn is followed by intermediary stages, such as the *rating* and *feedback phases*, in which said entries are evaluated and commented on mainly by the *crowd community* (all registered members), and at times also by customers, a jury or platform guides. These phases often also allow for rectification and adjustment of submissions. The last step is the *curation phase*, in which the customer selects the winner(s) (mainly based on the preceding rating). A quote from a staff member of a US design platform accurately sums up the way that macrotask platforms standardise and rationalise creative work: '[Our] platform adds considerable structure to the design process [...] in that we ask very specific questions and indicate deadlines. Halfway down the line, after four days, they have to select a group of finalists [...] And to be honest, we try to speed matters up even more [and] make the process even more efficient.' By specifying standardised and short-cycle project schedules, platforms determine the work schedule and cycle at least in part, changing the labour process in real terms, too. Although a first draft is produced entirely autonomously on crowdworkers' own desktop PCs, and the work tools, such as software programmes and private files containing individually accumulated expertise or materials, belong to the producers, relevant work steps are then added subsequently, e.g. controlling, communication and collaboration. In order to become an end product, the drafts must first undergo these work steps. This part of the labour process is transferred to the platform, through which it becomes the actual site of production, at least in part.

Even on contest platforms, the control over the performed work can thus be organised in an efficient and decentralised manner by the crowd – in contrast to microtask platforms – in the form of unpaid extra work. The reason is that automated controlling solutions for the production of such subjective goods are very limited to begin with, e.g. to the testing of file formats. The crowd upload their intermediary results and final products to the platform where all registered members are then encouraged to report spam and plagiarism, provide feedback and criticism, and evaluate submitted entries. As a reward for this *community engagement* (or, rather *peer-to-peer* control), they receive reputation points. Given that neither customers nor the community can review hundreds of entries or profiles, macrotask platforms filter and draw up a limited shortlist of likely adequate entries or online workers via complex predictive algorithms. On the one hand, the underlying data for doing so come from the permanent tracking of the online workers that coalesces into their digital reputation. They include not only objective criteria (performance evaluation, certificates and skills, activity), but also subjective ones (community engagement, communication and collaboration with the community and customers, additional off-the-job experience). On the other hand, the algorithms are fed by the permanent interaction (likes, evaluations, reporting, comments) on the platform itself.

While communication during the labour process is hardly needed, nor is it technically possible on microtask platforms, lengthy discussion threads and countless 'likes' within the individual projects and personal profiles can be observed on contest platforms. On many of these platforms, lively – albeit project-centred – discussions ensue, in which problems in the labour process are considered and resolved collectively; submitted entries are debated and collaboratively refined. The implicit and subjective knowledge that is essential for the production of creative and complex goods may not be standardisable or generalisable, but at least it becomes visible and appropriable.

Contest platforms appropriate the experience-based expertise and the intelligence of the masses, referred to as *crowd wisdom.*

However, from this emerges another specific characteristic that makes the platform prone to error: the collaboration comes into conflict with the high degree of competitiveness. Contest platforms seek to resolve this contradiction through incentive systems and *gamification.* Many award reputation points for *collaboration* and *community engagement,* some even issue proper awards that may boost portfolios or constitute a separate financial incentive.

The form of short-cycle project work with intermediary stages and performance targets, the significance of implicit knowledge as well as the decentralised and indirect control through autonomous self-management, team collaboration and peer-to-peer control, resemble the agile work methods which have acquired wide popularity, particularly among white-collar office workers.[19] Although the required work-related knowledge cannot be standardised or codified, the underlying high-skill processes, which represent a black box to management, are to be made visible nonetheless. In contrast to microtasks, the required expertise on macrotask platforms cannot be standardised and codified; the opposite is the case, because subjective skills are essential. Indeed, a task may not be tied to any specific person, which would contradict the principle of crowdwork, but the person processing it does have to deploy their subjectivity.

In effect, a strongly individualised visibility and subjectivation can be observed on all kinds of macrotask platforms. A staff member describes the profiles on the contest platform she works for as follows:

> Here you see her badges [game elements used for behavioural control]. [...] [She] is particularly active, giving other creative workers feedback and constantly encouraging people. [...] That's a kind of social status on the platform. [She] earns [points] for each interaction. That is, whenever [she] gives feedback on an idea, evaluates an idea, submits ideas of her own or sets up a team.

The intention is to use recognition and praise as an incentive in order to attract professional freelancers; at the same time, precisely these subjective resources represent an important type of skill. In contrast to the often-claimed invisibility, the crowd on macrotask platforms have to present themselves as talented experts in order to set themselves apart from the mass of competitors.[20] For individuals, this work regime can lead to subjectivation and the pressure to market oneself: what is required is an 'entrepreneurial self' in order to sell one's own labour power on the online labour market.[21]

The specific form of subsumption found on contest platforms for macrotasks is not constituted by centralised instruction of the labour process, but rather by the networked, decentralised interaction, as a result of which the collaborative substance and the subjective resources are subjected to the conditions and dynamics of capitalism.[22]

OLD POWER IN DIGITAL GARB

The investigation shows that crowdwork marks the emergence of a novel but by no means consistent type of capitalist labour. Within this new set up, distinct processes and degrees of real subsumption are appearing which, depending on the respective complexity of a task, are comparable in many regards to existing workplace-based (in particular Taylorist and agile) labour processes. The form of subsumption that characterises microtask platforms is the fragmentation of the labour process, and the centralisation and standardisation of the work-related knowledge. Platforms thereby react to the constantly changing and anonymous workforce in order to let them produce simple digital goods in a proto-Taylorist labour process in a serial and standardised manner despite workers' physical and formal autonomy. At the same time, this form of work organisation severely limits the scope of application.

On macrotask platforms, by contrast, online workers retain their high degree of autonomy even in production, for the labour process cannot be broken down and objectified, and the work-related knowledge and expertise remains implicit. The task at hand is rather to subsume the individual's subjectivity in real terms by making communication and interaction integral parts of the labour process, which in turn take place in the production space of the platform. Regardless, it can be assumed that this work model will also remain confined to certain niche activities that do not require any business-specific knowledge or long-term responsibilities. Yet the complexity of the labour regimes on macrotask platforms in combination with the general normalisation of a neoliberal self-entrepreneurship suggests that platform-based online work may certainly represent a viable long-term rationalisation strategy in some areas of creative and more highly skilled tasks, for example, as the counterweight to agile management methods in white-collar occupations.

In both cases, the active structuring role played by platforms can be observed. While they radically marketise labour compared to workplace-based employment, they assume a role that is equivalent to the workplace in the socio-technical triangular relationship between capital and labour: they translate customer orders into a labour process which materialises labour in the form of use values. In this sense they organise *management functions as a commodity*. This may represent a sequence of (evolutionary) change in capitalism: from the early capitalist company patriarch via corporate management[23] to the external platform, capitals tend to manage *themselves* less and less. The emerging management regimes potentially rationalise not only workplace-based labour but are also themselves highly rationalised, for example, in the sense that the crowd is included in decentralised and mutual control.

What is new is the advanced and peculiar form in which workplace domination confronts the individual in a neutral, technological guise. Similar to the machine system, workplace domination is objectified in the materiality of the platform: its algorithms and designs constitute its political and social power, for whoever controls the space and interfaces and manages access determines action scope and thus rules. That said, positing the platform as equivalent to the Marxian machine system, as may be concluded following Andreas Boes and colleagues, appears to go too far: due to the formal independence and lack of direct access, platforms cannot directly subject the individual workers and their labour to their desired rhythm and thereby alienate them. Instead, they govern through *infrastructural power*: a more restrained power that structures space, interests and preferences instead of bodies; a power that rules without ruling.[24]

213

This gives rise to a number of fundamental *implications for those offering their labour*. What emerges is a hybrid labour regime that can be characterised as dependent independence: online workers are formally self-employed, highly mobile and flexible – and yet, their working conditions depend on the platforms. The technological form lets domination appear as absent and as an indisputable order. The workplace conflict is anonymised, dispersed and individualised. Instead, fragmented and de-collectivised 'solo capitalists'[25] are needed who self-economise and, especially on macrotask platforms, market themselves in order to sell their labour power. However, platforms are by no means ironclad, and the field of tension between radical market dependence and the construction of autonomy is at times resolved in the form of problems of acceptance, deviant work behaviour and practices of resistance.[26] In addition to this, the crowd's high mobility represents a considerable power resource.

Crowdwork underscores the labour-intensive flip side of digitalisation. The generalisation of the work model seems limited due to the specific problems of management and control. Crowdwork ought to be seen mainly as a field of experimentation for new forms of administration of capital as well as workplace domination via digital, infrastructural power, which may rule certain layers of the workforce in the future and will by no means necessarily remain limited to self-employed platform work.

14

The Machine System of the Twenty-first Century?

On the subsumption of communication by digital platform technologies

Felix Gnisa

According to various pundits, the advent of digital technologies has heralded a phase of economic reproduction with particularly favourable conditions for the overcoming of capitalist societies. Big Data analyses and additive production processes such as 3D printers are hoped to allow for the management of economic processes via decentralised planning instead of the market.[1] The immaterialisation of the means of production, for example in the form of software codes, is to render the distribution principle of private property redundant.[2] Projected advances in automation may in fact pave the way towards transcending the work-centred society.[3] Such considerations build on the notion that the plausibility of post-capitalist ambitions is substantiated not least by the existence of conceivable efficient alternatives to a market-organised economic mode that exercises control over labour. Another important criterion of such a post-capitalist economy is the extent to which digital technologies enable the immediate producers to organise the production process independently. For there is no justification for planning fantasies that concern society as a whole if they are not supported by the *democratic control over production* and thus run the risk of cultivating bureaucratic rule even beyond the market-based organisation of social reproduction – a fact evidenced by the tragedy of state-bureaucratic socialism.[4]

The digital platform economies that have emerged over the past 15 years represent a suitable object of study to discuss this problem. As digital pioneer industries, they reflect a new productive logic of capitalism in which the objective for companies is less the manufacturing of products than making communication infrastructures available in which users, workers, retailers and companies can interact with one another.[5] Consequently, they differ considerably from the kind of work organisation which led to rather pessimistic verdicts regarding the possibilities of the democratic organisation of work: the industrial factory *subsumed in real terms*. Against the backdrop of this pessimistic comparative screen, these verdicts help emphasise how digital capitalism establishes a new quality of labour subsumption – and thus a new relation between production, the technological control over labour and the conditions of appropriating technology – that differs from its industrial predecessor.

REAL SUBSUMPTION AS A PRAGMATIC PROBLEM OF TECHNOLOGICAL APPROPRIATION

Marx introduces the concept of the formal and real subsumption of labour under capital in order to describe transformations of organisational forms and technologies motivated by the structural dynamics of the capitalist mode of production. Marx describes artisanal production in the putting-out system of mercantile capitalism as subsumption in formal terms. Although the labour of craftsmen was integrated into the value-creation cycle of capital, their specific organisation of work was left untouched. In the process of real subsumption, however, the mode of work is itself reorganised so as to meet the requirements of an economy based on market competition.[6] The result is the kind of industrial work organisation for which studies in the sociology of work based on the theorem of real subsumption[7] issued a sobering productivity diagnosis. What was fundamental in these studies was the observation that the rationalisation of industrial labour occurred essentially via gains in time efficiency, and that the *economy of time* was implemented via the separation of conceptual labour and the actual performance of work tasks: work-related knowledge and expertise were concentrated in the work and planning offices of the factories, and the majority of producers were instructed in the detailed work steps which had been devised beforehand. Subdividing labour and training workers to be specialised in one task meant they completed monotonous work more quickly than the skilled craftsman who had the ability to complete all individual production steps. This *technique of rationalisation* found its material embodiment in the technology of the industrial factory, the *machine system*: the specific skills expropriated from manufacturing workers were inscribed into tools and moving machinery which determined the rhythm of work, and the majority of producers were accordingly forced to follow the production flow. In the process of real subsumption, two structural characteristics of capitalist societies thus become inscribed in the form of productive technology: the dimension of the centralisation of work-related knowledge reflects the *class structure*, and the dimension of cycle time reflects the *exchange-value imperative*, as market advantages for individual companies are essentially achieved via the reduction of living labour. However, both the domination of labour *and* productivity are established simultaneously in this process: domination, because the majority of workers no longer possess the knowledge concerning the labour process; productivity, because that is what accelerated the serial production of standardised goods and made mass production possible in the first place.

The process of real subsumption thus poses a pragmatic problem for a progressive transformation of society that prefers not to abandon the wealth potentials it has developed. The coupling of efficient economic reproduction with a means of production that cements the disenfranchisement of the majority of workers can cause serious problems for the project of a democratic organisation of the labour process. After all, what is relevant for the latter is the knowledge pertaining to the production process.[8]

PRODUCTIVITY: ALLOCATION AND EFFICIENT INFORMATION REGIMES

The factory subsumed in real terms organises productivity through the centralisation of work-related knowledge and expertise. Digital platforms, by contrast, are only functional because they allow companies to access and extract productive knowledge that is not located within their organisational boundaries, but instead with scattered producers. This is illustrated by four platform types which organise productive activity.[9]

1) Platforms in the gig economy such as Uber, Helpling or Airbnb allocate jobs to self-employed taxi drivers or cleaners or allow individuals to list private holiday lets.[10] The platforms possess neither the material resources nor the labour forces to offer certain services, but rather provide a digital infrastructure in order to connect work orders, resources and labour. As such, they rely both on the producers' material resources and the knowledge about the existence of certain resources and labour forces that can only be provided by the producers.

2) On microtask platforms like Amazon Mechanical Turk or Clickworker, low-complexity tasks are tendered for bids. The portfolio ranges from text production for product descriptions, the transcription of audio clips, or the tagging of pictures to the translation of short text content. The work is particularly low-skilled. The companies placing the orders, however, not only rely on the knowledge of producers for the completion of tasks, they also have no idea who a certain assignment should be completed by. The matching up of talent and tasks is organised via the independent acceptance of projects by the labour forces.[11] As workers themselves thus contribute the knowledge concerning the effective matching up of capacity and orders, it is possible to oversee a high number of clickworkers with only a few staff members. On the largest microtask platform, Crowdflower, 5 million registered workers are managed by 100 employees.[12]

3) On creative platforms such as Jovoto, which coordinate product innovation or the design of brand logos,[13] or the software development platform Topcoder,[14] orders are also tendered to a large crowd. In contrast to the microtask platforms, however, this is high-skilled, creative work, which means these platforms make highly implicit knowledge accessible for companies. Yet, here too, crowdworkers decide individually whether they are adequately skilled for a task that is tendered. On German-language crowdworking platforms for high-

skill tasks, around 94,000 registered members are supervised by only 23 internal platform staff.[15]

4) Social media platforms like Facebook or Google allow users to socially interact with one another so that the platforms can target them with personalised advertisements. By posting content and comments, making friends or joining groups, users produce a network of cultural knowledge which, when analysed, forms a cartography of needs, preferences and lifestyles. Although it may appear somewhat strange to refer to the users' behaviour as labour,[16] their communication, in terms of its relevance to the dimension of advertising, by all means constitutes productive activity within the value-creation cycle of capital and can thus be interpreted in terms of subsumption.

What all these platforms have in common, despite the different 'labour processes' they organise, is that they collect information on productive capacities, resources and needs which are used for the coordination of production. The knowledge accumulated on platforms, then, is not relevant for the immediate production process itself – the platforms do not organise or supply the driving of cars or the programming of software – but for the coordination of producers. The platforms make it possible for an Uber driver to be made aware of a passenger in need of a ride, for the cultural artefacts produced by users on Facebook to be exposed to rating by digital communities, or for companies to source the specifically qualified labour force who can contribute productive knowledge. The information condensed in digital infrastructures therefore rather constitutes allocative knowledge, and platforms are in this sense *allocative means of production*, as they allow for the allocation of required tasks, resources and capacities.

As the allocative means of production that they are, platform technologies constitute a fundamentally different form of productivity than the industrial machine system. Marx considered productivity to be the cheapening of goods, in the sense that 'more commodities [are produced] with a given quantity of labour'.[17] This entails a certain logic of production which assumes that labour does not mainly consist of designing products but of materialising them. In standardised industrial production, products are designed by research and development (R&D) departments, after which engineers in equipment construction design corresponding production systems; work offices then define individual work steps, and workers complete these tasks. Here, rationalisation means giving the intellectually conceived product a material body with as little expenditure of labour as possible. That is the path of real subsumption: a production logic in which engineers and management possess the knowledge about the product, and the bulk of manufacturing workers materialise it.

Another notion of productivity is put forward by Yochai Benkler, a theoretician of network production: productivity is the *function of labour capacity and the resources to which it has access*.[18] It assumes that the product is *non-standardised, immaterial or dynamic*, and labour therefore in this case consists primarily of conceptually devising the product.

The different types of platforms are good examples of this: neither the client nor the management of crowdworking platforms know what a code for a certain program or an advertising campaign they commission is supposed to look like. Similarly, the Big Data analysts of social media platforms cannot decide which cultural practices enjoy most popularity, as the ad-placing companies, for whom the datasets are evaluated, rely precisely on users revealing their preferences so that advertisements can be personalised. *The product is non-standardisable.*

Likewise, on platforms in the gig economy, in which no creative labour is sourced, the product ultimately cannot be determined: the management of Uber, for example, cannot plan which demand for a ride shall be attended to by which driver. The product, that is, the *matching* of resource and demand, is temporally and spatially dynamic and therefore relies on the informational contribution of the drivers.

At first glance, microtask platforms offer an update to the Taylorist system of industrial labour, as they are marked by the tendering of extremely fragmented sub-tasks.[19] That said, this subdivision of the process as a whole is not accompanied by a knowledge of the desired product on the part of the commissioning party. This is a significant difference to labour in the industrial factory and results from the *immaterial* character of the labour product. In the industrial production of material goods, work offices were able to determine the result even of individual sub-tasks because workers ultimately only serially materialised the pre-existing non-material concept of a product. If, by contrast, the translation of a text already existed in the head of the person or company placing the order on a microtask platform, there would be no task to be completed; yet by actually completing it, its producer creates new knowledge. The fact that clients know nothing about the product they are pursuing is evidenced by the model of control through which they ensure the adequate completion of a task. Most of the time, tasks are performed by several clickworkers at once, and algorithms identify individual deviations as dysfunctional solutions. The uncertainty about the final form of the labour product is to be reduced by a comparison of the knowledge supplied by the involved clickworkers, and yet it cannot simply be resolved through the absolute transfer of the production-related knowledge to the commissioning client.[20]

If the product is in fact conceptualised and designed by the producer in all of these cases, then for a company that does not know whose labour capacity is best suited to resolving a production problem, the most effective procedure is to address this problem to the greatest possible number of producers so that an adequate labour capacity becomes aware of it. This is the essence of Benkler's productivity logic: the greater the potential functions of labour capacity and resources, the greater the benefit of the digital infrastructures. In contrast to the materialising productivity of the machine system, allocation is thus largely immaterial productivity, as an effective matching relation is the result of the condensation of information.

ALIENATION: THE SUBSUMPTION OF COMMUNICATION

Proceeding from allocative-immaterial productivity, as opposed to the materialising productivity of the machine system, a new form of labour subsumption can be identified. Platforms conduct allocation in a way that subordinates producers to *independent communication*, just as manufacturing workers are subjected to the independent tool machines. This circumstance is illustrated quite pointedly by two platforms and their algorithmic mechanisms: the gig platform Uber, and the microtask platform Amazon Mechanical Turk.

Uber

Uber organises living labour through three algorithmic tools.

Firstly, an algorithm automatically matches up drivers and pas-sengers. Drivers do not have the option to preselect preferences for passengers but have to decide, based on the information provided by Uber regarding location, name and rating of the passengers, whether or not they wish to accept a request. After a deadline of 15 seconds has passed without the request being accepted, the ride is automatically allocated to another driver. The criteria for this allocation remain unknown to the drivers. Frequently, they receive requests for an area which could be reached more quickly by another driver. Apart from the criterion of distance, the mutual rating of drivers and passengers or the log-in duration may serve as the underlying data that is used for *matching*. For example, drivers who activate their app for a longer period of time may be allocated rides with a greater distance.[21]

Through the so-called *surge-pricing* algorithm, secondly, dynamic prices are calculated for highly frequented areas and times. As soon as demand in a given area exceeds supply, these zones are displayed as *surge-pricing zones* in the drivers' app. Aggressive incentives such as sending push messages even when the app is turned off, repeated notifications of potential surge-pricing zones when a driver logs out, or sending emails regarding predicted high-demand volumes all serve to stimulate drivers' financial motivation. The predictions concerning peak hours are based on the evaluation of previous trip data.[22] For drivers, by contrast, it is uncertain whether they will profit from the surge-pricing periods, as the allocation algorithm may just as well direct them to passengers outside those zones. What is more, Uber threatens exclusion from the platform if drivers reject requests outside the surge-pricing zones. That is to say, on the one hand, the placement of algorithmically calculated incentives activates the pool of living labour in order to compensate for frictions in demand cycles. On the other hand, the algorithmic allocation mechanism ensures that messages that make drivers aware of higher earning opportunities are not used against Uber's matching logic.

Thirdly, allocation is managed based on the mutual *rating* of drivers and passengers and the calculation of request-acceptance rates. Uber pays a guaranteed hourly wage for a minimum acceptance rate, but also 'deactivates' drivers whose rate is too low. A value of 4.5 out of 5 can be enough to be deactivated. Drivers are thus under constant pressure to receive favourable customer ratings and develop a 'service mindset'[23] in order to increase customer satisfaction – for example, by detecting, via subtle conversation and eye contact, whether a passenger wishes to engage in conversation, which music is desired, or whether the air conditioning is too cold.[24] The algorithmic performance evaluations and acceptance rates are sent to drivers on a weekly basis in order to encourage them to adopt a work attitude that is conducive to the platform's objectives.[25]

Amazon Mechanical Turk

A number of crowdsourcing tools have been developed for the microtask platform Amazon Mechanical Turk which companies can use for the automatic management of clickworkers who perform complex tasks. One of them is Turkomatic,[26] which organises the coordination of a subdivided labour process via the independent cooperation between algorithms and producers. The programme first creates a form for the task definition – for example, writing a product description for an online retailer – which is filled in by the commissioning client and in which a fixed price for the completion of a HIT (Human Intelligence Task) is tendered. Subsequently, different segments of the task are presented to the crowd following a pre-programmed procedure. The crowd then returns solutions, on the basis of which further production steps are tendered.

The first HIT consists of assessing whether the complexity of the task is adequate for the tendered price. Should a clickworker decide that this is not the case, Turkomatic devises another HIT in order to partition the task. This process is repeated until the complexity of the task falls to a level that matches the fixed price, upon which Turkomatic asks a clickworker to decide, in the form of a HIT, whether the sub-tasks should be completed sequentially, that is, building on one another, or in a parallel process. After all fragmented HITs have been completed, Turkomatic composes a so-called *merge*-HIT which asks clickworkers to piece together the sub-tasks. The preliminary results of the sub-tasks are tendered for assessment by other workers in all stages of the process. Should preliminary results be marked as entirely dysfunctional, the algorithm automatically tenders once more all tasks that are in need of review.

In both cases, all the knowledge conflated in the product is provided by the workers, yet, as the dispersed crowd that they are, they do not consciously engage in this cooperation but are subjected to the work steps and coordination methods determined by algorithmic trajectories. Producers do not cooperate with each other, but with the algorithmic machine, serving it as communicators who send information so that it can plan the subsequent labour process. In this sense, they enter into a dynamic managerial relationship with technology, in which, however, workers are deployed as elements of an overall system whose management targets are defined by automated communication methods. Producers participate in a jointly constituted pool of allocative information, yet the circulation of this information – *its communication* – is structured via expropriated channels that are not controlled by workers, but serve capital-functional criteria: at Uber, information concerning requested rides in combination with surge-pricing information serves the swift matching of demand with supply, while the rating mechanisms serve to foster a disciplined, functional work attitude. The self-management and fragmentation of work on crowdworking platforms serve the cheapening of labour,[27] the reduction of internal management costs,[28] and the protection of internal knowledge resources of the companies placing orders.[29]

Considering the two dimensions of real subsumption – class structure and the economy of time – we can identify a specific form of subsumption. In the dimension of class structure, the platforms expropriate work-related knowledge – in the form not of immediate production-related knowledge, but of *allocative knowledge*. A reorganisation of this knowledge according to the provisions of the economy of time and thus a timing of production, however, cannot be attributed to platforms. Platforms create matches, but not the acceleration of production. In order to cope with the uncertainty as to whether the labour intensity exerted for a product corresponds to the socially given productivity level, the (commercial) platforms all rely on the financial constraints of the piecework rate. Here we find a parallel to the historical stage of formal subsumption. As a result of the lack of knowledge regarding the labour process, the owners of manufactories and factories were unable to enforce their performance expectations through work instructions, but had to try to implement them using financial power – for example, by coupling the wage of industrial workers to the volume of manufactured products through subcontracts.[30]

The fact that the time dimension of real subsumption is irrelevant to the dominant character of technology is illustrated, on the one hand, by the distinct production logic and thus the non-standardised dynamic and immaterial character of labour products that are generated by platforms and for which timing specifications are difficult to implement. On the other hand, and when following the notion of online platforms as pioneer industries of digital capitalism, it is somewhat indicative that time efficiency, in an economy in which digital platforms appear to become expedient, plays a less important role than favourable matching relations.

APPROPRIATION: A TECHNOLOGY FROM THE WORKERS' PERSPECTIVE AND THE WEIGHT OF THE IMMATERIAL

The specific quality of subsumption, finally, allows for conclusions regarding the extent to which an efficient work organisation is necessarily accompanied by an expropriation of work-related knowledge and expertise. The concept is thus useful for fathoming the possibility of the transformation of technology in favour of a democratic organisation of work. In principle, such a technology would have to express that the work-related knowledge is controlled by producers. With regard to the organisation of work in an industrial context, this means that the work-related knowledge which producers are subjected to by the machines must be shifted back to the workers. From the perspective of workers, technology would have to regain the status of a tool and be subjected to their control. However, this also points to a pragmatic appropriation dilemma for the technology of the factory subsumed in real terms, in which productivity and domination are closely coupled: the restitution of work-related knowledge and expertise runs the risk of straying into a return to artisanal forms of production and thereby neutralising the time efficiency gained through the previous expropriation. One example of such an attempt was the proposal for *Telechiric* (remote control) devices developed by shop stewards at the UK-based Lucas Aerospace Corporation in the 1970s, which were intended to allow workers to control robotic tools via gear sticks and TV cameras instead of having to adjust to the movements of automated tool machines.[31] Telechirics would have been subjected to the control of workers and would certainly have expanded their physical and optical capacities; whether they would have been capable of making production more time-efficient, however, is questionable.

The subsumption of communication, by contrast, may well hold more favourable conditions for such a project of appropriation. Finally, let us turn to three indicators that support the notion that the effectiveness of allocative productivity is not dependent on the disenfranchisement of producers.

Firstly, allocative knowledge is constituted as a *common* pool of information. The task at hand is thus no longer one of returning this allocative work-related knowledge to producers. Rather, an alternative technology would require a method of communicating information that accommodates the needs/expectations of all producers; the criteria of allocation would have to be the result of a democratic negotiation process. Existing concepts in computer sciences concerning platforms, which allow for decentralised power supply in *smart grids*[32] and allocate the provided resources based not only on efficiency criteria but also on fairness criteria, point to the plausibility of such possibilities. The crucial aspect is that such an alternative organisation of allocative professional expertise need not prevent the possibility of effective allocation.

Secondly, the principal character of platform technologies consists in the fact that they cope with uncertainties in the labour process; they make it possible to organise a labour process in which it is unclear *what* the product should look like, or at *what time* and *which location* it will be needed. This uncertainty also leads to an irreducible residue of control on the part of producers within the labour process – it is not the algorithmic tool Turkomatic that determines the specific fragmentation of the labour process, but clickworkers. This suggests the fundamental possibility of organising labour processes through platforms which proceed from far-reaching controlling opportunities for producers – for example, in the sense that all those involved in the translation of a text have an overview of the process as a whole and thus decision-making competencies in individual work steps – *without* neutralising the effective achievement of matching relations.

The fact that the relation between productivity and dominance is no longer constitutive, is ultimately also illustrated by the lack of a link between capitalist *Landnahme*[33] and the development of productivity. The machine system was the peak of a development that began with the independent craftsman and ended with industrial production. The development of wealth and capitalist *Landnahme* were closely intertwined. The platforms' productivity logic, by contrast, was detected by Yochai Benkler in the context of the Free Software movement of the 1990s, which was able to develop software products that are essential for today's network infrastructure.[34] Today's platforms thus emulate a work method which represented an efficient organisational form under non-capitalist conditions. It is therefore questionable whether the dominance over labour has actually injected new productive dynamics into this particular mode of work.

Should these assumptions be accurate, efficient economic reproduction and workers' control over their own work environment would no longer be a contradiction. The productive logic of capitalism may thereby open up a new scope for a democratisation of work organisation, which could form part of a societal transformation strategy as a whole.

15

Digital Labour and Prosumption under Capitalism

Sebastian Sevignani

The term 'digital labour' is on everyone's lips these days. Broadly speaking, it denotes the most diverse activities, such as the extraction of rare earths for the information and communication industries (ICT), industry and services supported by digital technologies (Labour and Industry 4.0), or the production of hardware and software. This chapter focuses on the (core) area of digital labour that is most interesting and challenging in terms of a theory of capitalism: the production of information and data that occurs during the use of information technologies such as the internet and 'social' media.

The term 'social media' is to be understood as all those socio-technical arrangements that are not exclusively the means of human cognition but allow for mutual communicative relationships which may also form cooperative structures between human beings. For example, there are countless subjective reasons why Facebook users share their views (cognition) with a large number of other users on the platform, exchange feedback (communication), perhaps set up a group in the long term (cooperation) and become active on behalf of certain issues even outside of Facebook. The internet, as a system of globally connected computers, is engendering a new social action space.[1]

The concept of prosumption underscores the synchronicity of processes of production and consumption. This movement of thought, which considers distinct functional economic realms in their necessary interconnectedness, is nothing unusual when proceeding from a Marxian perspective.[2] Prosumption, then, serves to describe the conflation of distinct areas and roles that were originally conceived separately, in the sense that the behaviour of consumers is harnessed for the production of goods and services, and consumers assume productive roles. This feature existed even in the pre-digital era of the consumer society.[3] For instance, consumers engage in productive activities when they clear their tables in fast food restaurants or recycle supposed 'waste products' from their own household.

In the information space, digital prosumption acquires a decisive new quality: due to the particular characteristics of information, namely that other consumers can hardly be excluded from its use and it is not used up when consumed, production and consumption roles can immediately coincide temporally and spatially (and often do so unnoticed by the 'prosumer'). Given that each and every consuming act leaves a trace in the information space, which can then be used for production, and more and more actions are linked to the information space, these supposed 'waste products' of digital prosumption constitute a new sphere of accumulation for capital, as represented by tech giants like Google or Facebook.

The precise role of the phenomenon of prosumption in the theory of informational capitalism has been and continues to be the subject of a controversy (conducted mainly in the English-speaking world) that we know as the *Digital Labour Debate*.[4] In the following, I would like to substantiate which approach to the problem of prosumption, in terms of social theory and capitalist theory, I consider to be conducive. I begin by addressing the question of whether it is justified to speak of digital prosumption as actual labour. I then discuss whether digital prosumption can be exploited, before finally situating the debate around the economic value of digital prosumption in a broader theory of capitalism that takes into account the articulation of distinct modes of production.

PROSUMPTION AS DIGITAL LABOUR

If you ask internet users to describe their online activities, very few would refer to it as 'work'. The reasons often stated are that the use of social media takes place during one's free time, that it is regarded as a fun activity, that no (tangible) product emerges, and that it is not remunerated. However, proceeding from this everyday understanding does not explain the matter in any great depth. Our experience in capitalism narrows our understanding of what actually constitutes work (e.g. that only wage labour can be considered 'real' work). If this everyday notion of work is simply reproduced, the result is an analytical blind spot when critically reflecting on activities that deviate from this norm. The political conclusion one may then draw is perhaps the idea put forward by the early socialist Charles Fourier, namely to abolish work as such, which was criticised by Marx.[5]

A critical theory therefore begins by seeking to expand the common concept of work. Marx provides several starting points for doing so, and this expansion has been further refined by neo-Marxist approaches. Marx's point of departure for political economy is the distinction between concrete useful work, which produces use values, and its capitalist form of abstract labour.[6] Moreover, he emphasises that even if work does not dissolve into play, it can be the source of pleasure nonetheless. The expansion of the concept of work has since been emphatically recommended by a whole range of different authors and theoretical schools: Marxist feminists have pointed to the problems of a wage-centred notion of work and the corresponding privatisation and concealment of the production of life and female labour power.[7] Proceeding from Fourier and psychoanalytical considerations, Herbert Marcuse discussed the possibility of a sensuous quality of work.[8] The works produced by Marxist-oriented cultural studies have redefined the relation between base and superstructure, considering communication as a process associated with the social base.[9] Critical psychology, basing itself on Activity Theory, has reconstructed the link between work and language from an evolutionary point of view.[10] Critical linguistics and semiotics argue that communication is a form of production (of signs).[11] And, finally, the post-workerist (or 'post-operaist') tradition, which is today more broadly discussed in the context of informational capitalism, has popularised the concept of immaterial, communicative and affective labour.[12]

Similar to the theory of social informatisation,[13] I propose to conceptualise digitalisation as a development of the system of human productive forces and part of the broader process of informatisation. In this sense, prosumption can be understood as informational work. The system of human productive forces consists of the active subjects who use means of labour to work on objects; in the process, the subjects also develop and take shape while redesigning both themselves and the external natural world. They objectify the capacities and skills they have acquired in previous activities in the form of labour products and (re-)appropriate them in renewed work processes. Each of these tasks requires cognitive skills. What distinguishes the skills of human beings from the impressive architectural skills of bees, according to Marx, is the fact that bees cannot visualise and plan their construction, their hives, beforehand.[14]

This act of intellectually preconceiving a work process assumes an independent material shape in the form of information and, subsequently, machine-processable data. To illustrate this, take the following example: data, which are nothing but electronic impulses or digits, become information once they acquire a certain meaning. The number 37.9 becomes information when it is displayed on a (Celsius) temperature scale that ends at 45. In that case, 37.9 is a high temperature, indicating fever and an illness within the human body. The process of informatisation occurs in a reverse manner: knowledge and experience are reduced to information, detached from their context and thereby become shareable between different individuals. Compared to the broader process of informatisation, digitalisation signifies further reduction, an even stronger detachment of experience in the form of data.[15] In this way human experience can, firstly, be shared more quickly. Secondly, at an informational level, it can be modified as well as combined and integrated with other bodies of knowledge available in the form of data and information – and this can be done without a renewed appropriating reference to a world of experience that (in the meantime) may have changed. Information and data represent objectified human cognitive capacities and thus labour products, albeit not those that are tangible in the traditional sense.

Analogous to this broader understanding of work, it seems appropriate to also expand the objective elements of the system of productive forces and thus the concept of the means of production. Raymond Williams suggested construing means of communication as means of production.[16] They include information (or formalised data) as means of labour and media as socio-technical arrangements in which the information can be modified, combined and processed through human labour power and knowledge.[17] From this perspective, prosumption means working with means of communication and producing information.

Digital informatisation as the development of productive forces, for instance, creates the potential to discuss and compare situational knowledge and experience with general social requirements at a very fast pace and with the inclusion of all those affected. In other words: the opportunity arises to connect many (partial) production publics with a largely general and democratic public. This emancipatory perspective, however, is obstructed by the predominant conditions in capitalist societies. On the one hand, there is structural inequality; on the other hand, the objectified human capacities turn against their own creators, which can be described as alienation. This raises the question as to what extent both – exploitation and alienated socialisation through value – apply to the phenomenon of prosumption in informational capitalism.

EXPLOITED DIGITAL PROSUMPTION

In its more general meaning, exploitation signifies a social mechanism that ties the 'good fortune of the strong' to the 'misery of the weak'.[18] The connecting element between the two antagonistic 'classes' is the circumstance that the exploited are excluded from the productive resources and the appropriation of the proceeds generated through their labour. The exploiters, by contrast, own the relevant means and the products of labour. In this general use, the concept of exploitation can certainly be applied to digital prosumption.[19]

What is crucial for this purpose is that the means of communication in their function as means of production must not be exclusively equated with control over a technical device and access to an information space. Nor does the concept neatly fit into an ownership relations model. Adopting a perspective inspired by Marx, the primary objective is not to define the 'legal term' of ownership, but rather to characterise relations of production[20] which regulate control over the reproduction and means of life. This includes functional equivalents to private ownership, such as the network effects associated with social media that must be taken into consideration when it comes to control over the relevant means of communication. Private ownership of, say, technical communication infrastructure certainly plays a role here, but it is not an exclusive role. A smartphone with a Facebook app only becomes a relevant means of communication in combination with a data centre, which allows for centralised social media, as well as the resources of attention and reach. If these resources are distributed unevenly, there is social pressure for internet users to use one of the available and popular social media services, as they would otherwise risk social and communicative exclusion in a digitally connected world. Based on the secured control (at least in terms of ownership) over technical infrastructure (software, servers) and labour forces (innovation, marketing, etc.), a small number of commercial enterprises manage to take advantage of network effects and channel attention and communication processes. Correspondingly, the most used global online services are all operated by private companies seeking to make a profit,[21] with only one exception (Wikipedia).

Different business models are conceivable in the information space. For example, direct payment for internet services (such as online newspapers with a paywall), which is, however, rarely the case with the more popular services that are mostly accessible free of charge (e.g. YouTube, Google's search engine and Facebook). In the case of these cost-free services, the business model consists of either adding the option for users to purchase additional services/features or generating income through the sale of advertising placement.

We may speak of exploitation when the users' activities, their prosumption of information, is used for this business model. Their cognition, communication and cooperation are harnessed for valorisation purposes. This requires surveillance through which users and their activities can be identified, classified and assessed in a comparative manner.[22] In the advertising model, surveillance is most evident as the results are offered to advertising clients.

Surveillance always involves the exchange of private data, legitimised through a privacy policy.[23] A central passage of Facebook's Terms of Service reads:

> You own all of the content and information you post on Facebook
> [...] For content that is covered by intellectual property rights,
> like photos and videos (IP content), you specifically give us the
> following permission, subject to your privacy and application
> settings: you grant us a non-exclusive, transferable, sub-licensable,
> royalty-free, worldwide license to use any IP content that you
> post on or in connection with Facebook (IP License). (Clause 2 of
> Facebook's 2015 Statement of Rights and Responsibilities)

In the context of this privacy policy agreement, I would like to draw
an analogy between Marx's workers who are free in the double sense,
and internet users who also enjoy two freedoms. They are free from
the ownership of the means of communication (first freedom), yet,
in legal terms, are the owners of their data, which is at their own free
disposal (second freedom). This way, the exchange of private data
in return for the services offered by online platforms is legitimised,
which includes the surveillance of prosumer activities and the appropriation of the data they generate.

Contrary to the notion that prosumptive activities are only formally
subsumed under (communicative) capital – that is to say, the actual
activities are harnessed for valorisation purposes but not transformed
by them – there is good reason to assume that the exploitation of
prosumption does not leave these activities unaffected.[24] Precisely
because surveillance-based business models rely on their users' prosumptive activities, the owners of the means of communication
interfere with the cognitive, communicative and cooperative processes in the information space. Surveillance-based business models
become more profitable as users reveal more valorisable data or
generate more valuable information. Due to their control over the
means of communication, commercial social media, unlike alternative, non-commercial social media, heavily influence user activities
to this end. The fact that informational capitalism frequently causes
crises of privacy may be considered evidence of the subsumption of
prosumption under capital, as users experience the development of
social media oriented towards commodity production as a breach of
their autonomy.[25] According to this analysis, (class) struggles against

exploitation can today manifest themselves in struggles for data protection and privacy, and against surveillance.

PROSUMPTION AND VALUE IN AN EXPANDED THEORY OF CAPITALISM

Among the most controversial questions discussed in the context of a critical theory of informational capitalism is the analysis of the economic valorisation of prosumption. This is about, firstly, the question as to whether prosumption actually entails the production of value and how it is distributed among distinct classes. Secondly, the question emerges about an expanded theory of capitalism that goes beyond the narrow Marxist definitions in *Capital*: capitalism appears as a complex structure of interplay between distinct modes of appropriation and production.

Activities can, firstly, contribute to capital accumulation or be a functional element thereof. Marx differentiates between different means of capital accumulation in the form of profit, rent and commercial revenue. Rent represents a form of income that can be realised through the monopolisation of productivity-enhancing means, say, through the leasing of land. Commercial revenue is achieved by taking advantage of price levels. To Marx, both forms ultimately constitute deductions of profit produced elsewhere and are thus a form of inner-economic redistribution between distinct capital classes. Activities that enable profit-making contribute directly to capital accumulation, while those that make rents and commercial revenue possible do so only indirectly. Functional activities for capital accumulation, then, are those which create the conditions for these valorisation opportunities. They can be referred to as reproductive activities.[26] This includes, for example, care activities that reproduce labour power as well as activities which produce and ensure the natural and political[27] and – relevant to this study – informational or knowledge-related[28] preconditions for capital accumulation. The creation of these enabling opportunities may follow other logics than that of capital accumulation and can be organised, say, in a commons-based form,[29] such as the production of free software on which alternative social media can be based.

Secondly, all these activities can be paid or unpaid. In value-theoretical terms, there is a controversy here – in reference to Marx – about how to measure value. A substantialist labour theory of value associated with classical political economy is confronted with a theory of a logic of validity that strictly ties value to monetary exchange and thus to the wage form.[30] While the former position allows for value to be measured in terms of (labour) time expended at the site of production, the latter position emphasises that value is a social relation which cannot be directly measured but is expressed only through money. Expended labour has no value if its products cannot be realised on markets and in the form of monetary values. In my view, the second of these two positions more accurately takes into account the circumstance that something is today considered valuable only if it features in a number of official statistics, such as on gross domestic product (GDP), while it emphasises the important role of money. Under capitalism, all produced values aspire to being realised in the form of money.

In my understanding, this outlined political-economic set of tools can only inadequately be represented by the distinction between productive and unproductive labour – which Marx did indeed make but used too inconclusively.[31] Capitalism consists of a complex and crisis-prone articulation of different modes of production. With regard to digital capitalism, this insight – which is quite widespread in critical development theory in peripheral countries[32] – also manifests itself very clearly in the capitalist centres. On the one hand, we can observe capital strategies that rely increasingly on the '*Landnahme*'[33] of the results of prosumption whenever informational products are appropriated. Such *Landnahme*, however, also occurs where commodity production is coupled with an alternative mode of production that remains intact. Interaction in commercial social media, which is based on the philosophy of giving or a commons model rather than on exchange, can, for example, be 'tapped' for the purpose of commodity production.

Against this theoretical background, the limitation of Marx's analysis in *Capital*, namely that the exploitation of labour is forced into the wage form, i.e. the commodity form, becomes clear.[34] His main interest here lies in the continued existence of the exploitation mechanism under the political and economic conditions of wage labour that is free in the double sense, and the (incomplete) generalisation of a mode of production in which the wealth of a society appears in the form of commodities. Moreover, in Volume One of *Capital* his main focus is on the production of profit and not on processes of inner-economic redistribution. When Ursula Huws, proceeding from that analysis,[35] defines this form of labour – in terms of a theory of capitalism and class – as labour 'inside the knot', she does justice, in analytical terms, to the structuring role of capitalist wealth, which can only be measured in money. However, she underestimates the fact – which is rather significant with regard to the transformation of capitalism – that capitalism can face challenges from outside the realm of productive wage labour as well. Contradictions and frictions can be found not only 'inside the knot' of capitalism, but also in relation to the 'outside' that facilitates it. Experiences, values and norms that are acquired from the appropriated outside can come into conflict with the capitalist 'logic of value'.[36]

Capitalist development occurs as a complex inside-outside movement.[37] It always entails the internalisation of external elements, the inclusion of externalised areas, the occupation of a not (or not *yet*) fully commodified outside. Class struggle is therefore not only about the intensification, limitation or even cancellation of capitalist exploitation. Class action is also always aimed at shifting the boundaries between areas of inclusion and exclusion in society, paid and unpaid labour, exploitation and over-exploitation, etc. For example, in some fields of prosumption it is not the struggles around and for a (better) wage that take centre stage, but, say, in the case of social media, the infringement of privacy standards (negotiated between users) by commercial actors whose access to private data cannot be prevented by the privacy regulations built into the technological structure of these media. That said, the social debate around privacy – and this once again underscores the particular social significance of the 'knot' of paid productive labour under capitalism – is strongly oriented by the discourse of (capitalist) private ownership and the market, as even a wage for Facebook users is being demanded.

Digital prosumption, to build on Alvin Toffler in making reference to (Marx's) theory of capitalism, is therefore not only the temporal and spatial coincidence of production and consumption in a certain mode of production, but also that of reproduction and production, and of several modes of production. Proceeding from the deliberations presented here, it can assume various forms of activity. Its 'nature' does not allow for a conclusion regarding its political-economic role in capitalism. Prosumption can be paid or unpaid, it can directly contribute to capital accumulation or be a functional element thereof in various ways.

DIGITAL PROSUMPTION AND FACEBOOK

To conclude, I would like to illustrate the presented reflections based on the example of Facebook. Facebook is a stock-market listed commercial enterprise that runs an online service which generates profit for the company, largely through advertising. The social network and everything that occurs within it serves the purpose of capital accumulation. Advertising clients are offered the opportunity to target their ads directly at potential customer groups that are compiled using highly refined criteria. The advertising firms invest in Facebook ads either to increase the sale of their own goods or to establish market barriers for their competitors by channelling the audience's attention. Today a growing share of advertising spending is invested in online ads. This allows some social media to be profitable, while other, traditional recipients of ad spending (the 'old' mass media) are thrown into a funding crisis.

The use of Facebook constitutes prosumption. User interactions (liking, sharing, commenting, etc.) can be understood as the objectification of knowledge into information and the renewed appropriation and integration of this information into subjective knowledge. The formalisation of information into data so characteristic of the information space allows for a new mode of network formation (that is, e.g., more independent of specific locations), and this itself, in turn, does not follow the logic of capital accumulation. Although what takes place on social media has often been described – in reference to Pierre Bourdieu – as a competition for symbolic and social 'capital', i.e. for recognition and prestige, the purpose of social network building is not monetary return. I regard prosumption on social media as a non-capitalist mode of production which certainly allows for cooperative elements alongside the competition-driven allocation of recognition. The deployment of the products and means of prosumption does not, in the interaction between users, follow the logic of exclusion and exploitation.

Yet prosumption on Facebook is permanently monitored, which serves two objectives that can be attributed to two distinct modes of production. On the one hand, there is horizontal surveillance, the precondition for social network building. It allows users to keep themselves informed about each other's activities. Vertical surveillance, then, aims at integrating prosumption into a mode of production oriented towards capital accumulation. This marks the moment of exploitation of users, which then feeds back into their social network building. The aim of vertical surveillance is to identify, classify and comparatively assess the prosumption data in view of marketable goods. Access to the collected data may be made available to interested parties directly for a fee, which, however, would somewhat limit Facebook's special role as custodian of the access to users and thus, ultimately, the valorisation opportunities. In the dominant business model, the prosumption data (most of which is automated and only some of which is processed in the form of wage labour) constitutes the raw material for the creation of user profiles, which allow advertising clients targeted access to the attention of certain customer groups. Vertical surveillance constitutes exploitation because Facebook's financial income correlates with the duration, but also with the intensity, of digital prosumption and network building and thus, consequently, also the unequal distribution of the means of communication.[38] Facebook's interest in the valorisation of social network building in turn engenders a structuring effect. Correspondingly, ever since the company's stock-market launch, there have been numerous interventions into the process of objectification and appropriation of prosumption at the level of data extraction, and the data collected on the platform has been combined with data generated elsewhere in the information space in order to satisfy shareholder expectations. For example, Facebook increases the volume and quality of monitored data through 'like' buttons which can be found on many different websites. User data are not only collected on Facebook's own website but throughout the entire internet, promising valuable insights into consumer preferences. Another example of the influencing of user activity are the so-called *sponsored stories* that are placed prominently in the user's timeline (Facebook's homepage), as a result of which the user's intended communication is interrupted by advertising messages.

User prosumption on Facebook is unpaid and, as an activity, does not contribute directly to capital accumulation. Yet, given the surveillance, it is tied to the accumulation of capital and a functional element thereof. Without the exploitation of prosumption Facebook would have no valorisation opportunities. Facebook's current earnings represent an inner-economic redistribution of profits from advertising capital to commercial social media. While it makes perfect sense to speak of the exploitation of users of commercial social media, it is a form of exploitation that differs from the reproduction of social inequality through wage labour analysed by Marx.

CONCLUSION

In pursuing an expanded theory of capitalism as outlined in this chapter, the task at hand is to take struggles that occur in external functional areas, such as the struggle for privacy, more seriously in class-theoretical and political terms. But what exactly does that imply? I would like to close with a few brief remarks on this. One strength of the concept of exploitation is that it focuses on the disadvantaged as producers of their own misery. Applying the concept of exploitation to prosumption means that it is users' activities that substantiate the power of the tech companies in the first place. From this perspective, we may assume an objective interest in organising the legitimation of existing power structures in the information space in a more decentralised and egalitarian way, given the potential inherent in the means of communication – a task which, needless to say, must be politically organised. While the question of whether users can (objectively) be ascribed an interest in change must be answered in the affirmative, the significance of these struggles for the production of capitalism as a whole seems more difficult to determine. On the one hand, it certainly depends on the share in globally earned profits of those companies whose business models are based on the exploitation of prosumption, and is, in this sense, rather something of a side issue.[39] On the other hand, it would be a mistake to measure the significance of communicative struggles exclusively based on their economic weight.[40] After all, relations of communication constitute and provide a space in which (class) struggles can emerge. In this sense, struggles for a non-commercial, non-exploitative, decentralised and democratically organised information space should not be underestimated.[41]

16

Artificial Intelligence as the Latest Machine of Digital Capitalism – For Now

Timo Daum

Although the debates surrounding the discipline may have fallen quiet for a few decades, Artificial Intelligence (AI) is currently seeing an unprecedented renaissance. The public debate is dominated by notions of general artificial intelligence, i.e. machines whose cognitive capacities are comparable to those of human beings in terms of both quality and quantity. They are thought to be capable of either triggering a Third World War, as Tesla founder Elon Musk seems to be convinced of, or, alternatively, peacefully taking over power, as German AI guru Jürgen Schmidhuber believes.[1]

The implementation of such 'strong AI', however, does not appear to be on the agenda anytime soon. On closer inspection, the reality is far more tenuous. No matter whether it is image recognition, the preselection of applicants, driverless vehicles or social scoring, AI is always involved – but in its 'weak' variant. In some very limited areas of application, it may indeed be able to perform certain cognitive tasks, automate processes and even improve over the course of its use – no more, but no less either.

There has been a maturation of AI methods which enable digital capital to optimise its data extraction. The leading companies in digital capitalism have specialised in the generation of valorisable information from vast amounts of data and turned this activity into a profitable business model. Capital is thereby establishing a new form of business in which the extraction, evaluation and valorisation of data constitute the essence of economic activity.

The extraction, processing and analysis of these raw data increasingly occur via AI-based software. In many areas, AI applications owned by tech corporations are on the brink of mass marketisation and becoming everyday phenomena.

AI is a little bit like God: although there is no tangible proof of its existence, it does cause an awful lot of commotion. This holds true at least for 'strong AI', which is all about automats that can comprehensively compete with human cognitive capacities. Strong AI rests on the notion that human cognitive capacities – consciousness, empathy, morals – and higher cerebral functions are not tied to a certain biological materiality, but may just as well be copied by sufficiently powerful computers. Particularly in Silicon Valley hopes run high that artificial and natural intelligence will merge in the none-too-distant future.[2]

The mission statement devised at the 1956 Dartmouth Conference, which established the discipline, expressed the conviction 'that every aspect of learning or any other feature of intelligence can in principle be so precisely described that a machine can be made to simulate it'.[3] Initially, the preferred method – favoured, for example, by AI pioneer Marvin Minsky – was a top-down approach, in terms of an attempt to program the rules underlying human behaviour.

Weak AI, by contrast, is limited to developing trained cognitive systems for specialised tasks such as the categorisation of image content. In reference to Patrick Langley, such systems could be termed 'idiots savants',[4] which may display a talent in a given area but are utterly useless beyond this field. Here, a bottom-up approach was followed, in the sense of an emulation of neural networks that simulate brain cells and learn new behaviours.

The early days of 'good old-fashioned AI', as Hector J. Levesque refers to the euphoric beginnings of AI research, were marked by boundless optimism.[5] Constructing learning, thinking machines that were on a par with human beings seemed not only desirable and feasible, but was thought to be a goal that was only a few computer generations away from becoming a reality.

In 1959, the American AI pioneer Arthur Samuel coined the term 'machine learning' to describe software with built-in self-learning processes, i.e. that was able to independently develop models from large datasets.[6] Deep learning, in turn, represents a subdomain of machine learning; it is based on artificial neural networks that emulate the human brain in order to achieve highly efficient learning. The aim of neural networks is to identify and evaluate structures within the data that are fed into the system (input), and to autonomously generate results (output) through many repeated runs of those data. Deep learning proceeds from statistical data analysis, not a deterministic algorithm. Initial successes with neural networks were achieved as early as the 1970s. Following a highly critical report by the mathematician Sir James Lighthill in 1973 and the termination of funding by US Congress, AI research-related activities noticeably ebbed away: the so-called 'AI winter' had begun.

When AI is talked or written about today, it is usually with regard to machine learning applications. AI expert Alpaydin summarises the current situation: 'As it currently stands, the vast majority of the AI advancements and applications you hear about refer to a category of algorithms known as machine learning. These algorithms use statistics to find patterns in massive amounts of data.'[7] Why is it, then, that we are currently witnessing the renaissance of decades-old technologies?

On the one hand, methods of machine learning have reached the brink of profitable application thanks to cheap and efficient computer hardware and the refining of certain methods. The Taiwanese-born American venture capitalist and AI specialist Kai-Fu Lee considers AI technologies to be approaching mass marketability, as profitable business models are within reach and there are no longer any technical obstacles to their widespread application. He thus speaks of an 'age of implementation': products employing AI, such as personal assistants, chatbots and automated driving software, are reaching product maturity and are about to conquer the mass market.

Added to this is the existence of colossal amounts of data in many applications, which are usually collected automatically and at no cost (Big Data), and made available as training data for machine learning. In contrast to previous stages of the discipline, in which scientific advances took centre stage, we have now entered the 'age of data' (Kai-Fu Lee). The volume of training data determines the quality of the AI applications into which they are fed. As a result, those who have the most data in a given field of application today stand the best chance of providing high-quality AI-based applications.

The data corporations from Silicon Valley have a significant edge in this regard. The major tech enterprises, which have managed to secure a dominant position in the past, increasingly rely on AI technologies. These corporations possess the largest data collections worldwide, have the most capital at their disposal to hire the best talent in the business and, at the same time, have the greatest base of both users and data suppliers for their AI applications. Apple, Amazon, Alphabet, Microsoft, Facebook and IBM are the names of those who share the AI pie – outside of China. In China, the situation is similar. Here, the *Big Three* – search engine Baidu, internet company Tencent and Amazon clone Alibaba – have the largest data collections, most user profiles, strong cloud-computing infrastructures, immense financial resources and sufficient computing power to dominate AI.

The deep learning pioneer Andrew Ng compares the current wave of AI-driven software with the emergence of electricity. 'About a century ago, we started to electrify the world through the electrical revolution. By replacing steam powered machines with those using electricity, we transformed transportation, manufacturing, agriculture, healthcare and so on. Now, AI is poised to start an equally large transformation in many industries.'[8] Like electricity, AI will become a base technology, powering a multitude of digital applications. In sum, AI-related technologies are on the path to becoming the most important processing and valorisation machine in a data-extracting model of capitalism.

THREE VALORISATION MECHANISMS

Tech corporations have become the most profitable and powerful enterprises in the world – Alphabet, Amazon, Apple, Facebook and Microsoft top the list of the most valuable firms. All the companies listed are digital tech enterprises, i.e. organisations whose business relations with employees, customers, suppliers and other external partners are organised via digital networks.[9] They embody a type of capitalism in which information – its generation, distribution via networks and, ultimately, capitalisation – takes centre stage.

Big Data, that is, the automatic accumulation of vast amounts of data in digital form, represents the raw material of this capitalist valorisation model. The capitalism critic Evgeny Morozov refers to this functional principle as 'data extractivism'.[10] In digital capitalism information has moved to the centre of economic and social activity and, in many respects, has either marginalised or left behind traditional goods, services and the associated business models. Everywhere we look today there is talk of data extraction, Big Data and algorithm-controlled data mining.

The corporations of digital capitalism establish platforms,[11] i.e. infrastructures, which they provide to third-party users while determining the rules for and making a profit off each and every action occurring. The network effect, as a result of which the use value of a product increases with the number of users, creates these companies' steadfast monopoly. Platforms strategically build on permanent user participation, constant redesigns and optimised user experience in order to extract ever more data from their users. Just to keep with the extraction analogy: the iron ore that is mined corresponds to the raw data that is mainly generated from the bustling activity on the platforms. The high market capitalisation of these companies, matched, as it were, by a tiny amount of material value, rests on a valorisation promise that is based on the immense number of users and the data generated as a result.

This model is catching on. The data and information economy is becoming increasingly significant in all economic sectors – manufacturing, agriculture, finance and healthcare, to name but a few. In all these areas, data collection and analysis via AI-based technologies are becoming essential. The critic Nick Srnicek emphasises how the significance of the platform model goes beyond the online economy in the narrower sense: 'On the one hand, platforms increasingly dominate strategically important positions in the economy. On the other hand, platform companies increasingly also pervade traditional economic sectors.'[12] The respective relevant players attempt to establish platforms of their own – such as, say, Siemens, in the area of industrial networking.

Are we, then, witnessing a new phase in the history of capitalism? In that case, industrial capitalism would appear as an historical stage that has been replaced, or complemented, by new forms in different waves since the 1970s. There is much to indicate that the old accumulation model is on the retreat. Three new forms of accumulation are emerging; they were described long ago, but are only now converging into a new phase.

General knowledge as a service[13]

Industrial era capitalism revolved around the exploitation of human labour in the production process. Marx writes of the 'productive expenditure of human brains, muscles, nerves, hands etc'. The labour that is embodied in finished commodities, 'that forms the substance of value, is equal human labour, the expenditure of identical human labour power'. Actual performed labour always only appears subsequently as the average labour power of society.[14] The entire logic of capitalist economic activity lies in the extraction of surplus value, i.e., the unpaid share of living labour in the direct production process.

Likewise, capital's operations are 'state of the art' insofar as it employs knowledge as a production factor. In doing so, it drives scientific discoveries, which even come to appear as an inherent characteristic of capital itself. As the science-fiction author Stanisław Lem wrote: 'No living person today understands the design principles of all the devices at the disposal of our civilization. Yet there is someone who has such understanding: society'.[15] For this 'someone', i.e., this social function of general knowledge, Marx uses the term *general intellect*.[16]

In his famous 'Fragment on Machines', Marx traces a scenario in which the progressive rationalisation of production and the automation of processes cause the share of directly objectified manual and intellectual labour to fade increasingly into the background. As a final consequence, direct work input is displaced from the production process while the general intellect, i.e., technology based on general knowledge, becomes a decisive production factor. Marx's hypothetical automated factory is comparable to the asymptotic approximation of a singularity: the political-economic division by zero. After all, in his scenario, there is no more living labour, and hence no more exploitation, surplus value or profit – capital loses its *raison d'être* and disappears.

Parallels between the scenario in 'Fragment on Machines' and contemporary digital capitalism have often been observed. In this vein, Nick Dyer-Witheford praises the prognostic quality of the techno-futurist 'Fragment': 'as if Karl Marx had written a science fiction novel and precisely described our current information economy'.[17] The French economist Yann Moulier-Boutang also sees the general intellect at work in contemporary 'cognitive capitalism', describing it as 'a mode of accumulation in which the object of accumulation consists mainly of knowledge, which becomes the basic source of value, as well as the principal location of the process of valorisation'.[18]

However, the dominance of the general intellect has not spelled the end of capitalist relations, as Marx had hoped in his 'Fragment'. Although the general intellect has in fact already been socialised, it has been successfully packaged as a proprietary service and exploited for profit by the *general intellect industry*, as one could quite justifiably label the tech corporations. Both of these processes – the constantly growing share of collective social knowledge within capitalist production on the one hand, and the continuous striving of capital to privatise the end products of this process on the other – are common threads throughout the entire history of capitalism.

The British Marxist historian Tessa Morris-Suzuki describes this phenomenon as follows:

> Once more we are confronted with the fact that, in the production of information, free social knowledge is appropriated and turned into a source of private profit. We have moved away from Marx's picture of the classical capitalism where inputs to production are bought at competitive prices on the market, and where the sources of exploitation can therefore lie only in the labor process itself. It is now theoretically possible for corporations to reap profits without the direct exploitation of their workforce, by making use of a free good to create a product which then temporarily becomes the private monopoly of the corporation.[19]

Slavoj Žižek also sees at work a new accumulation model in which rent is extracted in the form of a monopolistically mediated usage charge. This charge is levied on a general intellect that is actually already a commons:

> To grasp these new forms of privatization, one should critically transform Marx's conceptual apparatus: because of his neglect of the social dimension of 'general intellect' (the collective intelligence of a society), Marx didn't envisage the possibility of the privatization of the 'general intellect' itself – this is what is at the core of the struggle for 'intellectual property'.[20]

In a sense, the platforms of digital capitalism already approximate this scenario remarkably closely. After all, data as well as algorithms are to a large extent publicly accessible – as *open source*, created by us all, i.e. as a social product, as general knowledge. This is precisely what Google transforms into a service when it indexes the content of websites, the usage of which Google then valorises.

The stores of data which feed AI applications – the millions of images, texts, voice commands – have also been collectively created by us all. Although they constitute a social commons, a handful of private actors generate proprietary services with them in order to secure their own profitability. General knowledge is becoming the most important productive force of digital capitalism, yet the latter has paradoxically succeeded in valorising this free social knowledge in the proprietary service form.

User-driven capitalism

In industrial capitalism, the exploitation of living labour in the immediate production process – the predominant form of appropriating the fruits of labour – was the result of an historical development which is far from complete. Today we are seeing the emergence of various new forms of exploitation, such as the exploitation of labour performed via platforms and of the labour required to train AI applications to identify various objects, which users are forced to perform for free.

On the platforms of digital capitalism, the raw data that is constantly being generated represents base material to be refined by algorithms and AI. Yet the mining of these data resources is performed not for a wage by miners whose surplus value is appropriated by capital. Rather, it is the users of platforms, exhibiting a double character as consumers and workers, who produce the never-ending stream of data which can therefore be viewed as the result of unpaid user labour.

New forms of exploitation are joining the appropriation of surplus value in the form of wage labour, which appears as only one specific form of labour exploitation in the immediate production process. In this respect, as Maurizio Lazzarato emphasises, these new forms of exploitation follow from 'different forms of value production'.[21] Exploitation is thus being expanded beyond the sphere of wage labour and the limits of the factory. Indeed, this idea has already been articulated by Deleuze and Guattari. Guattari writes that

> the very notion of the capitalist corporation should be broadened so as to include collective equipments, and the notion of work position, as well as most non-salaried activities. In a way, the housewife occupies a work position in her home, the child holds a work position at school, the consumer at the supermarket, and the television viewer in front of the screen.[22]

Today the model of *user-generated content* enjoys widespread implementation: billions of people are bound up in the process of user-generated capital valorisation, working directly for capital. Negri and Hardt are also convinced that value is produced by biopolitical labour in the production of social life itself.[23] Finally, Paul Mason sees the general intellect at work in social cooperative labour, such as in the sphere of the commons.[24]

This is particularly evident in current AI applications: when users buy a product which contains AI applications, such as a smart home device or virtual assistant hardware equipped with speech recognition, they buy a product for which they themselves constitute a resource. Buyers become a resource insofar as they turn into a constant source of new speech commands providing training data to optimise the system.

Tech corporations take our labelled and contextualised data, which we ourselves have 'uploaded into the cloud', and send it back as applications. Users simultaneously perform unpaid labour by providing free feedback on the functioning of AI. They are consumers but also products insofar as their actions, decisions and preferences can be registered and used to create custom advertising profiles.

Accumulation by innovation

Rationalisation in production has always been the method of choice used by capital to edge out competitors. This encompasses both producing more cheaply and capturing market share through product innovation. Hence, competition is the driving force behind capitalism's historically unprecedented power to innovate, to creatively destroy and to disrupt as desired. Mark Zuckerberg's widely known motto, 'move fast and break things', could well have come from Schumpeter ('creative destruction') or Clayton Christensen ('disruptive innovation').[25] Capitalism is the most innovative social order which humanity has brought forth thus far, and at the same time the most destructive: when people speak of the Anthropocene, the era of human mastery over the planet, they should actually speak of the Capitalocene.[26] After all, only after industrialisation did humanity manage to permanently alter the earth's surface.

In the Marxian critique of political economy, innovation exhausts itself because it is external to the 'normal' production process; it does not initially play a role in the capitalist production process. Innovation by itself does not produce value and does not concern the labour theory of value. Here, innovation remains a special case, an exception, a coup scored by a single capital against the competition.

Can innovation go from being the exception to the norm? Morris-Suzuki puts forth the thesis that this can indeed happen given two conditions: the marginalisation of the significance of direct human labour input in the production process, simultaneously accompanied by the creation of information products becoming the central object of profit generation, in which case 'innovation becomes the core of the company's profit-making activity'. Under these conditions, companies would be forced to shift 'the center of gravity of surplus value creation [...] away from the production of goods and towards the production of innovation – that is, of new knowledge for the making of goods'.[27]

The unchanging production of the same physical object is the norm in the production of material goods. The xth copy of a specific model of chair may well find a buyer, as concrete labour has been expended to produce said copy. With digital information, this is no longer the case. Once information has been created, it need not be produced from scratch again; as far as business is concerned, it has been burned.

The consequence of this situation is the generation of an *ever-changing product*, a product which constantly and continuously modifies itself and thus always stays a step ahead of the competition. In Morris-Suzuki's scenario, the exception becomes the rule as occasional leaps in innovation are replaced by a continuous ramp. Innovation takes on a new meaning: no longer just a weapon against the competition, it becomes the core of a company's profitable activity.

Morris-Suzuki refers to this principle as the 'perpetual innovation economy'.[28] Here, 'surplus knowledge' is central to the 'incessant generation of new products and new methods of production'.[29] Perpetual innovation abolishes a linear accumulation model which continuously aggregates individual elements of labour as a labour product, replacing it with a non-linear model. Increasingly often, repetitive labour processes are automated, almost without resource expenditure (such as with the streaming of digital content), and at zero marginal cost.

AI-based products in particular are characterised by constant self-improvement. The South Korean electronics corporation LG has launched an entire product line around this characteristic: marketed under the heading 'Evolve', products are advertised which supposedly not only do not age, but remain forever young, changing with and being educated by the user almost as if they were children being raised by parents. As LG's Technical Director I. P. Park explains: 'The age of artificial intelligence allows us to go even further. Information will now get better, richer, and deeper with usage and time.'[30]

THE LATEST MACHINE OF CAPITAL, FOR NOW

Ernst Bloch once remarked that it was not disputed in Marxist circles 'that each latest machine which late-bourgeois technology produces is the best'.[31] With good reason, artificial intelligence can be described as the latest machine of digital capitalism, at least for the time being. With its help, digital capitalism has succeeded in consolidating a new social operating mode in which the extraction, evaluation and valorisation of data has become the focus of economic activity.

Given the current wave of new applications that are being labelled 'Artificial Intelligence', we are essentially dealing with data-driven software that can be successfully used in certain closely limited areas of application. We are witnessing a phase of AI development in which the technologies owned by the tech corporations have become mass marketable and thus turned into everyday products. Their function is limited to specific tasks such as the categorisation of images, the detection of patterns in large amounts of data, the representation of human–machine interfaces and the like. The construction of thinking machines is (still) not on the agenda – the current task at hand for the relevant actors is rather to consolidate the data-extracting business models.

In many areas, user reactions are fed back into the system in real-time, i.e. without any noticeable delay between input and output, between action and reaction, which in turn contributes to optimising the system's runtime. User signals, i.e. user behaviour patterns, are used for personalised responses, error recovery and the incremental product improvement in a cybernetic control loop. AI-driven services are optimised through the consumers themselves while being fed by their user data. All this occurs within a circuit of perpetual innovation with the simultaneous goals of optimisation and innovation as well as the monetisation of the consumers' activities – with a constantly improving user experience. The user becomes a three-headed being: he or she is at once the customer, the supplier and the product.

AI represents a technology that serves the aims of analysing Big Data, efficiently valorising the free labour of users and monitoring the digital workforce, just like the assembly line was (and continues to be) both a means of rationalisation and an instrument of power in

253

the factory. Artificial Intelligence is, at least for now, the latest innovation of digital capitalism, one through which it seeks to expand its globally dominant role in economy and society, consolidate its business models and secure its valorisation model.

All three mechanisms of capital valorisation – the valorisation of general knowledge as a service, the exploitation of the gratuitous labour of users, and perpetual innovation as a source of profit – are realised in contemporary digital capitalism. Multiple forms of 'a productive expenditure of human brains, muscles, nerves, hands [and hearts, T.D.]'[32] beyond the wage labour form create labour products that are useful for capital. As a result, while actions and reactions are fed back into the system, all areas of life come to serve as a resource for generating profit.

17

Forces and Relations of Control

On the possibility of sustainable and democratic economic planning in the digital age

Georg Jochum and Simon Schaupp

The central role digitalisation plays in the social change we are currently witnessing is increasingly being recognised in political and economic debates. Frequently, however, this recognition is linked to a doctrine of inevitability that makes digitalisation appear as a kind of natural force somehow descending on society – a force that can be embraced or demonised, but not shaped politically. And despite the often-invoked disruptive force of technological development, it is usually considered self-explanatory that the process of digitalisation will take place within the framework of a growth-oriented capitalist economy and therefore no fundamental break with the existing economic and social order will occur.[1]

Considering the current systemic social and ecological crises, we view such assumptions as rather problematic. Even though the extent and imminence of these crises have been sufficiently documented scientifically,[2] the control and steering mechanisms of the capitalist economy prove incapable of responding with adequate measures. As the failure of efforts for an energy transition to reduce worldwide CO_2 emissions illustrates, the reasons for this inability are rooted not only in the unwillingness to act on the part of the decision-makers in charge. Above all, it is inscribed in the systemic growth imperative of the capitalist economy itself.

In the following, we shall therefore outline a possible way of dealing with the social-ecological crisis that transcends this imperative. Specifically, our focus is on the potential that the rapid development of digital technologies offers for sustainable and democratic economic governance. Digital governance and control provide new possibilities of planning that could help solve the problems of previous and existing non-capitalist economies, particularly with regard to deficits of efficiency and democracy. Goods production, for example, could be coordinated directly via the digital matching of human needs and available resources. This would, firstly, mitigate the ecological blindness of capitalist market coordination and, secondly, open up the prospect of economic democracy.

This 'utopia' is based on real current developments. In times of Big Data and an ever-expanding 'surveillance capitalism',[3] which provides companies with comprehensive knowledge about the preferences and needs of (potential) customers (and allows for their intensified manipulation), market mechanisms are systematically replaced by new forms of cybernetic economic governance and control: supply chains, labour markets, work processes and even prices are controlled digitally. Although this does not create a new central planning authority, neither does this type of capitalism correspond to the neoliberal fiction of market regulation unfettered by any form of planning. Correspondingly, the 'development of the forces of control' increasingly comes into conflict with the 'relations of control'. While this contradiction by no means automatically leads to the overcoming of the capitalist economic order, it certainly provides the objective conditions for a decidedly political transformation, which we refer to as a '*control transition*'.[4]

HISTORICAL AND THEORETICAL BACKGROUND

Before presenting our deliberations on digital technology's potential for a reorganisation of society, we would first like to reflect on the technological developments that have taken place thus far and the various associated forms of society.

The inextricable link between technological and social development was made plain by Karl Marx in a rather famous passage of his text *The Poverty of Philosophy*:

Social relations are closely bound up with productive forces. In acquiring new productive forces men change their mode of production; and in changing their mode of production, in changing the way of earning their living, they change all their social relations. The hand-mill gives you society with the feudal lord; the steam-mill, society with the industrial capitalist.[5]

By citing the 'hand-mill' and 'steam-mill' as the leading technologies of two distinct historical epochs, Marx focused on the means of production and labour, which in each case, through a specific combination with human labour power, allowed for a specific appropriation of nature. The term 'production' (from the Latin *'pro-ducere'*: yield, generate, create; *ducere* = 'lead, pull')[6] points to the process of 'yielding', 'leading' or 'drawing' nature's potential via the labour process, as becomes particularly clear in *Capital*: 'The process is extinguished in the product. The product of the process is a use-value, a piece of natural material adapted to human needs.'[7] As we argue in the following pages, Marxist theory, and particularly the claim that '[a]t a certain stage in their development, the material productive forces of society come into conflict with the existing relations of production,'[8] can contribute, even today, to a deeper understanding of socio-technical dynamics and the development of the potential for a profound political-economic change. However, we see the need for an analytical and terminological reformulation. For it is not physical labour being supplemented and replaced by the mechanical productive power of machines, allowing for new ways in which nature can be appropriated, but rather the development of cybernetic technologies of control that lies at the heart of the technological change which has occurred in recent years over the course of what is referred to as digitalisation.

Following Norbert Wiener, who derived the term 'cybernetics' from the Greek word κυβερνητικός (steersman),[9] we conceive of cybernetic technologies as a specific form of productive forces, the central feature of which is the capacity for controlling mechanical and social processes.

Due to this centrality of governance, control and regulation, we refer to these technologies not as productive forces, but as forces of governance and control.[10] By doing so, we aim to point out a central difference between the classic Industrial Revolution and the cyber-technological revolution that has occurred in the high-tech societies of 'cybernetic capitalism'[11] over the past decades.[12]

We proceed from the assumption that the central hypothesis in Marxian theory of an increasing contradiction between the development of the productive forces and the relations of production can be redefined on the basis of the reformulation outlined above and in light of current developments. In cybernetic capitalism, the forces of control have developed to a point where the overcoming of the capitalist relations of control that have existed thus far is not only possible, but in fact necessary in order to avoid grave social-ecological crises. We start by elaborating our understanding of the 'forces of control' before discussing the levels on which a radical development of these forces has occurred.

PRODUCTIVE FORCES AND FORCES OF CONTROL

In his Foreword to the *Critique of Political Economy*, Marx postulated that the contradiction between the development of productive forces and the dominant relations of production would increasingly intensify and the transition to a socialist mode of production would eventually become inevitable. 'The bourgeois relations of production are the last antagonistic form of the social process of production [...] the productive forces developing within bourgeois society create also the material conditions for a solution of this antagonism.'[13]

In state-socialist Marxism-Leninism, the Marxian reflections were interpreted as meaning that the contradiction between the social character of production based on the division of labour and the continuing private command over the developing forces of production would lead to the capitalist mode of production becoming increasingly inefficient. In this view, due to the 'law of the correspondence between the relations of production and the character of the level of development of the productive forces', the end of the contradictory capitalist mode of production is inevitable, as 'the working class seizes political power'.[14]

The hope that the development of the productive forces would take on a 'naturally inherent' tendency towards overcoming capitalism ultimately proved too optimistic. The attempt to build a socialist society failed in the long term, alongside other factors that were prevalent in (far-from-)real socialism, because of the inefficiency of the planned economy. The triumph of neoliberal capitalism after the collapse of the Eastern Bloc resulted in the increasingly marginal significance of orthodox Marxism and of alternative, heterodox interpretations of Marxian theory. Over the past few years, however, we have been witnessing a renaissance of Marxian-inspired concepts – accelerated by the refinement of digital technologies and their application – that consider the overcoming of capitalism as both likely and possible due to its contradictions. Correspondingly, Paul Mason writes in his book *Postcapitalism*: 'The main contradiction today is between the possibility of free, abundant goods and information and a system of monopolies, banks and governments trying to keep things private, scarce and commercial. Everything comes down to the struggle between the network and the hierarchy.'[15]

In our view, Mason correctly points out the potential of digital network technologies for a post-capitalist organisation of production and consumption. That said, it appears rather reductionist to transfer, as Rifkin does, the characteristic 'abundance' of digitally produced, or rather shared, goods to the entire productive sphere and thus to link the digital revolution to the 'eclipse of capitalism' and the utopia of an 'economy of abundance' and a 'sustainable cornucopia'.[16] Given the likeliness of an increasing scarcity of material and energy resources propelled by the ecological crisis, such simplistic productive-force optimism may justifiably be regarded as overly naive. Moreover, Rifkin and Mason seem to forget, in a technology-deterministic manner, the inherently political aspect of economic transformations. We thus call for a transcendence of the mere postulation of a contradiction between the development of productive forces and the relations of production, as is essentially still put forward by both Mason and Rifkin. Instead, the question of the potential for post-capitalist forms of economic governance provided by the digital-cybernetic means of control ought to be put at the heart of the analysis. We see the need for such an approach arising not least from the already mentioned problems of economic governance in '(not) actually existing socialism' and the emergence of a totalitarian form of rule in the corresponding systems.

By 'means of control' we understand a whole range of technologies that may be beneficial to the governance of the economy and society. This includes, firstly, political steering mechanisms in the narrower sense and, in particular, the techniques of controlling labour within workplaces. Finally, technologies such as writing or money and their use as a means of domination and control can be included in the list.

In this regard, we share the Habermasian view that '[t]he capitalist economic system marks the breakthrough to this level of system differentiation; it owes its emergence to a new mechanism, the steering medium of money'.[17] This 'steering medium' acquired increasing dominance over other means of control as a result of the 'dis-embedding'[18] of the markets. Political counter-movements with the aim of re-embedding markets have led to social regulation and the limitation of the power of money. The Fordist mode of regulation in particular may be regarded as such an attempt at re-embedding that was based on a specific compromise: a politically regulated capitalism emerged, which retained the role of money as a central means of control, but also strengthened the role of the state. In our view, the emergence of the so-called post-Fordist mode of regulation is to be understood as a transition to a neoliberal-cybernetic mode of control that reduced the influence of the state and is characterised by the use of new cybernetic technologies and the new forms of division of labour it allows for.[19]

In the following section, we first present the main characteristics of the cybernetic paradigm and subsequently demonstrate that there have by all means been attempts at a non-capitalist form of adapting cybernetic ideas, and that the potential for an emancipatory cybernetic mode of control and production certainly exists today.

CYBERNETICS – THE SCIENCE OF CONTROL
BETWEEN DOMINATION AND EMANCIPATION

Norbert Wiener is commonly regarded as the father of modern cybernetics. He defined the new field of research as the 'science of communication and control'.[20] Its objective was no less than the development of a universal science through which all other systems, be they living or technological, could be understood and ultimately controlled. In this sense, cybernetic thinking consists mainly of models, analogies and other abstract representations with the purpose of rendering complex and diverse systems comparable with one another. Correspondingly, for example, the human brain was interpreted as an electrical circuit.[21]

Cybernetic theory is based on the principle of feedback-based self-organisation. This concept was originally deduced from observations of biological systems that adapt to changes in their environment instead of first devising a cognitive plan or hierarchical instructions. Feedback loops are supposed to place a system in a state of dynamic equilibrium, which cyberneticians refer to as 'homoeostasis'.

The nucleus of the cybernetic revolution emerged from the rapid advances in the development of self-controlling and information-processing technologies. As a result of the creation of the cyberspace through the networking of computers (i.e. the virtual space created by cybernetic machines), the cybernetic revolution entered into a stage in which it transformed society as a whole and the world of work in particular. In the process, this 'cybernetisation of labour'[22] in 'cybernetic modernity'[23] did not simply result from the increasing dissemination of information and communication technologies in production. Another crucial factor was that the new forms of flexible production made possible by cybernetic technologies were accompanied by a cybernetisation of human subjectivity, which finds its main expression in various forms of digital self-surveillance, or *self-tracking*.[24] The genesis of a neoliberal-cybernetic capitalism made possible as a result in recent years, however, was by no means inherent in cybernetics as such; instead, cybernetics must be regarded as politically contingent.

From the outset, the founders of cybernetics were in disagreement over the relation between cybernetics and the market economy. Pioneers of the discipline like Ross Ashby and John von Neumann thought about ways to conflate cybernetics and neoliberalism, which can be understood as the embryonic form of today's ideology of cybernetic capitalism. Norbert Wiener, by contrast, argued that the capitalist accumulation dynamic contradicts the social homoeostasis in the sense of cybernetics.[25] Stafford Beer, the originator of *management cybernetics*, in fact conceived the infrastructure for a cybernetic economic democracy in socialist Chile (1970–73).[26]

The tradition of market-oriented cybernetics would not become dominant until the mid-1970s, after the more emancipatory, socialist schools of thought had been pushed back. Proceeding from Boltanski and Chiapello,[27] we may say that neoliberalism adapted the cybernetic utopia by discarding the associated hope for an emancipatory governance of society and transforming it into the new spirit of cybernetic capitalism through its connection with the neoliberal market utopia. The coup d'état in Chile and the violent destruction of the vision of a democratic-socialist form of cybernetics could be considered a paragon of this transformation.

In the following, we outline how cybernetic capitalism has developed over the past decades and show how capitalism simultaneously develops forces of control as a result, seemingly rendering the abandonment of the market principle a real option.

Cybernetic capitalism developed within the neoliberal system, yet simultaneously implicitly led to the challenging of its axiomatics. For the apologists of neoliberalism, the superiority of the free-market economy is based on its capacity to efficiently manage and control complex systems of production and distribution. According to Hayek, all forms of economic governance based on targeted social planning are ultimately constrained by the given knowledge:

> the conflict between, on the one hand, advocates of the spontaneous extended human order created by a competitive market, and on the other hand those who demand a deliberate arrangement of human interaction by central authority based on collective command over available resources is due to a factual error by the latter about how knowledge of these resources is and can be generated and utilised.[28]

Ultimately, only '[i]nformation-gathering institutions such as the market enable us to use such dispersed and unsurveyable knowledge to form super-individual patterns.'[29] The assumption that all alternative forms of gathering information about (individual and collective) needs and the correspondingly oriented control of production should prove inefficient due to the complexity of the economy may have been somewhat plausible at the time Hayek was writing his theses. Yet, the illusion that this form of market-mediated information gathering still represents the only and essential form of controlling the production process even today certainly ought to be put aside. After all, in current cybernetic capitalism, a fundamentally new form of information acquisition and the corresponding control of production and distribution has asserted itself – alongside the continuing prevalence of the capitalist logic of profit maximisation – which has only little in common with the ideology of pure market regulation and its superiority.

DIGITAL CUSTOMER RELATIONS AND GLOBAL SUPPLY CHAINS

Far-reaching information gathering both about global supply chains and individual customers can be observed in the spheres of distribution and consumption. As Fredric Jameson demonstrates,[30] one example of advanced cybernetic economic planning based on such information processing is the Walmart corporation. As early as the mid-2000s, Walmart's datacentre registered more than 680 million products per week and over 20 million customer transactions per day. Barcode scanners and computer systems in the stores identify each article sold and store this information. Satellite telecommunication links are established directly between individual stores and the central computer system and from this system with the computers of suppliers to allow for automatic (re-)orders. As the individual identifiability of every product was required, the corporation decided to use RFID (Radio Frequency Identification) tags in all products. These tags allow the tracking of all raw materials, workers and consumers within and outside of Walmart's global supply chains. As a result, the resource and goods logistics can be linked directly with consumption, and, theoretically, even with the wear and tear of products in use.[31]

The business models of internet companies like Google, Amazon and Facebook, of course, go even further, as they *rely* on the collection of user data in order to enable targeted digital advertising. As Zuboff argues, the aim of the tech corporations is not only to obtain information about the behaviour and preferences of consumers, but to actually create them via 'instrumentarian power', with the result that in 'surveillance capitalism [...], the means of production are subordinated to an increasingly complex and comprehensive "means of behavioral modification".[32]

Regarding pricing, Amazon, for example, does not trust the mechanisms of supply and demand. Instead, a system of *dynamic pricing* is used which issues individual prices per customer. While market prices are the result of the relation between aggregate demand and aggregate supply, *dynamic pricing* is based on information about individual customers. Pricing is thus the result of a surveillance process. Quite tellingly, this breach of the neoliberal dogma has sparked some outrage.[33] It appears that it is dawning even on the ideologues of neoliberalism that the largest corporations in the world would prefer to leave the management and control of their economic processes entirely to digital data processing than to the market mechanisms of supply and demand. Digital technology simply allows for more efficient information about what is needed at what time than the price system – as the exclusive means of market information – ever could.

One perhaps even more far-reaching transformation of the capitalist mode of production can currently be observed in the use of Big Data in connection with blockchain[34] and other cybernetic technologies. In the agricultural sector, major corporations collect data on past harvest yields or weather as well as information on the cost of seeds and fertilisers, which are then analysed via computerised algorithms. Satellites allow for the mapping of cultivated areas and contribute to precision farming and Smart Farming.[35] Moreover, blockchain technologies form the basis of new forms of accounting, which make the secure storage and control of all transactions along the value and supply chains possible.

However, critics point out that the use of these new technologies increases the power held by big corporations and displaces smallholding farmers.[36] The dominance of the market principle as an element of control in an economy geared towards growth and profit maximisation currently stands in the way of a socially and ecologically sustainable use of cybernetic technologies. A small number of major corporations are gaining control over entire supply chains and markets. In the process, a cybernetic monopoly capitalism is emerging that essentially contradicts the principle of the free market.

New technologies of control are not inherently designed to be used solely to the disadvantage of mankind and nature. Today, we are already seeing blockchain technologies being used to prevent the trade of 'blood diamonds' extracted from war zones or to ensure compliance with social and environmental standards in cobalt mining. This shows that the demand for social and ecological sustainability, at least in some sub-areas, can by all means lead to a limitation of market principles – albeit, of course, within the capitalist economy.

In sum, we can establish that the basic assumption of neoliberal ideology, namely that only the market allows for a comprehensive information collection process, and the corresponding 'contention that we are constrained to preserve capitalism because of its superior capacity to utilise dispersed knowledge',[37] today – in the age of Big Data – proves to be obsolete. Capitalism develops forces of control that decisively qualify the assumption – which has always been ideologically motivated – of a need for the free market as a central mechanism of information gathering and control. At the same time, the ecological crisis requires a kind of economic governance that limits or even ends capitalism's expansive logic of *Landnahme*.[38] The development of the forces of control is currently increasingly coming into conflict with the capitalist relations of control due both to the opportunities offered by new digital technologies and to ecological requirements.

What is needed is a new social use of the forces of control in order to harness their potential. The technology-deterministic and market-oriented discourse about the future of work under the term 'Industry 4.0', however, rather ignores these questions of control, and for the most part considers political intervention into technology development as imperative in order to secure a leading position for Germany in the global race for digitalisation.[39]

This could be countered by a vision of using cybernetic technologies to completely reinvent politics and the economy. What is required is a control transition, which puts the cybernetic technologies at the service of society and nature. Moreover, a new, second-order cybernetics is needed for the purpose of democratically deliberating the ways in which control technologies ought to be applied.

THE CONTROL TRANSITION

With the phrase 'control transition' we refer to the utopia of a social appropriation of the developed forces of control that would allow us to overcome the socially and ecologically problematic capitalist relations of control.

In current debates on the social and ecological future of society, a fundamental energy transition is being called for that replaces the fossil fuels characteristic of modern industrial society with alternative, renewable energies. By analogy, we may speak of the need for a control transition, as a result of which money, the means of control dominating capitalist modernity, forfeits its significance and is complemented and replaced by alternative forms of control. This is not to imply any kind of return to state-centred planned-economy models of governance. Rather, it would mean proceeding from the unexploited potential of cybernetics and debates surrounding collective forms of governance.

Elinor Ostrom has demonstrated that collective forms of regulation often lead to more efficient resource management than those centred on the state and/or the market.[40] The new digital technologies and platforms offer new opportunities to modernise and expand these collective forms of governance and control; this includes, above all, the possibility of generating a vast number of plans for democratic deliberation instead of a single bureaucratically imposed economic plan. Software agents, i.e. computer programs capable of autonomous behaviour, may indeed play a central role in this scenario. In a post-capitalist society, they would be relieved from computation-intensive tasks such as algorithmic trading[41] and could instead be used to automatically preprocess vast amounts of aggregate economic data for democratic decision-making. They would make it possible to calculate multiple planning options together with their respective ecological and social impacts, and put them to a vote. Basic configurations – an algorithmic constitution, so to speak – could be preprogramed (e.g. CO_2 emissions must remain within a certain limit and working hours must not exceed 30 per week). These plans could then, as Nick Dyer-Witheford proposes, be discussed and put to a vote on social media platforms that have been brought into public ownership, i.e. when 'Facebook, Twitter, Tumblr, Flickr and other Web 2.0 platforms not only themselves become operations self-managed by their workers (including their unpaid prosumer contributors), but also become fora for planning: Gosplan[42] with "tweets" and "likes"'.[43] This would render a central planning authority, which devises and implements a single, binding plan, obsolete once and for all.

OUTLOOK

As we have demonstrated, the means of control have developed within cybernetic capitalism to the point that they allow for new forms of needs-based and democratic economic governance. At the same time it is clear, given the ecological crisis, that the expansive dynamic of capitalism is reaching external boundaries. The development of new forms of economic governance is thus both possible and necessary.

Needless to say, replacing a neoliberal despotism with one based on a digital planned economy is not desirable – nor is the algorithmic automation of decisions concerning inherently political matters. Instead, digital communication infrastructures, such as social media, could form the technological basis for radically democratic economic governance. This would eliminate the need for a central planning authority. Autonomous software agents could instead calculate myriad potential plans, including their ecological and social impacts. These plans could then be put to a vote digitally. This in turn would dramatically reduce the cost and effort associated with democratic economic governance (e.g. via workers' councils), so that a radically democratic deliberation of complex economic questions could actually become material reality.

This control transition could also coincide with a fundamental social reorientation towards the abandonment of the objective of profit maximisation that is the core purpose of the 'steering medium' we call money. The orientation towards the common good would allow for a fundamental change of direction and thus a cybernetic course correction towards an economy based on social and ecological solidarity. Such a change, of course, will not be accomplished through the development of the forces of control themselves, but relies crucially on a political movement.

Notes on Contributors

Florian Butollo is a researcher at the WZB – Berlin Social Science Center, and heads the 'Working in Highly Automated Digital-Hybrid Processes' research group at the Weizenbaum Institute for the Networked Society in Berlin. His recent publications include a volume edited together with Prof. Dr Oliver Nachtwey: *Karl Marx. Kritik des Kapitalismus. Schriften zu Philosophie, Ökonomie, Politik und Soziologie*, Berlin 2018.

Timo Daum is a university lecturer and author. He recently published *Die Künstliche Intelligenz des Kapitals*, Hamburg 2019.

Kristina Dietz heads the 'Global Change – Local Conflicts?' (GLOCON) junior research group at the Free University of Berlin (FU Berlin). Her recent publications include 'Direct Democracy in Mining Conflicts in Latin America: Mobilising Against Colombia's La Colosa Project' in the *Canadian Journal of Development Studies*, 2018.

Franza Drechsel is the Senior Advisor and Project Manager for West Africa in the Africa Unit of the Rosa Luxemburg Foundation. Together with Bettina Engels and Mirka Schäfer, she recently published '"The Mines Make Us Poor": Large-Scale Mining in Burkina Faso', *GLOCON Country Report*, No. 2, Berlin 2019.

Christine Gerber is a researcher and PhD student working in the 'Globalisation, Work and Production' research group at the WZB – Berlin Social Science Center. Together with Martin Krzywdzinski, she recently published 'Arbeiten immer und überall? Entgrenzung von Arbeit am Beispiel von Crowdwork', in Hans Hanau and Wenzel Matiaske (eds.), *Entgrenzung von Arbeitsverhältnissen*, Baden-Baden 2019.

Felix Gnisa is a researcher at the Institute of Sociology, specialising in the Sociology of Work & Industrial and Economic Sociology, at the Friedrich Schiller University in Jena, Germany.

Frigga Haug is a writer and editor. She co-edits the *Historical-Critical Dictionary of Marxism* and the journal *Das Argument*, and lectures on topics related to Marxist feminism at many national and international events. Her recent publications include *Selbstveränderung und Veränderung der Umstände*, Hamburg 2018.

Jan-Peter Herrmann (translator) holds an MA in Social and Cultural Anthropology and Linguistics from the Free University of Berlin. Since 2012, he has translated a broad range of books and articles both into German and English, mostly in the areas of labour market and trade union research, the sociology of work, Marx studies, and history.

Georg Jochum is a researcher at the Sociology of Science department at the Technical University of Munich (TUM). His research focus includes the sociology of work and technology, sustainability research and the critique of coloniality. His recent publications include 'Wie werden wir arbeiten? Die sozio-öko-technologische Transformation der Arbeitsgesellschaft', in *Smartopia. Geht Digitalisierung auch nachhaltig? politische ökologie*, Vol. 155, Munich 2018.

Elena Louisa Lange is a Senior Research Fellow and lecturer at the Institute of Asian and Oriental Studies at the University of Zurich. She recently published 'The Proof is in the Pudding: On the Necessity of Presupposition in Marx's Critical Method', in *Consecutio Rerum*, No. 5, 2019.

Christian Meyer is a PhD student at the Friedrich Schiller University in Jena, Germany, and a Rosa Luxemburg Foundation scholarship holder. He recently published 'Ambivalenzen der Digitalisierung und gesellschaftliche Kräfteverhältnisse', in *Ökologisches Wirtschaften*, No. 3, 2017.

Kim Moody is a Senior Research Fellow at the University of Hertfordshire and has focused on issues related to the labour movement for many years. In 1979, he was among the founders of the US-based journal *Labor Notes*, serving on the editorial board until 2001. His recent publications include *On New Terrain: How Capital is Reshaping the Battleground of Class War*, Chicago 2017.

Phoebe V. Moore is Associate Professor of Political Economy and Technology at the University of Leicester's School of Business. Her recent publications include *The Quantified Self in Precarity: Work, Technology and What Counts*, London 2018.

Nadine Müller is the head of the department for Innovation and Good Work at the service union ver.di. Her latest publications include 'Die nächste Gestaltungsherausforderung: Künstliche Intelligenz – wozu, was und wie sollen Algorithmen lernen?', in *Zeitschrift Gute Arbeit*, April 2019.

Sabine Nuss is the managing director of Karl Dietz Verlag Berlin. She is a columnist for the journal *OXI. Wirtschaft anders denken*, and more recently edited the collected volume *Der ganz normale Betriebsunfall. Viermal Marx zur globalen Finanzkrise*, Berlin 2018.

Sabine Pfeiffer holds the Chair of Sociology (Technology – Work – Society) at the Nuremberg Campus of Technology of the Friedrich Alexander University Nuremberg-Erlangen. She recently published 'Digitale Arbeitswelten und Arbeitsbeziehungen: What You See Is What You Get?', in *Industrielle Beziehungen*, Special Volume Digitale Arbeitswelten und Arbeitsbeziehungen: Direkte und indirekte Effekte digitaler Technik, 2019.

Simon Schaupp is a sociologist and works as a postdoctoral researcher at the University of Basel. His current focus is on the effects of digitalisation on power relations. Together with Anne Koppenburger and Paul Buckermann, he has edited the collected volume *Kybernetik, Kapitalismus, Revolutionen. Emanzipatorische Perspektiven im technologischen Wandel*, Münster 2017.

Dorothea Schmidt is professor emeritus for economic and social history at the Berlin School of Economics and Law. She regularly publishes articles in the journal *Prokla*, including 'Mythen und Erfahrungen: die Einheit der deutschen Arbeiterklasse um 1900', No. 175, 2014.

Sebastian Sevignani is currently completing his postdoctoral habilitation in theoretical and general sociology at the Friedrich Schiller University in Jena, Germany. He is a member of the Netzwerk Kritische Kommunikationswissenschaft (Network of Critical Communication Studies), the Centre for Emancipatory Technology Research (ZET), and a board member of the Institute for a Global Sustainable Information Society (gsis). He recently published 'Historisch-Materialistische Medien- und Kommunikationstheorie 2.0', in *Maske und Kothurn*, No. 64, 2019.

Karsten Uhl is the Director of the Mittelbau-Dora Concentration Camp Memorial and teaches modern history at the Technical University of Darmstadt (TU Darmstadt). Together with Nina Kleinöder and Stefan Müller, he is the co-editor of *Humanisierung der Arbeit. Aufbrüche und Konflikte in der rationalisierten Arbeitswelt des 20. Jahrhunderts*, Bielefeld 2019.

Judy Wajcman is Professor of Sociology at the London School of Economics and visiting professor at the Oxford Internet Institute. Her research focuses on the political implications of artificial intelligence, robotics and machine learning. She is considered one of the most eminent scholars on feminist sociology of technology. Together with Nigel Dodd, she published *The Sociology of Speed: Digital, Organizational, and Social Temporalities*, Oxford 2017.

Notes

INTRODUCTION

1. Andreas Boes, Tobias Kämpf, Barbara Langes and Thomas Lühr, 'Lean' und 'agil' im Büro. Neue Formen der Organisation von Kopfarbeit in der digitalen Transformation, Bielefeld 2018.
2. Erik Brynjolfsson and Andrew McAfee, The Second Machine Age: Work, Progress, and Prosperity in a Time of Brilliant Technologies, New York/London 2014.
3. Kevin Drum, 'You Will Lose Your Job to a Robot – and Sooner Than You Think. Automation Helped Bring On the Age of Trump. What Will AI bring?', Mother Jones, November/December 2017, at www.motherjones.com/politics/2017/10/you-will-lose-your-job-to-a-robot-and-sooner-than-you-think.
4. Paul Mason, Postcapitalism: A Guide to Our Future, London 2016; Nick Srnicek and Alex Williams, Inventing the Future: Postcapitalism and a World Without Work (revised and updated edition), London/New York 2016.
5. Karl Marx, A Contribution to the Critique of Political Economy, in Karl Marx and Frederick Engels, Collected Works (MECW), Vol. 29, New York 1987, p. 91. Whether or not this is the ideal conclusion from the Marxian perspective remains highly controversial. The later analytical writings no longer contain such apodictic demands. See Michael Heinrich, 'The Fragment on Machines: A Marxian Misconception in the "Grundrisse" and its Overcoming in "Capital"', in Riccardo Bellofiore, Guido Starosta and Peter D. Thomas (eds.), In Marx's Laboratory: Critical Interpretations of the Grundrisse, Leiden 2013, pp. 197–212.
6. Karl Marx, Capital: A Critique of Political Economy, Volume One, translated by Ben Fowkes, London 1976, p. 130.
7. Ibid., p. 431.
8. Ibid., p. 617.
9. Simon Schaupp, 'Vergessene Horizonte. Der kybernetische Kapitalismus und seine Alternativen', in Paul Buckermann, Anne Koppenburger and Simon Schaupp (eds.), Kybernetik, Kapitalismus, Revolutionen. Emanzipatorische Perspektiven im technologischen Wandel, Münster 2017; Nick Srnicek, Platform Capitalism (Theory Redux), Cambridge 2017; Oliver Nachtwey and Philipp Staab, 'Das Produktionsmodell des digitalen Kapitalismus', in Sabine Maasen and Jan-Hendrik Passoth (eds.), Soziologie des Digitalen – Digitale Soziologie, Special Volume No. 23 of the Journal Soziale Welt, Baden-Baden 2020, pp. 285–306; Shoshana Zuboff, The Age of Surveillance Capitalism: The Fight for the Future at the New Frontier of Power, New York 2019.

10. See the chapters by Dorothea Schmidt, Sabine Pfeiffer and Nadine Müller in this volume.
11. Marx, *Capital, Volume One*, pp. 781–802.
12. Konrad Fischer, 'Vorwärts in die Vergangenheit', *Wirtschaftswoche*, 18 January 2019.
13. Philipp Staab, *Falsche Versprechen. Wachstum im digitalen Kapitalismus*, Hamburg 2016.

1 AUTOMATION: IS IT REALLY DIFFERENT THIS TIME?

1. This chapter was originally published as a review article: Judy Wajcman, 'Automation: Is It Really Different This Time?', in *The British Journal of Sociology*, Vol. 68 (March 2017), No. 1, pp. 119–27, published by John Wiley & Sons Ltd., Oxford. Reprinted with kind permission of the publisher.
2. Singularity being the term for Ray Kurzweil's prediction that machines will soon be smarter than humans.
3. Carl Benedict Frey and Michael A. Osborne, 'Technology at Work: The Future of Innovation and Employment', *Citi GPS: Global Perspective & Solutions*, February 2015.
4. Melanie Arntz, Terry Gregory and Ulrich Zierahn, 'The Risk of Automation for Jobs in OECD Countries: A Comparative Analysis', *OECD Social, Employment and Migration Working Papers*, No. 189, OECD Publishing, Paris 2016.
5. Andrew Abbott, *The System of Professions: An Essay on the Division of Expert Labor*, Chicago 1988.
6. Harry Braverman, *Labor and Monopoly Capital: The Degradation of Work in the Twentieth Century*, New York 1998 (1974).
7. Malte Ziewitz (ed.), Special Issue: Governing Algorithms, *Science, Technology, & Human Values*, Vol. 41 (2016), No. 1; Heather Ford and Judy Wajcman, '"Anyone Can Edit", Not Everyone Does: Wikipedia and the Gender Gap', *Social Studies of Science*, Vol. 47 (2017), No. 4, pp. 511–27.
8. See https://www.sciencemuseum.org.uk/what-was-on/robots.
9. Lilly Irani, 'Difference and Dependence among Digital Workers: The Case of Amazon Mechanical Turk', *South Atlantic Quarterly*, Vol. 114 (2015), No. 1, pp. 225–34.
10. Lucy Suchman, *Human-Machine Reconfigurations: Plans and Situated Actions*, Cambridge 2007.
11. See the excellent special section of the *Journal of Economic Perspectives*, Vol. 29 (2015), No. 3, where David Autor reminds us how regularly concerns about automation and joblessness recur.
12. Sheila Jasanoff and Kim Sang-Hyun (eds.), *Dreamscapes of Modernity: Sociotechnical Imaginaries and the Fabrication of Power*, Chicago 2015.
13. See the MIT Press book series on Infrastructures.

2 'VORACIOUS APPETITE FOR SURPLUS LABOUR'

1. For the 'Automatic Cash Register and Self-Checkout' made by the company SFOUR, see http://sfour.ru/en/solutions/selfcheckout.html.
2. Matthias Becker's book on the subject is well worth reading: *Automatisierung und Ausbeutung. Was wird aus der Arbeit im digitalen Kapitalismus?*, Vienna 2017, pp. 140–9.
3. Felix Klopotek, 'Hammer und Pixel', *Konkret*, 10/2018, p. 23.
4. Karl Marx, *Capital: A Critique of Political Economy, Volume One*, translated by Ben Fowkes, London 1976, p. 252.
5. Ibid., p. 349.
6. Karl Marx, *Capital: A Critique of Political Economy, Volume Three*, translated by David Fernbach, London 1981, p. 966.
7. Marx, *Capital, Volume One*, p. 345.
8. Karl Marx, *Outlines of the Critique of Political Economy*, in Karl Marx and Frederick Engels, *Collected Works* (MECW), Vol. 28, New York 1986, p. 31. Some pages on, Marx continues: 'It is a long-established view that at certain periods people lived exclusively by plunder. But to be able to plunder, there must be something to plunder, and this implies production. Moreover, the manner of plunder is itself determined by the manner of production, e.g. a stock-jobbing nation cannot be robbed in the same way as a nation of cowherds' (p. 35).
9. The Labour Theory of Value is presented as a *quantitative* theory in most of the literature, explaining that production and market prices are not based on labour values. Yet that is only one side of the central Marxian theorem. The *qualitative* side, however, is ignored for the most part.
10. Marx, *Capital, Volume One*, p. 126.
11. Ibid., p. 127.
12. Ibid.
13. Ibid., p. 128.
14. A fact of which, however, Adam Smith was also already aware. See Smith, *An Inquiry into the Nature and Causes of the Wealth of Nations*, Edinburgh 1846, p. 13.
15. Marx, *Capital, Volume One*, p. 129.
16. Ibid., p. 168.
17. Ibid., p. 132.
18. On the unequal exchange between capital and labour as the precondition of the theory of surplus value, see Elena Louisa Lange, 'Capital', in Jeff Diamanti, Andrew Pendakis and Imre Szeman (eds.), *The Bloomsbury Companion to Marx*, London 2018, pp. 273–80.
19. Marx, *Capital, Volume Three*, p. 270.
20. Michael Heinrich, *Kritik der politischen Ökonomie. Eine Einführung*, Stuttgart 2005, p. 100.
21. Marx, *Capital, Volume Three*, p. 966, author's emphasis.

22. Marx, *Capital, Volume One*, p. 341.
23. Ibid., p. 430.
24. Ibid., p. 432.
25. Ibid., p. 433.
26. There is fierce controversy in the literature as regards the significance of this law within the writings of Marx, which cannot be portrayed in any greater detail here. A more recent, influential controversy is that between Michael Heinrich, who views the role of the law critically, on one side, and Guglielmo Carchedi, Michael Roberts, Fred Moseley and Shane Mage, on the other. See monthlyreview.org/commentary/critique-heinrichs-crisis-theory-law-tendency-profit-rate-fall-marxs-studies-1870s.
27. Marx, *Capital, Volume Three*, p. 318.
28. Ibid., p. 319.
29. Karl Marx, *A Contribution to the Critique of Political Economy*, in MECW, Vol. 29, New York 1987, pp. 91–2.
30. Ibid., p. 92.

3   INDUSTRIAL REVOLUTION AND MECHANISATION IN MARX

1. For such a depiction of Marx, see, e.g., Martin Burckhardt, 'Ungeheure Apparate', in Marx und die Geburt des modernen Kapitalismus, *ZEIT-Geschichte*, 3/18, pp. 66–9, here: p. 68. On earlier debates about whether Marx ought to be regarded as a 'technological determinist', see Donald MacKenzie, 'Marx and the Machine', *Technology and Culture*, Vol. 25 (1984), No. 3, pp. 473–502. On the degradation thesis, see in particular Harry Braverman, *Labor and Monopoly Capital: The Degradation of Work in the Twentieth Century*, New York 1974.
2. Karl Marx, *A Contribution to the Critique of Political Economy*, in Karl Marx and Frederick Engels, *Collected Works* (MECW), Vol. 29, New York 1987, p. 82.
3. Karl Marx, *Economic Manuscript 1861–1863*, in MECW, Vol. 33, New York 1991, p. 495. Marx's own emphasis in this and all other Marx quotes in this chapter.
4. Ibid., p. 392.
5. Ibid., p. 423.
6. Karl Marx, *Capital: A Critique of Political Economy, Volume One*, translated by Ben Fowkes, London 1976, p. 492.
7. Ibid., p. 599.
8. Ibid., p. 590.
9. Ibid., 505.
10. Ibid., p. 506.
11. Ibid., p. 601.
12. Ibid., p. 534.
13. Ibid., p. 563.

14. Ibid., p. 563.
15. Ibid., p. 545.
16. Ibid., p. 548.
17. Ibid., pp. 548, 559.
18. David Landes, *The Unbound Prometheus: Technological Change and Industrial Development in Western Europe from 1750 to the Present*, second edition, Cambridge 2003 (1969), p. 41.
19. Raphael Samuel, 'Workshop of the World: Steam Power and Hand Technology in Mid-Victorian Britain', *History Workshop Journal*, No. 3, 1977, pp. 6–72, here: p. 7.
20. Ibid., p. 8.
21. Ibid., p. 11.
22. Ibid., p. 17.
23. Ibid., pp. 17–18.
24. Ibid., p. 21.
25. Ibid., pp. 19, 31.
26. Ibid., p. 24.
27. Ibid., pp. 20, 26, 27.
28. Ibid., p. 27.
29. Ibid., p. 37.
30. Ibid. p. 39.
31. Ibid., pp. 40–2.
32. Ibid., p. 45.
33. Ibid., p. 48.
34. Ibid., p. 50. Similar developments occurred in cutlery production in small workshops in Sheffield.
35. Ibid., p. 51.
36. Ibid., p. 34.
37. Ibid., p. 35.
38. Ibid., pp. 54–5.
39. Ibid., p. 58.
40. Population of European cities, see www.atlas-europa.de/to4/bevoelkerung/europ_staedte/pdf/BevStaedte-Tabelle_dt.pdf.
41. Hans-Peter Müller, 'Zur Problematik einer historisch-kritischen Edition', in *Karl Marx: Die technologisch-historischen Exzerpte*, transcribed and edited by Hans-Peter Müller, Frankfurt am Main 1981, pp. I–CXX, here: pp. IV, LXX; Rainer Winkelmann, 'Kommentar: Materialistische Geschichtsauffassung versus technokratisches Gesellschaftsbild', in *Karl Marx: Exzerpte über Arbeitsteilung, Maschinerie und Industrie*, transcribed and edited by Rainer Winkelmann, Frankfurt am Main 1982, pp. I–CXCII, here: pp. VI–XII.
42. Marx, *Economic Manuscript 1861–1863*, MECW, Vol. 33, p. 489.

43. Andrew Ure, *Philosophy of Manufactures. Or, an Exposition of the Science, Moral, and Commercial Economy of the Factory System in Great Britain*, London 1835, p. 329.
44. William Lazonick, 'The Self-acting Mule and Social Relations in the Workplace', in Donald MacKenzie and Judy Wajcman (eds.), *The Social Shaping of Technology*, Milton Keynes/Philadelphia 1985, pp. 93–108.
45. Winkelmann, *Exzerpte über Arbeitsteilung*, pp. V–VII, CXI; Charles Babbage, *On the Economy of Machinery and Manufacture*, London 1832.
46. Babbage, *On the Economy*, Chapter 19.
47. Marx, *Capital, Volume One*, p. 470, footnote 23.
48. Müller, 'Zur Problematik', pp. XLVII ff., LXVIII; Samuel, 'Workshop of the World', p. 14. In this regard, more generally, see David Edgerton, *The Shock of the Old: Technology and Global History since 1900*, London 2006. Edgerton criticises the tendency to assess the technological state of a given time by spectacular innovations, while *technology-in-use*, that is, the more widespread technology based on older developments, is often ignored. In this sense, steam power, which is generally regarded as the trademark feature of the Industrial Revolution, did not reach the pinnacle of its significance – in both absolute *and* relative terms – by 1800, but by 1900 (p. xi).
49. Marx, *Economic Manuscript 1861–1863*, MECW, Vol. 33, pp. 425–40.
50. Marx, *Capital, Volume One*, pp. 353–67.
51. Marx, *Economic Manuscript 1861–1863*, MECW, Vol. 33, pp. 393–421.
52. Marx, *Capital, Volume One*, pp. 573–74, 590, 592, 595.
53. Ibid., pp. 515–17.
54. MacKenzie, 'Marx and the Machine', p. 493.
55. Marx, *Capital, Volume One*, pp. 617–18.
56. Ibid., pp. 618–19.
57. Daniel Liebhardt, 'Das Märchen von den gescheiterten IT-Projekten', *netzwoche* 6/2009, p. 41; Michael Kroker, 'Die lange Liste schwieriger und gefloppter SAP-Projekte', *Wirtschaftswoche*, 17 December 2018.
58. Christian Rammer et al., *Innovationsverhalten der deutschen Wirtschaft*, Mannheim 2017, p. 7f.; Julian Müller, 'Das Verhältnis von Industrie und Finanzsektor unter der Finanzialisierung', *Prokla*, Vol. 42 (2012), No. 169, pp. 557–78.

4 A LONG HISTORY OF THE 'FACTORY WITHOUT PEOPLE'

1. The research producing the findings presented here was supported by the German Research Foundation (DFG) (UH 229/2–1).
2. In German, the term 'Fourth Industrial Revolution' is used to depict the era of advanced digital technologies (artificial intelligence, cyber-physical systems [or IoT], the Industrial IoT, etc.) as opposed to the 'Third Industrial Revolution'

of earlier IT-based or -aided industrial processes (e.g. Computer Numerical Control [CNC], early industrial robotics and automation) during the twentieth century. In the English-speaking world, the term 'Third Industrial Revolution' commonly includes this 'fourth' stage in the general emergence of digital technologies. For more detail, see Jeremy Rifkin, *The Third Industrial Revolution: How Lateral Power is Transforming Energy, the Economy, and the World*, London 2011.

3. See Peter Ittermann and Jonathan Niehaus, 'Industrie 4.0 und Wandel von Industriearbeit. Überblick über Forschungsstand und Trendbestimmung', in Hartmut Hirsch-Kreinsen, Peter Ittermann and Jonathan Niehaus (eds.), *Digitalisierung industrieller Arbeit. Die Vision Industrie 4.0 und ihre sozialen Herausforderungen*, Baden-Baden 2015, pp. 33–51, here: p. 35.

4. See Daniela Ahrens and Georg Spöttl, 'Industrie 4.0 und die Herausforderungen für die Qualifizierung von Fachkräften', in Hirsch-Kreinsen et al. (eds.), *Digitalisierung*, pp. 185–203, here: p. 190–1.

5. See Peter Brödner, 'Industrie 4.0 und Big Data – wirklich ein neuer Technologieschub?', in Hirsch-Kreinsen et al. (eds.), *Digitalisierung*, pp. 231–50, here: p. 238; Jürgen Howald, Ralf Kopp and Jürgen Schultze, 'Zurück in die Zukunft? Ein kritischer Blick auf die Diskussion zur Industrie 4.0', in ibid., pp. 251–68, here: p. 254.

6. See Hartmut Hirsch-Kreinsen, 'Einleitung. Digitalisierung industrieller Arbeit', in Hirsch-Kreinsen et al. (eds.), *Digitalisierung*, pp. 9–30, here: pp. 9–10, 20.

7. Martina Heßler, 'Zur Persistenz der Argumente im Automatisierungsdiskurs', *Aus Politik und Zeitgeschichte*, Vol. 66 (2016), No. 18–19, pp. 17–24, here: p. 19.

8. See ibid., pp. 20–1.

9. Andrew Ure, *The Philosophy of Manufactures. Or, an Exposition of the Scientific, Moral, and Commercial Economy of the Factory System in Great Britain*, second edition, London 1835, p. 18.

10. Karl Marx, *Capital: A Critique of Political Economy, Volume One*, translated by Ben Fowkes, London 1976, pp. 503, 544.

11. Ibid., p. 536. Marx distinguishes between 'machinery as such' and 'the capitalist application of machinery'. Ibid., p. 568.

12. Quoted in Patrick Fridenson, 'Die Arbeiter der französischen Automobilindustrie 1890 bis 1914', in Detlev Puls (ed.), *Wahrnehmungsformen und Protestverhalten. Studien zur Lage der Unterschichten im 18. und 19. Jahrhundert*, Frankfurt am Main 1979, pp. 228–61, here: p. 249. Apart from this, the majority of trade unions were in favour of rationalisation measures; see Gunnar Stollberg, *Die Rationalisierungsdebatte 1908–1933. Freie Gewerkschaften zwischen Mitwirkung und Gegenwehr*, Frankfurt am Main/New York 1981, pp. 13–14.

13. Adolf Wallichs, *Die Psychologie des Arbeiters und seine Stellung im industriellen Arbeitsprozeß* (Technische Abende im Zentralinstitut für Erziehung und Unterricht, Issue 3), Berlin 1917, p. 7.

14. See J. Ronald Shearer, 'Talking about Efficiency: Politics and the Industrial Rationalization Movement in the Weimar Republic', *Central European History*, Vol. 28 (1995), No. 4, pp. 483–507, here: p. 485.
15. See Bianca Westermann, *Anthropomorphe Maschinen. Grenzgänge zwischen Biologie und Technik seit dem 18. Jahrhundert*, Paderborn 2012, pp. 98–101.
16. Fritz Kummer, 'Die Maschinenmenschen. Als Verkehrspolizisten, Rechenmeister und Warenverkäufer', *Metallarbeiter-Zeitung. Wochenblatt des Deutschen Metallarbeiter-Verbandes*, Vol. 47 (1929), No. 20, p. 155.
17. Hanns Günther, *Automaten. Die Befreiung des Menschen durch die Maschine*, third edition, Stuttgart 1930, p. 5. The author's real name was Walter de Haas.
18. See ibid., p. 80.
19. See John J. Brown and Eric W. Leaver, 'Machines without Man', *Fortune* 5/1946 (November), pp. 165, 192, 194, 196, 199–200, 203–4; Martina Heßler, *Kulturgeschichte der Technik*, Frankfurt am Main/New York 2012, pp. 60–1.
20. Helmut Stein, 'Menschenleere Fabriken', *Völkischer Beobachter*, 27 February 1944.
21. See Moritz Kahn, *The Design and Construction of Industrial Buildings*, London 1917, p. 63.
22. See Karsten Uhl, *Humane Rationalisierung? Die Raumordnung der Fabrik im fordistischen Jahrhundert*, Bielefeld 2014, pp. 114, 146, 178.
23. See Martin Schwarz, '"Werkzeuge der Geschichte". Automatisierungsdiskurse der 1950er und 1960er Jahre im deutsch-deutschen Vergleich', *Technikgeschichte*, Vol. 82 (2015), No. 2, pp. 137–56, here: p. 139.
24. See ibid., p. 142. The end of the major automation euphoria was marked in West Germany by the 1973 oil crisis and in East Germany by the transition of power from Ulbricht to Honecker in 1971; see ibid., p. 143.
25. See Martin Schwarz, 'Fabriken ohne Arbeiter. Automatisierungsvisionen von Ingenieuren im Spiegel der Zeitschrift "automatic" 1956–1972', in Uwe Fraunholz and Sylvia Wölfel (eds.), *Ingenieure in der technokratischen Hochmoderne*, Münster i.a. 2012, pp. 167–78, here: p. 171.
26. See Johannes Platz, '"Revolution der Roboter" oder "Keine Angst vor Robotern"? Die Verwissenschaftlichung des Automatisierungsdiskurses und die industriellen Beziehungen von den 50ern bis 1968', in Laurent Commaille (ed.), *Entreprises et crises économiques au XXe siècle*, Metz 2009, pp. 36–59, here: pp. 39, 54.
27. See Uwe Fraunholz, '"Revolutionäres Ringen für den gesellschaftlichen Fortschritt". Automatisierungsvisionen in der DDR', in Uwe Fraunholz and Anke Woschech (eds.), *Technology Fiction: Technische Visionen und Utopien in der Hochmoderne*, Bielefeld 2012, pp. 195–219, here: p. 195.
28. See Karl Böhm and Rolf Dörge, *Unsere Welt von morgen*, Berlin 1960, pp. 54, 62.
29. See ibid., n.p. (between pp. 52 and 53).
30. See ibid., p. 56.

31. N.N., 'Die menschenleere Fabrik ist in zehn Jahren Wirklichkeit', in *Frankfurter Rundschau*, 7 June 1982.

32. Brödner, 'Industrie 4.0', p. 239.

33. See Karsten Uhl, 'Maschinenstürmer gegen die Automatisierung? Der Vorwurf der Technikfeindlichkeit in den Arbeitskämpfen der Druckindustrie in den 1970er und 1980er Jahren', *Technikgeschichte*, Vol. 82 (2015), No. 2, pp. 157–79; 'Die langen 1970er Jahre der Computerisierung. Die Formalisierung des Produktionswissens in der Druckindustrie und die Reaktionen von Gewerkschaften, Betriebsräten und Arbeitern', in Constanze Lindemann and Harry Neß (eds.), *Vom Buchdrucker zum Medientechnologen. Wege der Druckindustrie in die Welt der Digitalisierung*, Hamburg 2018, pp. 84–99.

34. IG Druck und Papier, *Notzeitung*, 6 March 1978. Archive in the House of the History of the Ruhr (Archiv im Haus der Gechichte des Ruhrgebiets), Bochum, file MüJe 140.

35. See John Diebold, 'Automation and the Editor: A Preview of Newsroom Procedures in 1973', in American Society of Newspaper Editors (eds.), *Problems of Journalism: Proceedings of the 1963 Convention*, New York 1963, pp. 140–50, here: p. 142. The first newspaper worldwide to introduce computerised typesetting was the *Los Angeles Times* in 1962; see Andrew Zimbalist, 'Technology and the Labor Process in the Printing Industry', in Andrew Zimbalist (ed.), *Case Studies on the Labor Process*, New York/London 1979, pp. 103–26, here: p. 108.

36. Richard Burkhardt, 'Die technische Entwicklung im grafischen Gewerbe und ihre Auswirkungen auf die Berufsausbildung und Beschäftigung', lecture delivered at the 4th Congress of the International Graphical Federation, Haus des Sports, Munich, on 19 September 1958, Heilbronn n.y. (1958), p. 9.

37. Richard Burkhardt, 'Die Entwicklung der grafischen Technik im Zeitalter der Automation', lecture manuscript, Congress of the International Graphical Federation, October 1964, Vienna, p. 25. Archive of Social Democracy (Archiv der sozialen Demokratie), file 5/MEDA 112041; see Diebold, 'Automation', p. 147.

38. See The Institute of Printing Limited (eds.), *Computer Typesetting Conference, London University July 1964. Report of Proceedings*, London 1965, pp. 14–15.

39. Erwin Ferlemann, Der technische Fortschritt und die Zukunftsaufgaben der grafischen Gewerkschaften. Referat beim IGF-Kongress vom 14. bis zum 19. September 1970 in Kopenhagen, Stuttgart 1970, p. 22. In a volume published in 1970, which compiled expectations for the future, however, the replacement of typesetters with 'digital typesetting machines' was predicted to happen as early as 1980. Admittedly, this book – just like the entire genre – was eager to present the most far-reaching and shocking forecasts; see Hagen H. Beinhauer and Ernst Schmacke, *Fahrplan in die Zukunft. Digest internationaler Prognosen*, Düsseldorf 1970, p. 66.

40. Detlef Hensche, 'Technische Revolution und Arbeitnehmerinteresse. Zu Verlauf und Ergebnissen des Arbeitskampfes in der Druckindustrie 1978', *Blätter für*

deutsche und internationale Politik, Vol. 23 (1978), No. 4, pp. 413–21, here:
p. 415.

41. Jürgen Alberts et al., *Zeitungsstreik*, Hamburg 1978, p. 71.
42. See Uhl, 'Maschinenstürmer', pp. 163–64, 170–71.
43. IG Druck und Papier, Executive Board, Notes for Lecturers (*Referentenmaterial*),
No. 167: Grenzenlose Rationalisierungsmöglichkeiten, Stuttgart, 16 January
1986, p. 3. Archive of Social Democracy (Archiv der sozialen Demokratie),
Bonn, file 5/MEDA423058.
44. See Fernand Braudel, 'History and the Social Sciences: The *Longue Durée*',
translated by Sarah Matthews, in *On History*, Chicago 1980. (Originally published as 'Histoire et sciences sociales: La longue durée', *Annales. Économies,
Sociétés, Civilisations*, Vol. 13 (1958), No. 4, pp. 725–53.
45. See Heßler, 'Zur Persistenz', p. 21.

5   THE JOURNEY OF THE 'AUTOMATION AND QUALIFICATION' PROJECT

1. See, for example, Wolfgang Jonas, Valentine Linsbauer and Helga Marx, *Die
Produktivkräfte in der Geschichte. Von den Anfängen in der Urgemeinschaft bis
zum Beginn der industriellen Revolution*, Berlin 1969.
2. Jürgen Kuczynski, *Vier Revolutionen der Produktivkräfte*, Berlin 1975.
3. See *Das Argument. Zeitschrift für Philosophie und Sozialwissenschaften*, No. 80
(special edition 1973), pp. 13–54.
4. Published as Frigga Haug (ed.), *Projektgruppe Automation und Qualifikation,
Bd. 2: Entwicklung der Arbeitstätigkeiten und die Methode ihrer Erfassung*, Berlin
1978 (second edition 1979).
5. Klaus Holzkamp, *Sinnliche Erkenntnis. Historischer Ursprung und gesellschaftliche
Funktion der Wahrnehmung*, Frankfurt am Main 1973; Ute Holzkamp-Osterkamp, *Grundlagen der psychologischen Motivationsforschung*, Vol. 1, Frankfurt
am Main 1975.
6. The 'biological, natural-historical development', the 'most general social characteristics' and the 'concrete features of the respective object as determined by
bourgeois society', ibid. p. 45.
7. Lucien Sève, *Man in Marxist Theory and the Psychology of Personality*, Hemel
Hempstead 1978.
8. We never understood bourgeois society simply as a hindrance, a wasted opportunity for potential human development (and neither did Marx), but as both a
captivation *and* unleashing of human development potential – as contradictory.
Critical psychology, as put forward by Holzkamp and Holzkamp-Osterkamp, by
contrast, views bourgeois society primarily as an institution for the suppression
of human development potential, neglecting any revolutionary potential.
9. In their study, *Industriearbeit und Arbeiterbewusstsein. Eine empirische Untersu-
chung über den Einfluss der aktuellen technischen Entwicklung auf die industrielle*

Arbeit und das Arbeiterbewusstsein (Industrial Labour and Workers' Consciousness. An Empirical Investigation into the Impact of the Current Technological
Development on Industrial Labour and Workers' Consciousness) (Frankfurt
am Main 1985), Kern and Schumann elaborated an investigation which claimed
to confirm, based on Marx, a link between work and consciousness. This study
became hegemonic for a trade union policy on work because it did not simply
conceive of workers as a community of sufferers, but, on the one hand, provided
a foundation for substantiating the thesis of deskilling through technological
development based on the fate of artisanal activities, and, on the other hand,
restricted the apparent increase in knowledge and skill to a very small class,
resulting in a polarisation and thus division of the working class.

10. Karl Marx, *Capital: A Critique of Political Economy, Volume One*, translated by
Ben Fowkes, London 1976, p. 275.
11. Projektgruppe Automation und Qualifikation, *Widersprüche der Automationsarbeit. Ein Handbuch*, Hamburg 1987, p. 31.

6 'FORWARD! AND LET'S REMEMBER'

1. This chapter focuses on the scientific debates taking place in the Federal
Republic of Germany from the 1950s onwards, as a reference to Marx was
largely common sense and there was considerable research on the role of technology here. While, even under this restricting condition, many other authors,
studies, institutes and schools of thought could also have been portrayed in
greater detail, the most important stages of the discussion and relevant focal
points can nevertheless be adequately reconstructed based on the approaches
depicted here.
2. Karl Marx, *Capital: A Critique of Political Economy, Volume One*, translated by
Ben Fowkes, London 1976, pp. 568–9.
3. Ibid., pp. 554–5.
4. Harry Braverman, *Labor and Monopoly Capital: The Degradation of Work in the
Twentieth Century*, New York 1998 (1974), pp. 5, 134.
5. Herbert Marcuse, *One-Dimensional Man: Studies in the Ideology of Advanced
Industrial Society*, Abingdon/New York 2002 (1964), p. xix; Otto Ullrich,
*Technik und Herrschaft. Vom Handwerk zur verdinglichten Blockstruktur indus-
trieller Produktion*, Frankfurt am Main 1979, pp. 104–5.
6. Karl Marx, *The Poverty of Philosophy*, in Karl Marx and Frederick Engels, *Collected Works* (MECW), Vol. 6, New York 1976, p. 166.
7. Robert Jungk, *Der Atom-Staat. Vom Fortschritt in die Unmenschlichkeit*, Reinbek
1979; Paul Mason, *Postcapitalism: A Guide to Our Future*, London 2015; for a
criticism of Mason, see Christian Fuchs, 'Henryk Grossmann 2.0. Eine Kritik
an Paul Masons Buch "Postkapitalismus: Grundrisse einer kommenden
Ökonomie"', *Z. Zeitschrift Marxistische Erneuerung*, No. 107, 2016, pp. 98–114.
8. Thomas Kuczynski, 'Zur Dialektik von Produktivkräften und Produktions-
verhältnissen in der Geschichte', in Dieter Janke and Jürgen Leibiger (eds.),

283

Digitale Revolution und soziale Verhältnisse im 21. Jahrhundert, Hamburg 2017, pp. 15–26, here: pp. 17–18; Marcuse, *One-Dimensional Man*, p. 158.

9. Karl Marx, *A Contribution to the Critique of Political Economy*, in MECW, Vol. 29, New York 1987, p. 92.
10. Wolfgang Fritz Haug, 'General Intellect', in Wolfgang Fritz Haug (ed.), *Historisch-kritisches Wörterbuch des Marxismus*, Vol. 5, Hamburg 2001, pp. 230–42, here: p. 237.
11. Michael Hardt and Antonio Negri, *Assembly*, New York 2017, pp. 118, 116.
12. Mason, *Postcapitalism*, Chapter 4.
13. Karl Marx, *The Eighteenth Brumaire of Louis Bonaparte*, in MECW, Vol. 11, New York 1979, p. 103.
14. Oskar Negt, *Lebendige Arbeit, enteignete Zeit*, Frankfurt am Main 1984, p. 239.
15. Gerhard Brand and Zissis Papadimitriou, 'Was trägt die industriesoziologische Forschung zur Entwicklung eines sozialwissenschaftlichen Technikbegriffs bei?' (1983), in Gerhard Brandt, *Arbeit, Technik und gesellschaftliche Entwicklung. Transformationsprozesse des modernen Kapitalismus. Aufsätze 1971–1987*, Frankfurt am Main 1990, pp. 189–209, here: p. 190.
16. Joachim Bergmann, 'Technik und Arbeit', in Burkart Lutz (ed.), *Technik und sozialer Wandel. Verhandlungen des 23. Deutschen Soziologentages in Hamburg 1986* (Technology and social change: discussions at the 23rd Conference of German Sociologists, held in Hamburg in 1986), Frankfurt am Main/New York 1987, pp. 114–34, here: p. 114.
17. Negt, *Lebendige Arbeit*, p. 240.
18. Brandt and Papadimitriou, 'Was trägt die industriesoziologische Forschung', p. 191; on cultural criticism, see Heinrich Popitz, Hans Paul Bahrdt, Ernst August Jüres and Hanno Kesting, *Technik und Industriearbeit. Soziologische Untersuchungen in der Hüttenindustrie*, Tübingen 1957, pp. 2–5.
19. Bergmann, 'Technik und Arbeit', p. 115.
20. The three German institutes abbreviated here are: Soziologisches Forschungsinstitut (Sociological Research Institute) at Georg August University in Göttingen (SOFI); Institut für Sozialwissenschaftliche Forschung (Institute of Social Scientific Research) in Munich (ISF), and Institut für Sozialforschung (Institute for Social Research) at Johann Wolfgang Goethe University in Frankfurt (IfS).
21. Brandt and Papadimitriou, 'Was trägt die industriesoziologische Forschung', p. 193.
22. Horst Kern and Michael Schumann, *Das Ende der Arbeitsteilung? Rationalisierung in der industriellen Produktion*, Munich 1985, p. 321.
23. Gerhard Brandt, 'Marx und die neuere deutsche Industriesoziologie' (1984), in Brandt, *Arbeit, Technik und gesellschaftliche Entwicklung*, pp. 254–80, here: p. 263.
24. Ibid., p. 255.
25. Brandt and Papadimitriou, 'Was trägt die industriesoziologische Forschung', p. 198.

26. Projektgruppe Automation und Qualifikation, *Widersprüche der Automationsarbeit. Ein Handbuch*, Berlin 1987, p. 179; on the PAQ, see also the chapter by Frigga Haug in this volume.

27. Ibid., pp. 181, 18–19.

28. Hartmut Hirsch-Kreinsen, 'Techniksoziologie', in Hartmut Hirsch-Kreinsen and Heiner Minssen (eds.), *Lexikon der Arbeits- und Industriesoziologie*, Berlin 2013, pp. 454–61, here: p. 455.

29. Bergmann, 'Technik und Arbeit', p. 115.

30. Burkart Lutz, 'Das Ende des Technikdeterminismus und die Folgen: soziologische Technikforschung vor neuen Aufgaben und neuen Problemen', in Lutz (ed.), *Technik und sozialer Wandel*, pp. 34–52, here: p. 35.

31. Bergmann, 'Technik und Arbeit', p. 115.

32. Sabine Pfeiffer, 'Technisierung von Arbeit', in Fritz Böhle, G. Günter Voß and Günther Wachtler (eds.), *Handbuch Arbeitssoziologie*, Wiesbaden 2010, pp. 231–61; Sabine Pfeiffer, 'Arbeit und Technik', in Hirsch-Kreinsen and Minssen (eds.), *Lexikon der Arbeits- und Industriesoziologie*, pp. 48–53; Fritz Böhle, 'Technik und Arbeit – neue Antworten auf "alte" Fragen', *Soziale Welt*, Vol. 49 (1998), No. 3, pp. 233–52; Michael Schumann, 'Das Ende der kritischen Industriesoziologie?', *Leviathan*, Vol. 30 (2002), No. 3, pp. 325–44.

33. Braverman, *Labor and Monopoly Capital*; for a critical approach on this, see Brandt, 'Marx und die neuere deutsche Industriesoziologie', p. 276.

34. Roger Häußling, *Techniksoziologie*, Baden-Baden 2014, p. 321.

35. Schumann, 'Das Ende der kritischen Industriesoziologie?', p. 326.

36. Helmut Martens, 'Industriesoziologie. Ende der Debatte heißt nicht Ende der Krise', *Soziale Welt*, Vol. 59 (2008), No. 1, pp. 79–100, here: pp. 85–6, 90.

37. Marx, *Capital, Volume One*, p. 617.

38. Friedrich Pollock, 'Die wirtschaftlichen und sozialen Folgen der Automatisierung', in Arbeitsgemeinschaft Sozialdemokratischer Akademiker (eds.), *Revolution der Roboter. Untersuchungen über Probleme der Automatisierung*, Munich 1956, pp. 65–105.

39. See Projektgruppe Automation und Qualifikation, *Widersprüche der Automationsarbeit*.

40. Braverman, *Labor and Monopoly Capital*, pp. 132–4.

41. Werner van Treeck, 'Automation', in Wolfgang Fritz Haug (ed.), *Historisch-kritisches Wörterbuch des Marxismus*, Vol. 1, Hamburg 2004; similar: PAQ.

42. Bergmann, 'Technik und Arbeit', p. 119.

43. Pollock, 'Die wirtschaftlichen und sozialen Folgen der Automatisierung', p. 93.

44. 'Here the candidate is immediately selected by unanimous choice: the "girl" machine operator who learns her job in a few days, attains optimum efficiency in a few weeks or months, and is drawn from a large pool at hardly more than half the pay of the machinist.' Braverman, *Labor and Monopoly Capital*, p. 139.

45. Projektgruppe Automation und Qualifikation, *Widersprüche der Automationsarbeit*, p. 176.

46. Rudi Schmiede, 'Informatisierung, Formalisierung und kapitalistische Produktionsweise: Entstehung der Informationstechnik und Wandel der gesellschaftlichen Arbeit', in Rudi Schmiede (ed.), *Virtuelle Arbeitswelten. Arbeit, Produktion und Subjekt in der 'Informationsgesellschaft'*, Berlin 1996, pp. 15–47; Kern and Schumann, 'Das Ende der Arbeitsteilung?'; Walther Müller-Jentsch, 'Technik als Rahmenbedingung und Gestaltungsoption industrieller Beziehungen', in *Arbeit und Bürgerstatus. Studien zur sozialen und industriellen Demokratie*, Wiesbaden 2009, pp. 213–37.

47. Joachim Hirsch and Roland Roth, *Das neue Gesicht des Kapitalismus. Vom Fordismus zum Post-Fordismus*, Hamburg 1986, pp. 114–15.

48. Kern and Schumann, 'Das Ende der Arbeitsteilung?', p. 24.

49. Schmiede, 'Informatisierung', pp. 20, 23.

50. Ibid., pp. 37, 39, 47; here, the influence of Marcuse – the analyses of whom Schmiede most certainly came across at the Frankfurt IfS – becomes apparent: 'The universal effectiveness and productivity of the apparatus [...] veil the particular interests that organize the apparatus.' Marcuse, *One-Dimensional Man*, p. 172.

51. Song on the first album, *Digital ist besser* ('Digital is better'), by the German band Tocotronic, 1995.

52. Sabine Pfeiffer, 'Warum reden wir eigentlich über Industrie 4.0? Auf dem Weg zum digitalen Despotismus', *Mittelweg 36*, Vol. 24 (2015), No. 6, pp. 14–36.

53. Florian Butollo and Thomas Engel, 'Industrie 4.0 – arbeits- und gesellschaftspolitische Perspektiven. Zwischen Dystopie und Euphorie', *Z. Zeitschrift Marxistische Erneuerung*, No. 103 (2015), pp. 29–41.

54. The topos of industrial revolutions and their consecutive numbering is nothing new. The subtitles of the two volumes of *The Outdatedness of Human Beings* by Günther Anders already point to a Second (1956) and Third (1980) Industrial Revolution, respectively. Braverman identifies a 'scientific-technical revolution' in the last decades of the nineteenth century which fundamentally changed the role of science (Chapter 7, pp. 107–16). In 1999, Müller-Jentsch writes of a 'third technological or industrial revolution'. Hirsch and Roth, as well as Rifkin, regard the combination of computers, information and communication technologies (ICT) and new techniques of control as constituting a Third Industrial Revolution. Brynjolfsson and McAfee, in contrast, speak of a *Second Machine Age*.

55. Nick Srnicek, *Platform Capitalism*, Cambridge 2017; Shoshana Zuboff, *The Age of Surveillance Capitalism: The Fight for a Human Future at the New Frontier of Power*, New York 2019.

56. Klaus Dörre, 'Digitalisierung – neue Prosperität oder Vertiefung gesellschaftlicher Spaltung?', in Hartmut Hirsch-Kreinsen, Peter Ittermann and Jonathan Niehaus (eds.), *Digitalisierung industrieller Arbeit. Die Vision Industrie 4.0 und ihre sozialen Herausforderungen*, Baden-Baden 2015, pp. 269–84.

57. Wolfgang Fritz Haug, 'Hightech-Kapitalismus an der Schwelle zur digitalen Schließung', in Janke and Leibiger (eds.), *Digitale Revolution*, pp. 61–73; Christian Fuchs, *Digital Labour and Karl Marx*, New York/London 2014, p. 144.
58. Simon Schaupp, 'Vergessene Horizonte. Der kybernetische Kapitalismus und seine Alternativen', in Paul Buckermann, Anne Koppenburger and Simon Schaupp (eds.), *Kybernetik, Kapitalismus, Revolutionen. Emanzipatorische Perspektiven im technologischen Wandel*, Münster 2017, pp. 51–73, here: p. 52.
59. See, for example, Jürgen Leibiger, 'Einführung', in Janke and Leibiger (eds.), *Digitale Revolution*, pp. 9–14; Dörre, 'Digitalisierung', p. 282.
60. Marx, *Capital: Volume One*, p. 505.

7   HIGH TECH, LOW GROWTH: ROBOTS AND THE FUTURE OF WORK

1. This chapter is an edited version of Kim Moody, 'High Tech, Low Growth: Robots and the Future of Work', *Historical Materialism*, Vol. 26 (2018), No. 4, pp. 3–34, published by Koninklijke Brill NV, Leiden. Reprinted with kind permission of the publisher.
2. Martin Ford, *The Rise of the Robots: Technology and the Threat of Mass Unemployment*, London 2016; Erik Brynjolfsson and Andrew McAfee, *The Second Machine Age: Work, Progress, and Prosperity in a Time of Brilliant Technologies*, New York 2014.
3. Ford, *The Rise of the Robots*, pp. 30–3.
4. Jeremy Rifkin, *The End of Work: The Decline of the Global Labor Force and the Dawn of the Post-Market Era*, New York 1995.
5. Ibid., pp. 9, 151; US Census Bureau, 'Statistical Abstract of the United States, 2012', Washington DC 2011, pp. 409–10; Bureau of Economic Analysis, Gross Output by Industry, 2017, at www.bea.gov.
6. Bureau of Economic Analysis, 'Current Cost Net Stock of Private Equipment by Industry, Table 3.1E', revised 23 August 2017, at www.bea.gov.
7. Carl Benedikt Frey and Michael A. Osborne, 'The Future of Employment: How Susceptible Are Jobs to Computerization?', *Technological Forecasting & Social Change*, Vol. 114 (2017), p. 265.
8. World Trade Organization, 'World Trade Report 2017', Geneva 2017, pp. 90–100.
9. World Economic Forum, *The Future of Jobs: Employment, Skills and Workforce Strategy of the Fourth Industrial Revolution*, Geneva 2016, pp. 3–28.
10. Daron Acemoglu and Pascual Restrepo, 'Robots and Jobs: Evidence from US Labor Markets', Cambridge 2017, p. 36, at https://www.nber.org/system/files/working_papers/w23285/w23285.pdf.
11. Bureau of Labor Statistics, 'The Employment Situation – July 2017', News Release, USDL-17-1070, 4 August 2017, Table A; US Census Bureau 2011, p. 377.

12. Lawrence Mishel and Josh Bivens, 'The Zombie Robot Argument Lurches On', Washington DC: Economic Policy Institute 2017, p. 6, at www.epi.org/publication/the-zombie-robot-argument-lurches-on-there-is-no-evidence-that-automationleads-to-joblessness-or-inequality.
13. International Federation of Robotics, 'Executive Summary World Robotics 2017, Industrial Robots', p. 23, at ifr.org/downloads/press/Executive_Summary_WR_2017_Industrial_Robots.pdf; Bureau of Labor Statistics, 'Employment, Hours, and Earnings from the Current Employment Statistics Survey (National), 2017, All Employees, Commercial Banking', at https://data.bls.gov/pdq/SurveyOurputServlet; Alison Sanders and Meldon Wolfgang, 'The Rise of Robotics', BCG Perspective, Boston Consulting Group 2014, at www.bcg.com/publications/2014/business-unit-strategy-innovation-rise-of-robotics.aspx.
14. International Federation of Robotics 2017, pp. 15, 23.
15. Mark Munro, 'Where the Robots Are', Brookings, 14 August 2017, at www.brookings.edu/blog/the-avenue/2017/08/14/where-the-robots-are; Gordon Hunt, 'GM's Robot Production Line Has its Head in the Cloud', Silicon Republic, 5 April 2017, at www.siliconrepublic.com/machines/gm-general-motorsrobots.
16. Acemoglu and Restrepo, 'Robots and Jobs', p. 41, p. A-14.
17. Bureau of Labor Statistics, 'Automotive Industry: Employment, Earnings, and Hours, 2017, National Employment', at www.bls.gov/iag/tgs/iagauto.htm; Paul S. Davies, 'Factors Influencing Employment in the U.S. Automobile Industry', *The Park Place Economist*, Vol. 1 (1993), No. 1, at digitalcommons.iwu.edu/parkplace/vol1/iss1/8.
18. Ford, *The Rise of the Robots*, pp. 54–5.
19. The argument against the role of imports in job loss is developed in detail in Kim Moody, *On New Terrain: How Capital Is Reshaping the Battleground of Class War*, Chicago 2017, pp. 8–13, 195.
20. Ibid., pp. 13–19; Mike Parker, 'Management-by-Stress: A Reply to Joshua Murray and Michael Schwartz', *Catalyst*, Vol. 1 (2017), No. 2, pp. 173–94. Despite high productivity, Toyota closed NUMMI in 2010 in order to go completely non-union in the USA.
21. Moody, *On New Terrain*, pp. 16–17; Kim Moody and Simone Sagovac, *Time Out: The Case for a Shorter Work Week*, Detroit 1995, pp. 15–17; Anwar Shaikh, *Capitalism: Competition, Conflict, Crises*, New York 2016, pp. 135–9.
22. Jose Ignacio Gimenez-Nadal and Alumdena Sevilla-Sanz, 'Job Polarization and the Intensification of Work in the United Kingdom and the United States over the Last Decades: Evidence from Time Diary Data', paper delivered at the Fourth Society of Labor Educators/European Association of Labour Economists Global Meeting, Montreal, Quebec, Canada, 26–28 June 2015, pp. 3–11.
23. Dianne Feeley, 'Big Three Contracts: Who Won?', *Against The Current*, No. 180 (2016), pp. 4–6.
24. Ford, *The Rise of the Robots*, p. 3.
25. Ibid., p. 5.

26. Robert J. Gordon, *The Rise and Fall of American Growth: The U.S. Standard of Living Since the Civil War*, Princeton 2016, pp. 588–99.

27. Brynjolfsson and McAfee, *The Second Machine Age*, pp. 28–9.

28. 'Humanoid Robots: After the Fall', *The Economist*, 13 June 2015.

29. Ford, *The Rise of the Robots*, pp. 5–6.

30. April Glaser, 'The Industrial Robotics Market Will Nearly Triple in Less than Ten Years: Collaborative Robots Are Expected to Account for a Third of that Market', *Recode*, 22 June 2017, at https://www.recode.net/2017/6/22/15763106/industrial-robotics-market-triple-ten-years-collaborative-robots.

31. Brynjolfsson and McAfee, *The Second Machine Age*, pp. 6–7, Figure 1.2 is misleading in that it neglects the social and cultural advances, periods of growth, and the huge scientific advances in math, navigation, ship construction, mechanics, astronomy, printing, artillery and firearms, etc., that preceded the Industrial Revolution by a century or more. These advances, however, were the results or enablers of the period of expanding trade and conquest by European powers, while the Industrial Revolution was made possible by capitalism's 'intensive as distinct from extensive expansion' that Wood points to. For those influenced by neoclassical-economic and technological determinism, there is no distinction between trade and commerce, which are ancient, and capitalism, which is not.

32. For an analysis of the rise of capitalism and its agrarian origins prior to the Industrial Revolution, see Ellen Meiksins Wood, *The Origin of Capitalism: A Longer View*, London 2002, pp. 67, 97–115, 174–5, *passim*.

33. Howard Botwinick, *Persistent Inequalities: Wage Disparity under Capitalist Competition*, Princeton 1993, pp. 124–33.

34. US Census Bureau 2011, pp. 409, 417.

35. Karl Marx, *Capital: A Critique of Political Economy, Volume One*, translated by Ben Fowkes, London 1976, p. 516.

36. David Cooper, 'A Majority of Low-Wage Workers Earn so Little that they Must Rely on Public Assistance to Make Ends Meet', Economic Policy Institute, 9 February 2016, at https://www.epi.org/publication/a-majority-of-low-wage-workers-earn-so-little-they-must-rely-on-public-assistance-to-make-ends-meet.

37. Marx, *Capital, Volume One*, p. 784.

38. Quoted in Michael Roberts, *The Long Depression: How It Happened, Why It Happened, and What Happens Next*, Chicago 2016, p. 263.

39. Ibid., p. 27.

40. Shaikh, *Capitalism*, p. 264.

41. Bryan Borzykowski, 'How Investors Can Profit from the Rise of the Robotics Industry', *Canadian Business*, 1 February 2016, at www.canadianbusiness.com/investing/how-investors-can-profit-from-the-rise-of-the-robotics-industry.

42. Shaikh, *Capitalism*, pp. 2–11, 66; Roberts, *The Long Depression*, pp. 223–4.

43. Gordon, *The Rise and Fall*, pp. 619–20; Bureau of Economic Analysis, 'Sources and Uses of Private Enterprise Income', Table 1.156, 3 August 2017.

44. Shaikh, *Capitalism*, pp. 616–18.
45. Gordon, *The Rise and Fall*, pp. 446–7, 458.
46. Shaik, *Capitalism*, pp. 810–2.
47. Bureau of Economic Analysis, 'Relation of Private Fixed Investment in Equipment in the Fixed Assets Accounts to the Corresponding Items in the National Income and Product Accounts', 7 September 2016, pp. 6.13–6.21. Editor's note: In the original article the corresponding figures are listed in Appendix II.
48. Roberts, *The Long Depression*, pp. 256–7; Mishel and Bivens, 'The Zombie Robot Argument Lurches On', pp. 8–10. Editor's note: At this point, the original article provides additional figures on the decline in investment growth in R&D and the low survival rate of business start-ups in information technology.
49. Andrew Hogan and Brian Roberts, 'Occupational Employment Projections to 2024', Monthly Labor Review, US Bureau of Labor Statistics, December 2015, at doi.org/10.21916/mlr.2015.49; US Census Bureau, 'Statistical Abstract of the United States, 2001', Washington DC 2001.
50. Roberts, *The Long Depression*, p. 106.
51. David Welch, 'Automakers' Overcapacity Problem', *Bloomberg Business Week*, 31 December 2008, at www.bloomberg.com/news/articles/2008-12-30/auto makersovercapacity-problem; Chris Bryant, 'Bosch Warns Industry on Over Capacity', *Financial Times*, 26 September 2012.
52. Federal Reserve, 'Industrial Production, Capacity, and Utilization', 2017, at www.federalreserve.gov/releases/g17/current/ipg1.svg; Council of Economic Advisers, 'Economic Report of the President', Washington DC 2011, p. 253.

8   PRODUCTIVE POWER IN CONCRETE TERMS

1. On the common distinction between these five types of interaction between humans and robots (Cell, Coexistence, Synchronised, Cooperation, Collaboration), see Wilhelm Bauer (ed.), Manfred Bender, Martin Braun, Peter Rally and Oliver Scholz, *Lightweight Robots in Manual Assembly – Best to Start Simply! Examining Companies' initial Experiences with Lightweight Robots*, Stuttgart 2016, pp. 8–9, at https://www.engineering-produktion.iao.fraunhofer.de/content/dam/iao/tim/Bilder/Projekte/LBR/Studie-Leichtbauroboter-Fraun-hofer-IAO-2016-EN.pdf.
2. Karl Marx, *Capital: A Critique of Political Economy, Volume* One, translated by Ben Fowkes, London 1976, p. 572.
3. Ibid.
4. Ibid., p. 549.
5. The most well-known lightweight robots include YuMi by ABB, Panda by Frank Emika, BionicCobot by Festo, iisy by KUKA or Sawyer by RethinkRobotics, now the Hahn Group.
6. Quoted in Bauer et al., *Lightweight Robots in Manual Assembly*, p. 6.

7. Bjoern Matthias, Hao Ding and Volker Miegele, 'Die Zukunft der Mensch-Roboter Kollaboration in der industriellen Montage' ('The Future of Human–Robot Collaboration (HRC) in Assembly'), International Forum on Mechatronics, 30–31 October 2013, Winterthur, Switzerland.
8. The questions asked are, in part, too vague. The German Trade Union Federation (DGB) 2016 index on 'Good Work' does not distinguish between computer-controlled machines and robots (operated by 24 per cent of workers); a wage-earner survey conducted by the Federal Institute of Education and Professional Training (BIBB) and the Federal Institute for Occupational Safety and Health (BAuA) in 2012 lists only activities related to 'monitoring and controlling of systems and machines' (39 per cent of respondents perform such tasks often or occasionally).
9. Robert Seamans and Manav Raj, *AI, Labor, Productivity and the Need for Firm-Level Data*, Cambridge 2018, pp. 5–8, at http://papers.nber.org/tmp/85128-w24239.pdf.
10. Angela Jäger, Cornelius Moll and Christian Lerch, *Analysis of the Impact of Robotic Systems on Employment in the European Union*, Karlsruhe 2016.
11. Wolfgang Dauth, Sebastian Findeisen, Jens Suedekum and Nicole Woessner, *German Robots: The Impact of Industrial Robots on Workers*, London 2017, at http://doku.iab.de/discussionpapers/2017/dp3017.pdf
12. International Federation for Robotics, *World Robotics: Industrial Robots 2018*, Frankfurt am Main/New York 2018.
13. On this basis, another study assesses labour market effects particularly with regard to service robots: Michael Decker, Martin Fischer and Ingrid Ott, 'Service Robotics and Human Labor: A First Technology Assessment of Substitution and Cooperation', *Robotics and Autonomous Systems*, Vol. 87 (2017), pp. 348–54.
14. Angela Jäger, Cornelius Moll and Christian Lerch, *Analysis of the Impact of Robotic Systems on Employment in the European Union*, Luxemburg 2016.
15. Dauth et al., *German Robots*.
16. Decker et al., 'Service Robotics'.
17. David E. Nye, *America's Assembly Line*, Cambridge 2013, p. 242.
18. Michael Haag, 'Kollaboratives Arbeiten mit Robotern – Vision und realistische Perspektive', in Alfons Botthoff and Ernst Andreas Hartmann (eds.), *Zukunft der Arbeit in Industrie 4.0*, Wiesbaden 2015, p. 60.
19. Ibid., p. 64.
20. Lars Windelband and Bernd Dworschak, 'Arbeit und Kompetenzen in der Industrie 4.0', in Hartmut Hirsch-Kreinsen, Peter Ittermann and Jonathan Niehaus (eds.), *Digitalisierung industrieller Arbeit*, Baden-Baden 2015, pp. 71–86.
21. Matthew Beane, 'Shadow Learning: Building Robotic Surgical Skill When Approved Means Fail', *Administrative Science Quarterly*, Vol. 64 (2018), No. 1, pp. 87–123.

22. Paul Windolf, 'Industrial Robots in the West German Automobile Industry', *Politics & Society*, Vol. 14 (1985), No. 4, pp. 459–95, here: p. 481.
23. Sabine Pfeiffer, 'Industry 4.0: Robotics and Contradictions', in Paško Bilić, Jaka Primorac and Bjarki Valtýsson (eds.), *Technologies of Labour and the Politics of Contradiction*, Cham 2018, pp. 19–36.
24. Windolf, 'Industrial Robots', p. 482.
25. Sabine Pfeiffer, 'Technisierung von Arbeit', in Fritz Böhle, Günter G. Voß and Günther Wachtler (eds.), *Handbuch Arbeitssoziologie. Band 1: Arbeit, Strukturen, Prozesse*, second edition, Wiesbaden 2018, pp. 321–58.
26. Windolf, 'Industrial Robots'.
27. See Bauer et al., *Lightweight Robots in Manual Assembly*.
28. All quoted interview passages are taken from the author's own qualitative empirical survey conducted with experts from German lightweight robot manufacturers in 2018.
29. Martin Naumann, 'Mensch-Maschine-Interaktion', in Thomas Bauernhansl, Michael ten Hompel and Birgit Vogel-Heuser (eds.), *Industrie 4.0 in Produktion. Automatisierung und Logistik. Anwendung – Technologien – Migration*, Wiesbaden 2014, p. 510.
30. The teach-in, moreover, is not a new concept but was already applied to industrial robots in the 1990s; see Gerd Hirzinger, 'Neue Teach-In-Verfahren in der Robotik', in Ingbert Kupka (ed.), *GI – 13. Jahrestagung* (Annual Meeting of the German Informatics Society), Hamburg, 3–7 October 1983, Proceedings, Vol. 73, Berlin/Heidelberg 1983, pp. 177–93.
31. Bauer et al., *Lightweight Robots in Manual Assembly*, p. 9.
32. See Erik Brynjolfsson, Daniel Rock and Chad Syverson, *The Productivity J-Curve: How Intangibles Complement General Purpose Technologies*, Cambridge 2018.
33. Ibid.
34. Marx, *Capital, Volume One*, pp. 562–3 (emphasis added).
35. Sabine Pfeiffer, 'The Vision of "Industrie 4.0" in the Making – a Case of Future Told, Tamed, and Traded', *Nanoethics* Vol. 11 (2017), No. 1, pp. 107–21.
36. See the study on AI-related media coverage in the UK: J. Scott Brennen, Philip N. Howard and Rasmus Kleis Nielsen, *An Industry-Led Debate: How UK Media Cover Artificial Intelligence*, Oxford 2018, at https://reutersinstitute.politics.ox.ac.uk/sites/default/files/2018-12/Brennen_UK_Media_Coverage_of_AI_FINAL.pdf.
37. Marx, *Capital, Volume One*, p. 443.
38. Ibid., p. 444.
39. Ibid., pp. 445–6.
40. Ibid., p. 447. With regard to digital transformation, the crowd and platform economy, for one, could be interpreted as an attempt to allow for this use of cooperation and its developed variants under capitalism even without the

physical production site and the manager (which Marx had considered essential) and using the means of production (financed by the capital of others).

41. Karl Marx, *A Contribution to the Critique of Political Economy*, in Karl Marx and Frederick Engels, *Collected Works* (MECW), Vol. 29, New York 1987, pp. 89–90 (section on 'Fixed Capital and the Development of the Productive Forces of Society', the so-called 'Machine Fragment').

42. All the theses presented here refer to the deployment of physical means of production in physical production environments. That is to say, I do not intend to formulate a general thesis about the effect of digitalisation *as such* on capitalism *as a whole*.

43. Christoph Tripp, *Distributions- und Handelslogistik. Netzwerke und Strategien der Omnichannel-Distribution im Handel*, Wiesbaden 2019, p. 38.

44. Marx, *Outlines*, MECW, Vol. 29, p. 90.

45. Ibid., p. 95.

46. Friedrich Krotz, 'Die Begegnung von Mensch und Roboter. Überlegungen zu ethischen Fragen aus der Perspektive des Mediatisierungsansatzes', in Matthias Rath, Friedrich Krotz and Matthias Karmasin (eds), *Maschinenethik. Normative Grenzen autonomer Systeme*, Wiesbaden 2019, p. 22.

47. Diane Coyle, 'Welcoming our Robot Overlords: The Disruptive Potential of Technological Progress', in Tony Dolphin (ed.), *Technology, Globalisation and the Future of Work in Europe*, London 2015, pp. 100–5, here: p. 104.

48. David Harvey, *Seventeen Contradictions and the End of Capitalism*, London 2014, p. 98.

9   DRONES, ROBOTS, SYNTHETIC FOODS

1. Erin Winik, 'New Autonomous Farm Wants to Produce Food without Human Workers', *MIT Technology Review*, 3 October 2018, at www.technologyreview.com/s/612230/new-autonomous-farm-wants-to-produce-food-without-humanworkers.

2. Michael Watts, 'The Southern Question: Agrarian Questions of Labour and Capital', in Haroon A. Akram-Lodhi and Cristóbal Kay (eds.), *Peasants and Globalization: Political Economy, Rural Transformation and the Agrarian Question*, London 2009, pp. 262–87.

3. Haroon A. Akram-Lodhi and Cristóbal Kay, 'Surveying the Agrarian Question (Part 2): Current Debates and Beyond', *The Journal of Peasant Studies*, Vol. 37 (2010), No. 2, pp. 255–84.

4. Chris Carlson, 'Rethinking the Agrarian Question: Agriculture and Underdevelopment in the Global South', *Journal of Agrarian Change*, Vol. 18 (2018), No. 4, pp. 703–21.

5. Markus Wissen, 'The Political Ecology of Agrofuels: Conceptual Remarks', in Kristina Dietz, Bettina Engels, Oliver Pye and Achim Brunnengräber (eds.), *The Political Ecology of Agrofuels*, London 2015, pp. 16–33.

6. Elmar Altvater, *Sachzwang Weltmarkt*, Hamburg 1987.
7. Kristina Dietz and Markus Wissen, 'Kapitalismus und "natürliche Grenzen". Eine kritische Diskussion ökomarxistischer Zugänge zur ökologischen Krise', *Prokla*, Vol. 39 (2009), No. 156, pp. 351–69.
8. Pat Mooney, 'Blocking the Chain: Industrial Food Chain Concentration, Big Data Platforms and Food Sovereignty Solutions', 2018, at https://www.etcgroup. org/sites/www.etcgroup.org/files/files/blockingthechain_english_web.pdf, p. 13.
9. Ibid., pp. 14–16.
10. Nils-Viktor Sorge, 'Restaurant feuert ersten Burger-Roboter', *Manager Magazin*, 19 March 2018.
11. Beate Friedrich and Sarah K. Hackfort, 'Konfliktfeld "neue Gentechnik". Regulierung landwirtschaftlicher Biotechnologien zwischen Innovation und Vorsorge', *GAIA Ecological Perspectives for Science and Society*, Vol. 27 (2018), No. 2, pp. 211–15, here: p. 211.
12. Transparenz Gentechnik, 'Gentechnik-Lachs. Zwanzig Jahre Zulassung, zögerliche Vermarktung', 18 September 2018, at www.transgen.de/tiere/392. gentechnisch-veraenderter-lachs.html.
13. Office of Technology Assessment at the German Bundestag (TAB), 'Synthetic Biology – the Next Phase of Biotechnology and Genetic Engineering', Working Report No. 164, November 2015, at https://www.tab-beim-bundestag.de/en/ pdf/publications/summarys/TAB-Arbeitsbericht-ab164_Z.pdf.
14. Miriam Boyer, personal communication, January 2019.
15. Lydia Mulvani and Deena Shanker, 'Why the "Bloody" Impossible Burger Faces Another FDA Hurdle', *Bloomberg*, 26 December 2018, at www.bloomberg.com/ news/articles/2018-12-26/why-the-bloody-impossible-burger-faces-another-fda-hurdle.
16. Chloe Cornish, 'Ag Tech Fundraising Doubles as Farmers Seek Disruptive Solutions', *Financial Times*, 8 January 2018.
17. FAO, *World Food and Agriculture. Statistical Pocketbook 2018*, at www.fao.org/ publications/highlights-detail/en/c/1164465.
18. Henry Bernstein, 'Rural Livelihoods and Agrarian Change: Bringing Class Back In', in Norman Long, Wang Yihuan and Ye Jingzhong (eds.), *Rural Transformations and Development: China in Context*, Cheltenham 2010, pp. 79–109.
19. Jan Brunner, 'Die Verhandlungsmacht von Arbeiter*innen und Gewerkschaften in landwirtschaftlichen Transformationsprozessen. Eine Analyse des Zuckerrohrsektors in Bundesstaat Sao Paulo', *GLOCON Working Paper Series*, Berlin 6/2017.
20. Matthias Martin Becker, 'Der Kardinalfehler der Debatte über Automatisierung', *OXI. Wirtschaft anders denken*, January 2019.
21. Monika Hoegen, 'Biopiraterie oder Saatgutklau. Hersteller und Kleinbauern bezichtigen sich gegenseitig', *Süddeutsche Zeitung*, 12 November 2003, at www.

deutschlandfunk.de/biopiraterie-oder-saatgutklau.697.de.html?dram:article_
id=72846.

22. Mooney, 'Blocking the Chain', pp. 12–13.

23. Tom Strohschneider, 'Zerschlagen, verstaatlichen, kontrollieren? Wie die Macht der Big-Tech-Konzerne begrenzt werden soll', in *OXI*, 26 February 2018, at oxiblog. de/zerschlagen-verstaatlichen-kontrollieren-wie-die-marktmacht-der-grossen-tectkonzerne-amazon-google-apple-facebook-baadd-begrenzt-werden-soll.

24. Mooney, 'Blocking the Chain', p. 35.

25. Rainer Behak, 'In Technik gegossener Anti-Institutionalismus', *OXI. Wirtschaft anders denken*, January 2019.

26. Tilman Santarius, 'Der Rebound-Effekt: Die Illusion des grünen Wachstums', in Blätter für deutsche und internationale Politik (eds.), *Mehr geht nicht. Der Post-wachstums-Reader*, Berlin 2015, pp. 167–74.

27. Tony Weis, 'The Accelerating Biophysical Contradictions of Industrial Capital-ist Agriculture', *Journal of Agrarian Change*, Vol. 10 (2010), No. 3, pp. 315–41.

28. Stephan Lessenich, *Living Well at Others' Expense: The Hidden Costs of Western Prosperity*, Cambridge 2019.

10 NETWORKED TECHNOLOGY AND PRODUCTION NETWORKS

1. See Dieter Sauer, 'Systemische Rationalisierung/Wertschöpfungsketten', in Harmut Hirsch-Kreinsen and Heiner Minssen (eds.), *Lexikon der Arbeits- und Industriesoziologie*, Berlin 2013, pp. 437–42.

2. Stefanie Hürtgen, Boy Lüthje, Peter Pawlicki and Martina Sproll, *From Silicon Valley to Shenzhen: Global Production and Work in the IT Industry*, Lanham 2013; Gary Gereffi, 'The Global Economy: Organization, Governance, and Development', in Neil J. Smelser and Richard Swedberg (eds.), *The Handbook of Economic Sociology*, Princeton 2005, pp. 160–82.

3. In the context of this chapter, the term 'Industry 4.0' serves merely as a reference to the corresponding debate. The aim is not to validate the notion of a Fourth Industrial Revolution as a coherent stage of industrial production. Rather, we should assume a bundle of '4.0 technologies' which are deployed selectively and depending on the respective context – and, for the most part, without any revolutionary effects on established manufacturing systems. For a criticism of the term, see Florian Butollo and Thomas Engel, 'Industrie 4.0 – arbeits-und gesellschaftspolitische Perspektiven. Zwischen Dystopie und Euphorie', *Z. Zeitschrift Marxistische Erneuerung*, No. 103 (2015), pp. 29–41; Florian Butollo, Ulrich Jürgens and Martin Krzywdzinski, 'Von Lean Production zur Industrie 4.0. Mehr Autonomie für die Beschäftigten?', *AIS-Studien*, Vol. 11 (2018), No. 2, pp. 75–90; Sabine Pfeiffer, 'Warum reden wir eigentlich über Industrie 4.0? Auf dem Weg zum digitalen Despotismus', *Mittelweg 36*, Vol. 24 (2015), No. 6, pp. 14–36.

4. The definition put forward, for example, by the business federation of the digital economy, BITKOM, reads: 'The term *Industrie 4.0* stands for the fourth industrial revolution, the next stage in the organisation and control of the entire value stream along the life cycle of a product. This cycle is based on increasingly individualised customer wishes and ranges from the idea, the order, development, production, and delivery to the end customer through to recycling and related services.' At https://www.bitkom.org/sites/default/files/pdf/NP-Themen/Branchen/Industrie-40/20160107-implementation-strategy-industrie40-en.pdf, p. 8.

5. These are platforms which centralise, process and evaluate data extracted through monitoring of the sensor-equipped processes in production, logistics and distribution. The analysis of these data can be used for the optimisation of processes in the sense of an increase of the relative rate of surplus value; it facilitates the coupling of production and distribution in terms of an improved coordination or timing of value chains.

6. Srnicek uses the term 'platform capitalism' to describe new value-creation models and concentration processes resulting from the centralisation of data, which permeate contemporary capitalism as a whole. See Nick Srnicek, *Platform Capitalism (Theory Redux)*, Cambridge 2017.

7. Translator's note: Incidentally, Adidas announced in late 2019 (after the publication of the original German edition of this volume) that it was closing its Speedfactories in Ansbach and Atlanta and moving production to Asia.

8. The Speedfactory is only one focal point of a more general debate about reshoring and regionalised, decentral production which is driven forward by specifically founded lobbying organisations and also discussed in academic literature; see, e.g., Jan Stentoft et al., 'Manufacturing Backshoring: A Systematic Literature Review', *Operations Management Research*, Vol. 9 (2016), No. 3–4, pp. 53–61; McKinsey & Company, *Is Apparel Manufacturing Coming Home? Nearshoring, Automation, and Sustainability – Establishing a Demand-Focused Apparel Value Chain*, 2018, n.p.

9. See the chapters by Kim Moody, Judy Wajcman and Sabine Pfeiffer in this volume.

10. Florian Butollo and Boy Lüthje, '"Made in China 2025": Intelligent Manufacturing and Work', Kendra Briken, Shiona Chillas, Martin Krzywdzinski and Abigail Marks (eds.), *The New Digital Workplace: How New Technologies Revolutionise Work*, London 2017, pp. 42–61.

11. Martin Krzywdzinski, 'Automation, Skill Requirements and Labour-use Strategies: High-wage and Low-wage Approaches to High-tech Manufacturing in the Automotive Industry', *New Technology, Work and Employment*, Vol. 32 (2017), No. 3, pp. 247–67.

12. Gary Herrigel, Volker Wittke and Ulrich Voskamp, 'The Process of Chinese Manufacturing Upgrading: Transitioning From Unilateral to Recursive Mutual Learning Relations', *Global Strategy Journal*, Vol. 3 (2013), pp. 109–25.

13. 'By its very nature, capital strives to go beyond every spatial limitatiøn. Hence the creation of the physical conditions of exchange – of the means of communication and transport – becomes a necessity for it to an incomparably greater degree: space must be annihilated by time. Insofar as the immediate product can be valorised on a mass scale in distant markets only to the extent that transport costs decline, and insofar as, on the other hand, means of transport and communication themselves can only function as spheres of valorisation, of labour organised by capital, to the extent that commercial traffic takes place on a massive scale – whereby more than the necessary labour is replaced – the production of cheap means of transport and communication is a condition of production based on capital, and therefore they are produced by it.' Karl Marx, *Outlines of the Critique of Political Economy*, in Karl Marx and Frederick Engels, *Collected Works* (MECW), Vol. 28, New York 1986, p. 448.
14. Srnicek, *Platform Capitalism*, pp. 39f.
15. 'But in the degree in which large-scale industry develops, the creation of real wealth becomes less dependent upon labour time and the quantity of labour employed than [...] upon the general level of development of science and the progress of technology, or on the application of science to production.' Marx: *Outlines of the Critique of Political Economy*, p. 90.
16. See Hürtgen et al., *From Silicon Valley to Shenzhen*.
17. Florian Butollo, Martin Ehrlich and Thomas Engel, 'Amazonisierung der Industriearbeit? Industrie 4.0, Intralogistik und die Veränderung der Arbeitsverhältnisse in einem Montageunternehmen der Automobilindustrie', *Arbeit: Zeitschrift für Arbeitsforschung, Arbeitsgestaltung und Arbeitspolitik*, Vol. 26 (2017), No. 1, pp. 33–59; see also Butollo, Jürgens and Krzywdzinski, 'Von Lean Production zur Industrie 4.0'.

11 COMPUTERISATION: SOFTWARE AND THE DEMOCRATISATION OF WORK AS PRODUCTIVE POWER

1. This and the following deliberations are based on my more elaborate depiction in Nadine Müller, *Reglementierte Kreativität. Arbeitsteilung und Eigentum im computerisierten Kapitalismus*, Berlin 2010 (new edition forthcoming).
2. Karl Marx, *The German Ideology*, in Karl Marx and Frederick Engels, *Collected Works* (MECW), Vol. 5, New York 1976, p. 34.
3. Karl Marx, *Capital: A Critique of Political Economy, Volume One*, translated by Ben Fowkes, London 1976, p. 775 (emphasis added).
4. Ibid., p. 325.
5. Ibid., p. 547.
6. 'The resulting increase of productivity is due either to an increased expenditure of labour-power in a given time – i.e. increased intensity of labour – or to a decrease in the amount of labour-power unproductively consumed' (ibid., p. 460). And: 'It is self-evident that in proportion as the use of machinery spreads,

and the experience of a special class of worker – the machine-worker – accumulates, the rapidity and thereby the intensity of labour undergoes a natural increase' (ibid., p. 533). What emerges is an average rate, or 'usual degree of intensity', and 'the capitalist is […] careful to see that this is done' (ibid. p. 303). The profit rate is also affected by the shortening of circulation time through improved communication (Karl Marx, *Capital: A Critique of Political Economy, Volume Three*, translated by David Fernbach, London 1981, p. 164).

7. Marx, *Capital, Volume One*, p. 513.

8. The term 'dominance shift' or 'shift in dominance' implies a reversal of relations: an initially secondary function becomes dominant, accompanied by the emergence of new qualities; see Klaus Holzkamp, *Grundlegung der Psychologie*, Frankfurt am Main/New York 1985, p. 80, at this point still synonymous with 'functional shift' (*Funktionswechsel*).

9. Projekt Automation und Qualifikation, *Automation in der BRD. Probleme der Produktivkraftentwicklung*, Berlin 1975, p. 81; Hermann May, *Arbeitsteilung als Entfremdungssituation in der Industriegesellschaft von Emile Durkheim bis heute*, Baden-Baden 1985, p. 50.

10. Manfred Burghardt, *Projektmanagement. Leitfaden für die Planung, Überwachung und Steuerung von Entwicklungsprojekten*, Berlin/Munich 1988, p. 10.

11. Lothar Hack and Irmgard Hack, *Die Wirklichkeit, die Wissen schafft. Zum wechselseitigen Begründungsverhältnis von "Verwissenschaftlichung der Industrie" und "Industrialisierung der Wissenschaft"*, Frankfurt am Main/New York 1985, pp. 468–9; Walter L. Bühl, *Wissenschaft und Technologie. An der Schwelle zur Informationsgesellschaft*, Göttingen 1995, p. 41.

12. Andrea Baukrowitz, 'Neue Produktionsmethoden mit alten EDV-Konzepten?', in Rudi Schmiede (ed.), *Virtuelle Arbeitswelten*, Berlin 1996, pp. 49–77, here: p. 57.

13. Hartmut Hirsch-Kreinsen and Beate Seitz, *Innovationsprozesse im Maschinenbau*, Dortmund 1999, pp. 20–1.

14. German Federal Ministry for Economic Affairs and Energy (BMWi), Monitoring-Report: Digital Economy 2014. ICT as Innovation Driver, at https://www.bmwi.de/Redaktion/EN/Publikationen/monitoring-digitale-wirtschaft-2014.pdf?__blob=publicationFile&v=1.

15. Press release No. 470 of 3 December 2018, German Federal Statistical Office (Statistisches Bundesamt), Wiesbaden.

16. Gerhard Bosch and Claudia Weinkopf, 'Arbeitsverhältnisse im Dienstleistungssektor', *WSI-Mitteilungen* 9/2011, pp. 439–49.

17. Statista 2019, at de.statista.com/statistik/daten/studie/3267/umfrage/anzahlder-erwerbstaetigen-in-deutschland-seit-dem-jahr-1991.

18. Statistisches Jahrbuch (Statistical Yearbook) 2018, at de.statista.com/statistik/daten/studie/1248/umfrage/anzahl-der-erwerbstaetigen-in-deutschland-nach-wirtschaftsbereichen.

19. Ines Roth, *Digitalisierung und Arbeitsqualität*, ver.di, Berlin 2017, p. 19.
20. Ibid., p. 21.
21. Frigga Haug, *Lernverhältnisse. Selbstbewegungen und Selbstblockierungen*, Hamburg 2003, p. 270. On the PAQ, see also the chapter by Frigga Haug in this volume.
22. Projekt Automation und Qualifikation, *Widersprüche der Automationsarbeit. Ein Handbuch*, Berlin 1987, pp. 179, 194–6; Müller, *Reglementierte Kreativität*, p. 55.
23. Andrea Baukrowitz and Andreas Boes, 'Arbeit in der "Informationsgesellschaft". Einige Überlegungen aus einer (fast schon) ungewohnten Perspektive', in Rudi Schmiede (ed.), *Virtuelle Arbeitswelten. Arbeit, Produktion und Subjekt in der "Informationsgesellschaft"*, Berlin 1996, pp. 129–58, here: p. 151.
24. PwC, 'Innovation – Deutsche Wege zum Erfolg', 2015, at https://www.pwc.de/de/publikationen/paid_pubs/pwc_innovation_-_deutsche_wege_zum_erfolg_2015.pdf.
25. Ines Roth, *Innovationsbarometer 2015. Digitale Innovationen im Dienstleistungssektor – Bedeutung und Folgen*, edited by ver.di (Bereich Innovation und Gute Arbeit – Department of Innovation and Good Work), Berlin 2015, p. 12, at innovation-gute-arbeit.verdi.de/innovation.
26. Andrea Baukrowitz, Andreas Boes and Bernd Eckhardt, *Software als Arbeit gestalten. Konzeptionelle Neuorientierung der Aus- und Weiterbildung von Computerspezialisten*, Opladen 1994; Marcel Christ, Detlef Krause, Arno Rolf and Edouard Simonm 'Wissen, wie alles zusammenhängt. Das Mikropolis-Modell als Orientierungswerkzeug für die Gestaltung von Informationstechnik in Organisationen und Gesellschaft', *Informatik-Spektrum*, Vol. 29 (2006), No. 4, pp. 263–73.
27. Fritz Böhle, Ursula Stöger and Margit Weihrich, *Interaktionsarbeit gestalten. Vorschläge und Perspektiven für humane Dienstleistungsarbeit*, Berlin 2014, p. 19; Nadine Müller and Anke Thorein, 'Arbeit mit Menschen humanisieren', in ver.di (ed.), *Arbeitspolitik von unten. 10 Jahre ver.di-Initiative Gute Arbeit*, Berlin 2018, pp. 41–4, at innovation-gute-arbeit.verdi.de/gute-arbeit/materialien-undstudien.
28. Jost Wagner, 'Die Kunst guter Dienstleistung – eine Strategie für innovative Dienstleistungsarbeit', in ver.di (ed.), *Dienstleistungsinnovationen*, Berlin 2013, pp. 49–56.
29. Ibid., p. 50.
30. Of the respondents in a study titled Status Quo Agile 2016/2017, 68 per cent stated that their projects were conducted in part through agile approaches, for 20 per cent this was consistently the case, while only 12 per cent of all projects were completed exclusively with the use of conventional methods (see Ayelt Komus et al., 'Status Quo Agile 2016/2017', Koblenz 2017, at https://www.process-and-project.net/studien/studienunterseiten/status-quo-scaled-agile-2020-en/); on agile work, see the Manifesto for Agile Software Development,

at http://agilemanifesto.org/iso/en/manifesto.html; Müller, *Reglementierte Kreativität*, pp. 119f.; and the chapter by Phoebe Moore in this volume.

31. Erik Brynjolfsson and Andrew McAfee, *The Second Machine Age: Work, Progress, and Prosperity in a Time of Brilliant Technologies*, New York 2014, p. 11.

32. Paul S. Adler, 'Practice and Process: The Socialization of Software Development', *Academy of Management Proceedings*, 2003 (1), at icos.groups.si.umich. edu/adlerpaper.pdf, p. 180.

33. Helmut Drüke, 'Internet. Technologie des Neo-Taylorismus oder Durchbruch zur Ent-Hierarchisierung in den Akteursbeziehungen', in Georg Schreyögg (ed.), *Wissen in Unternehmen: Konzepte, Maßnahmen, Methoden*, Berlin 2001, pp. 249–65, here: pp. 254–6.

34. 'Democratisation implies additional and more far-reaching participation. This would generalise the rights of disposition over the means of production so that workers and consumers would be included in decision-making concerning products, production lines, work organisation, market behaviour of business enterprises, etc.' (Alex Demirović, *Demokratie in der Wirtschaft. Positionen, Probleme, Perspektiven*, Münster 2007, p. 64.) According to Demirović, concepts seeking to theoretically develop economic democracy and, thereby, co-determination existed well into the 1980s: 'It was demanded that it be implemented at two additional levels: direct participation at the workplace level, and mechanisms for cross-business and cross-industry as well as global control at the macro-economic level [...] Both were intended to complement the existing institutions of workplace- and company-level co-determination' (ibid., p. 64).

35. Projekt Automation und Qualifikation, *Entwicklung der Arbeit*, Berlin 1978, p. 135.

36. Manfred Moldaschl and Dieter Sauer, 'Internalisierung des Marktes. Zur neuen Dialektik von Kooperation und Herrschaft', in Heiner Minssen (ed.), *Begrenzte Entgrenzungen. Wandlungen von Organisation und Arbeit*, Berlin 2000, pp. 205–24.

37. Kent Beck, *eXtreme Programming Explained: Embrace Change*, Reading, MA 2000.

38. Hartmut Seifert, 'Je länger, desto langsamer', *BöcklerImpuls* 20/2008, at boeckler. de/pdf/impuls_2008_20_6.pdf.

39. Nadine Müller and Ines Roth, 'Einleitung', in Roth, *Digitalisierung und Arbeitsqualität*, pp. 6–9, here: p. 8.

40. Some scholars estimate that digitalisation increased global economic output by 193 trillion US dollars in 2011. Karim Sabbagh et al., 'Digitalization for Economic Growth and Job Creation: Regional and Industry Perspectives', in Benat Bilbao-Osorio, Soumitra Dutta and Bruno Lanvin (eds.), *The Global Information Technology Report 2013: Growth and Jobs in a Hyperconnected World*, Geneva 2013, pp. 35–42. According to an analysis by Prognos, digitalisation contributed some 0.5 per cent of growth in value creation year upon year in the German service sector from 1998 to 2012. Around one third of the entire

tertiary growth in value creation in this period, the analysis continues, can be attributed to digitalisation – which, cumulatively and in absolute numbers, amounts to 95.1 billion euros. See Bitkom/Prognos (eds.), Digitale Arbeitswelt. Gesamtwirtschaftliche Effekte – Endbericht, 2013, n.p. Vereinigung der Bayerischen Wirtschaft: Digitalisierung als Rahmenbedingung für Wachstum. Eine vbw-Studie, erstellt von der Prognos AG, 2013, n.p.

41. Teresa Stiens, 'Mehr Jobs weniger Gehalt', *Süddeutsche Zeitung*, 16 April 2015.
42. IAB, Qualifikations- und Berufsfeldprojektion bis 2030, Kurzbericht 18/2012, at doku.iab.de/kurzber/2012/kb1812.pdf.
43. Carl Benedikt Frey and Michael A. Osborne, *The Future of Employment: How Susceptible are Jobs to Computerisation?*, Oxford 2013; Carsten Brzeski and Inga Burk, 'Die Roboter kommen. Folgen der Automatisierung für den deutschen Arbeitsmarkt', in IngDiBa, Economic Research, 30 April 2015; Tobias Kaiser, 'Maschinen könnten 18 Millionen Arbeitnehmer verdrängen', *Die Welt*, 2 May 2015.
44. See Adler, 'Practice and Process'.
45. Axel Zerdick et al., 'E-Conomics: Strategies for the Digital Marketplace' (European Communication Council Report), Berlin i.a. 2001, pp. 128f; Manuel Castells, *The Information Age: Economy, Society, and Culture, Volume 1: The Rise of the Network Society*, Malden 1996, p. 88.
46. In matrix project organisation, projects are managed alongside or within the line management structure. The line manager usually retains the authority to issue instructions, at least in a disciplinary sense. See Manfred Burghardt, *Projektmanagement. Leitfaden für die Planung, Überwachung und Steuerung von Entwicklungsprojekten*, Berlin/Munich 1988, p. 10.
47. Robert B. Reich, *The Work of Nations: Preparing Ourselves for 21st-Century Capitalism*, New York 1991, pp. 172–3ff; Elmar Altvater and Birgit Mahnkopf, *Grenzen der Globalisierung. Ökonomie, Ökologie und Politik in der Weltgesellschaft*, Münster 2007, p. 319.
48. Wolfgang Fritz Haug, *Politisch richtig oder richtig politisch. Linke Politik im transnationalen High-Tech-Kapitalismus*, Hamburg 1998, pp. 57–8.
49. The law concerning employees' inventions, for example, is supposed to ensure the inventor can secure the right to their own invention as a personal right. In the company, however, this collides with the employment contract: employees have to cede this right in return for a small remuneration. This leads to demotivation and conflicts among staff.
50. Boris Gröndahl, 'Die Tragedy of the anticommons. Kapitalistische Eigentumskritik im Patentwesen', *Prokla*, Vol. 32 (2002), No. 1, pp. 89–101, here: p. 97.
51. Copyleft licences such as the General Public Licence (GPL) are the most effective way to guarantee the long-term free availability of software and its modification.
52. Sabine Nuss, *Copyright & Copyriot. Aneignungskonflikte um geistiges Eigentum im informationellen Kapitalismus*, Münster 2006, p. 77.

53. Nadine Müller, 'Crowdwork und Mitbestimmung', *Zeitschrift Gute Arbeit*, No. 12 (2017), pp. 17–20, here: p. 17.

54. Ibid.

55. Gudrun Trautwein-Kalms, *Ein Kollektiv von Individualisten? Interessenvertretung neuer Beschäftigtengruppen*, Berlin 1995, p. 221.

56. Ibid., pp. 223–4.

57. ver.di (ed.), *Arbeitspolitik von unten. 10 Jahre ver.di-Initiative Gute Arbeit*, Berlin 2018.

58. Frank Bsirske, 'Transformation der Dienstleistungsarbeit. Leitbild Gute Dienstleistungen und Gute Arbeit', in Lothar Schröder and Hans-Jürgen Urban (eds.), *Jahrbuch Gute Arbeit 2019. Transformation der Arbeit – Ein Blick zurück nach vorn*, Frankfurt am Main 2019, pp. 36–50, here: p. 40.

59. ver.di, *Arbeiten 4.0 braucht gleichberechtigte Teilhabe! Mehr Mitbestimmung und Demokratie in der digitalen Arbeitswelt*, Berlin 2016, at verdi.de/themen/digitalisierungskongresse/kongress-2016; ver.di, *WOZU, WAS und WIE sollen Algorithmen lernen? Gute Arbeit und Künstliche Intelligenz* and *Beiblatt KI*, Berlin 2018, at innovation-gute-arbeit.verdi.de/themen/digitale-arbeit/beschluesse-und-positionen.

12 DESIGNING WORK FOR AGILITY AND AFFECT'S MEASURE

1. Affective and emotional labour are not identical, but for lack of space this chapter does not expand on this distinction. For further reading on affective and emotional labour see Phoebe Moore, 'Tracking Affective Labour for Agility in the Quantified Workplace', *Body & Society*, Vol. 24 (2018), No. 3, pp. 39–67; Arlie Russell Hochschild, *The Managed Heart: Commercialisation of Human Feeling*, Oakland 2012 (1983); Paul Brook, 'Emotional Labour and the Living Personality at Work: Labour Power, Materialist Subjectivity and the Dialogical Self', *Culture and Organization*, Vol. 19 (2013), No. 4, pp. 332–52; Antonio Negri, 'Value and Affect', *boundary*, Vol. 26 (1999), No. 2, pp. 77–88; Patricia T. Clough, 'The Affective Turn: Political Economy, Biomedia and Bodies', *Theory, Culture & Society*, Vol. 25 (2008), No. 1, pp. 1–22 (not a complete list).

2. Luis M. Sanchez and Rakesh Nagi, 'A Review of Agile Manufacturing Systems', *International Journal of Production Research*, Vol. 39 (2010), No. 16, pp. 3561–600, here: pp. 3562–3.

3. See https://agilemanifesto.org.

4. The Agile Movement, 2008, at agilemethodology.org/agile-methodology-what-is-it.

5. James A. Highsmith, *Agile Software Development Ecosystems*, Boston 2002 (emphasis added).

6. Sharon K. Parker, 'Beyond Motivation: Job and Work Design for Development, Health, Ambidexterity, and More', *Annual Review of Psychology*, Vol. 65 (2014), pp. 661–91, here: p. 666.
7. Ibid.
8. Michael L. Joroff et al., 'The Agile Workplace', *Journal of Corporate Real Estate*, Vol. 5 (2003), No. 4, pp. 293–311, here: p. 294.
9. Andy Danford et al., 'Partnership High Performance Work Systems and Quality of Working Life', *New Technology, Work and Employment*, Vol. 23 (2008), No. 3, pp. 151–66.
10. Steve Denning, 'How to Make the Whole Organisation Agile', *Forbes*, 22 July 2015, at www.forbes.com/sites/stevedenning/2015/07/22/how-to-make-the-wholeorganization-agile.
11. Jasmine Tata and Sameer Prasad, 'Cultural and Structural Constraints on Total Quality Management Implementation', *Total Quality Management*, Vol. 9 (1998), No. 8, pp. 703–10; Harvie Ramsay, Dora Scholarios and Bill Harley, 'Employees and High-Performance Work Systems: Testing inside the Black Box', *British Journal of Industrial Relations*, Vol. 38 (2000), No. 4, pp. 501–31.
12. Maurizio Lazzarato, 'Immaterial Labor', in Michael Hardt and Paolo Virno (eds.), *Radical Thought in Italy: A Potential Politics*, Minneapolis/London 1996, pp. 133–47.
13. Phoebe Moore, *The Quantified Self in Precarity? Work, Technology and What Counts*, London 2018.
14. Melissa Gregg, *Work's Intimacy*, Cambridge/Malden 2011.
15. Peter Fleming, *Resisting Work: The Corporatisation of Life and its Discontents*, Philadelphia 2015, p. 83.
16. Jason Read, *The Micro-Politics of Capital: Marx and the Prehistory of the Present*, Albany/New York 2003, p. 128.
17. Silvia Federici, 'On Affective Labour', in Michael A. Peters and Ergin Bulut (eds.), *Cognitive Capitalism, Education and Digital Labour*, New York 2011, pp. 57–74, here: p. 63.
18. William Bogard, 'Digital Resisto(e)rs', *CTheory*, 2010, pp. 4–21.
19. Marion Crain, Winifred R. Poster and Miriam A. Cherry (eds.), *Invisible Labour: Hidden Work in the Contemporary World*, Oakland 2016.
20. L. J. B. Hayes and Sian Moore, 'Care in a Time of Austerity: The Electronic Monitoring of Homecare Workers' Time', *Gender, Work and Organisation*, Vol. 24 (2017), No. 4, pp. 329–44.
21. Funded by the British Academy/Leverhulme small grant scheme, the author's role was to conduct independent academic research on the study via surveys and interviews. Co-investigators and the Primary Investigator (author) were also provided limited access to quantified and self-report data (where participants consented).
22. In the first interviews, three comments indicated a concern about what personal data management had access to, increasing to 21 in the final interviews.

23. David Beer, *Metric Power*, London 2016, p. 49.
24. Phoebe Moore, 'Work and the GDPR: The Future for Algorithms and People Analytics?', 7 November 2017, at phoebevmoore.wordpress.com/2017/11/07/the-gdpr-algorithms-and-people-analytics.
25. Carolyn Merchant, *The Death of Nature: Women, Ecology and the Scientific Revolution*, San Francisco 1990, p. 227.
26. Ruth Cain, 'Measure Your Own Misery: Self-quantification and the Techno-recovery Imperative in Mental Health "mHealth" Discourse'. Presentation, International Initiatives in Promoting Political Economy (IIPPE), Berlin, 13 September 2017.
27. Lazzarato, 'Immaterial Labor', p. 136.

13 OLD POWER IN DIGITAL GARB?

1. Different terms exist that denote the outsourcing of paid tasks via internet platforms, including *online gig work* or *on-demand work*. Platforms themselves rarely use the crowd terminology, referring instead to 'creative talent', 'experts', 'freelancers' or similar. The aim is to create an image of talented and independent freelancers instead of a digital factory.
2. Hans Pongratz and Robin Schenkewitz, Online-Arbeit auf Internet-Plattformen. Orientierungshilfe zum Nebenverdienst. *Handlungsbroschüre im Rahmen des Verbundprojekts 'Herausforderung Cloud und Crowd'*, at http://cloud-und-crowd.de/wp-content/uploads/2018/11/Orientierungshilfe-Online-Arbeit.pdf, p. 10.
3. Karl Marx, *Capital: A Critique of Political Economy, Volume* One, translated by Ben Fowkes, London 1976, pp. 283–93.
4. Andreas Boes, Tobias Kämpf, Barbara Langes and Thomas Lühr, *"Lean" und "agil" im Büro: Neue Formen der Organisation von Kopfarbeit in der digitalen Transformation*, Bielefeld 2018, pp. 41, 181.
5. Moritz Altenried, 'Die Plattform als Fabrik: Crowdwork, Digitaler Taylorismus und die Vervielfältigung der Arbeit', *Prokla*, Vol. 47 (2017), No. 187, pp. 175–92, here: p. 176; Aniket Kittur, Jeffrey Nickerson, Michael Bernstein, Elizabeth Gerber, Aaron Shaw, John Zimmerman, Matt Lease and John Horton, 'The Future of Crowd Work', *Proceedings of the 2013 Conference on Computer Supported Cooperative Work*, CSCW '13, New York 2013, p. 1303.
6. Lilly Irani, 'The Cultural Work of Microwork', *New Media & Society*, Vol. 17 (2015), No. 5, pp. 720–39.
7. Marx, *Capital, Volume One*, pp. 427–508.
8. See Felix Gnisa in this volume; Martin Kornberger, Dane Pflueger and Jan Mouritsen, 'Evaluative Infrastructures: Accounting for Platform Organization', *Accounting, Organizations and Society*, Vol. 60 (2017), pp. 79–95.
9. Nick Srnicek, *Platform Capitalism (Theory Redux)*, Cambridge 2017, pp. 48, 76, 84.

Notes

10. Also referred to as 'post-workerism' or 'post-operaismo'.
11. This chapter is based on the three-year research project 'Zwischen digitaler Boheme und Prekarität. Arbeit und Leistung in der Crowd' ('Between digital bohemianism and precarity. Labour and performance in the crowd') led by Prof. Dr Martin Krzywdzinski at the WZB Berlin Social Science Center. The quotes used in this chapter are taken from interviews with representatives of different platforms and the crowdworkers working for them. The interviews were conducted in the context of the research project.
12. Harry Braverman, *Labor and Monopoly Capital: The Degradation of Work in the Twentieth Century*, New York 1998 (1974); Michael Burawoy, *The Politics of Production*, London 1985.
13. Stephen Ackroyd and Paul Thompson, *Organizational Misbehaviour*, London 1999; Philip Edwards, *Conflict at Work: A Materialist Analysis of Workplace Relations*, Oxford 1986.
14. Boes et al., *"Lean" und "agil" im Büro*, pp. 22–30.
15. A platform's appeal for customers and the crowd in part depends on the number of transaction partners it enables interaction with. They therefore move to the platform that assembles a critical mass of desired users, i.e. customers or service providers (network effect), which in turn engenders monopoly tendencies. On this, see Srnicek, *Platform Capitalism*, pp. 45–6, 48.
16. Chris Smith, 'The Double Indeterminacy of Labour Power: Labour Effort and Labour Mobility', *Work, Employment & Society*, Vol. 20 (2006), No. 2, pp. 389–402.
17. See, for example, Jan-Marco Leimeister, Shkodran Zogaj, David Durward and Ivo Blohm, *Systematisierung und Analyse von Crowd-Sourcing-Anbietern und Crowd-Work-Projekten*, Düsseldorf 2016.
18. Justin Cheng, Jaime Teevan, Shamsi Iqbal and Michael Bernstein, 'Break It Down: A Comparison of Macro- and Microtasks', *Proceedings of the 33rd Annual ACM Conference on Human Factors in Computing Systems*, CHI '15, New York 2015, pp. 4061–4.
19. Boes et al., *"Lean" und "agil" im Büro*, pp. 28–30.
20. Hans Pongratz, 'Of Crowds and Talents: Discursive Constructions of Global Online Labour', *New Technology, Work and Employment*, Vol. 33 (2018), No. 1, pp. 58–73.
21. Alessandro Gandini, *The Reputation Economy: Understanding Knowledge Work in Digital Society*, London 2016; Ulrich Bröckling, *The Entrepreneurial Self: Fabricating a New Type of Subject*, Los Angeles/London 2016.
22. Jodi Dean, *The Communist Horizon*, London 2012, pp. 124ff.
23. Richard Edwards, *Contested Terrain: The Transformation of the Workplace in the Twentieth Century*, London 1979.
24. The Invisible Committee, *To Our Friends*, Semiotext(e) Intervention Series, Los Angeles 2014.
25. Timo Daum, *Das Kapital sind wir*, Hamburg 2017, p. 174.

26. Christine Gerber and Martin Krzywdzinski, 'Brave New Digital Work? New Forms of Performance Control in Crowdwork', *Research in the Sociology of Work*, Vol. 33 (2019), pp. 121–43.

14 THE MACHINE SYSTEM OF THE TWENTY-FIRST CENTURY?

1. Paul Mason, *Postcapitalism: A Guide to Our Future*, London 2016. See also the chapter by Schaupp and Jochum in this volume.
2. Jeremy Rifkin, *The Zero Marginal Cost Society: The Internet of Things, the Collaborative Commons, and the Eclipse of Capitalism*, New York 2014.
3. Nick Srnicek and Alex Williams, *Inventing the Future: Postcapitalism and a World Without Work*, revised and updated edition, London/New York 2016.
4. On the conceptual and historical tradition of workers' self-management, see Karl Korsch, *Arbeitsrecht für Betriebsräte* (Labor Law for Factory Councils), Berlin 1922; Dario Azzellini and Immanuel Ness (eds.), *Ours to Master and to Own: Workers' Councils from the Commune to the Present*, Chicago 2011.
5. Nick Srnicek, *Platform Capitalism (Theory Redux)*, Cambridge 2017; Oliver Nachtwey and Philip Staab, 'Die Avantgarde des digitalen Kapitalismus', *Mittelweg 36*, Vol. 24 (2015), No. 6, pp. 59–84.
6. Karl Marx, *Capital: A Critique of Political Economy, Volume One*, translated by Ben Fowkes, London 1976, pp. 429–508.
7. Joachim Bergmann, 'Reelle Subsumtion als arbeitssoziologische Kategorie', in Wilhelm Schumm (ed.), *Zur Entwicklungsdynamik des modernen Kapitalismus. Beiträge zur Gesellschaftstheorie, Industriesoziologie und Gewerkschaftsforschung. Symposium für Gerhard Brandt*, Frankfurt am Main 1989, pp. 39–48; Rudi Schmiede, 'Reelle Subsumtion als gesellschaftstheoretische Kategorie', in Schumm, *Zur Entwicklungsdynamik*, pp. 21–38.
8. Historically, this problem became relevant, for example, for the Soviets in revolutionary Russia, as their control over the factory consisted not of real decision-making power over production, but merely of supervising the engineers and former capital owners who continued to manage production. See David Mandel, 'The Factory Committee Movement in the Russian Revolution', in Azzellini and Ness (eds.), *Ours to Master*, pp. 104–29.
9. Not all platforms organise productive activity, which is why they are not mentioned here for pragmatic reasons. For an instructive overview, see Srnicek, *Platform Capitalism*.
10. Florian A. Schmidt, *Digital Labour Markets in the Platform Economy: Mapping the Political Challenges of Crowd Work and Gig Work*, Bonn 2017, pp. 18–19.
11. Jan-Marco Leimeister, Shkodran Zogaj, David Durward and Ivo Blohm, *Systematisierung und Analyse von Crowd-Sourcing-Anbietern und Crowd-Work-Projekten*, Düsseldorf 2016, pp. 44–5; Schmidt, *Digital Labour Markets*, pp. 15–16.

12. Schmidt, *Digital Labour Markets*, p. 15.
13. Leimeister et al., *Systematisierung*, pp. 46–8.
14. Karim M. Lakhani, David A. Garvin and Eric Lonstein, 'Topcoder (A). Developing Software through Crowdsourcing', in *Harvard Business School Case Study No. 610–032*, Cambridge 2010.
15. Volkmar Mrass, Christoph Peters and Jan-Marco Leimeister, 'Crowdworking Platforms in Germany: Business Insights from a Study & Implications for Society', in *82. Jahrestagung des Verbands der Hochschullehrer für Betriebswirtschaft* (82nd Annual Conference of the Association of University Professors of Business Administration [VHB]), Frankfurt am Main, Germany, pp. 6–7.
16. This assumption is prominently represented in Christian Fuchs and Sebastian Sevignani, 'What is Digital Labour? What is Digital Work? What's their Difference? And Why Do These Questions Matter for Understanding Social Media?', *Triple C*, Vol. 11 (2013), No. 2, pp. 237–93. The authors contend: 'Digital work is the organisation of human experiences with the help of the human brain, digital media and speech in such a way that new products are created. Digital labour is the valorisation dimension of digital work.'
17. Marx, *Capital, Volume One*, p. 486.
18. Yochai Benkler, 'Coase's Penguin, or, Linux and "The Nature of the Firm"', *Yale Law Journal*, Vol. 112 (2002), No. 3, pp. 369–446, here: pp. 415–17.
19. Moritz Altenried, 'The Platform as Factory: Crowdwork and the Hidden Labour behind Artificial Intelligence', Special Issue of *Capital & Class*, 'Machines & Measure', edited by Phoebe V. Moore, Kendra Briken and Frank Engster, 22 January 2020.
20. Schmidt, *Digital Labour Markets*, p. 16.
21. Min Kyung Lee, Daniel Kusbit, Evan Metsky and Laura Dabbish, 'Working with Machines: The Impact of Algorithmic and Data-Driven Management on Human Workers', in *Proceedings of the 33rd Annual ACM Conference on Human Factors in Computing Systems*, New York 2015, pp. 1603–12.
22. Ibid., pp. 1605–7; Alex Rosenblat and Luke Stark, 'Algorithmic Labor and Information Asymmetries: A Case Study of Uber's Drivers', *International Journal of Communication*, Vol. 10 (2016), pp. 3758–84, here: pp. 3766–9.
23. Lee et al., 'Working with Machines', p. 1608.
24. Rosenblat and Stark, 'Algorithmic Labor', p. 3772.
25. Ibid.
26. Anand Kulkarni, Matthew Can and Björn Hartmann, 'Collaboratively Crowdsourcing Workflows with Turkomatic', in *Proceedings of the ACM 2012 Conference on Computer Supported Cooperative Work*, New York 2012, pp. 1003–12.
27. Correspondingly, the labour price for an encyclopaedia entry was reduced in relative terms from US$3.05 for 393 words to US$3.26 for 658 words through task fragmentation. See Aniket Kittur et al., 'Crowdforge: Crowdsourcing Complex Work', in *Proceedings of the 24th Annual ACM Symposium on User Interface Software and Technology* (ACM, 2011), pp. 43–52.

28. Referring to the above-mentioned reduction of internal staff.
29. Jan Marco Leimeister, Shkodran Zogaj and David Durward, 'New Forms of Employment and IT – Crowdsourcing', in R. Blanpain, F. Hendrickx and B. Waas (eds.), *New Forms of Employment in Europe* (Bulletin of Comparative Labour Relations Series), Kluwer Law International BV, pp. 23–41, here: p. 39.
30. Harry Braverman, *Labor and Monopoly Capital: The Degradation of Work in the Twentieth Century*, New York 1974, pp. 42–4; Paolo Virno, *A Grammar of the Multitude*, Los Angeles/New York 2004, p. 62.
31. Peter Löw-Beer, *Industrie und Glück. Der Alternativ-Plan von Lucas Aerospace*, Berlin 1981, p. 94.
32. Jeremy Pitt and Andrzej Nowak, 'The Reinvention of Social Capital for Socio-Technical Systems', *IEEE Technology and Society Magazine*, Vol. 33 (2014), No. 1, pp. 27–80.
33. Translator's note: Literally translated, *Landnahme* means land grabbing, land appropriation or territorial gain. It refers to internal as well as external capitalist expansion. Theories of *Landnahme* argue that in the long run capitalist societies cannot reproduce themselves on their own foundations. In order to reproduce themselves, then, they continuously have to occupy and commodify a non-capitalist Other (i.e. regions, milieus, groups, activities) in, so to speak, ceaseless repetition of the act of primitive accumulation. See Klaus Dörre, 'Social Capitalism and Crisis: From the Internal to the External *Landnahme*', in Klaus Dörre, Stephan Lessenich and Hartmut Rosa (eds.), *Sociology – Capitalism – Critique*, London/New York 2015, pp. 247–77.
34. For example, the Apache web server.

15 DIGITAL LABOUR AND PROSUMPTION UNDER CAPITALISM

1. See Andreas Boes, Tobias Kämpf, Katrin Gül, Barbara Langes, Thomas Lühr, Kira Marrs and Alexander Ziegler, 'Digitalisierung und "Wissensarbeit": Der Informationsraum als Fundament der Arbeitswelt der Zukunft', *Aus Politik und Zeitgeschichte*, Vol. 66 (2016), No. 18–19, pp. 32–9.
2. Firstly, all labour 'uses up its material elements, its objects and its instruments. It consumes them, and is therefore a process of consumption' (Karl Marx, *Capital: A Critique of Political Economy, Volume One*, translated by Ben Fowkes, London 1976, p. 290). Secondly, a certain part of the economy is dedicated to the creation of means of production, that is to say, production for productive consumption. Thirdly, Marx also considers consumption processes from the perspective of the maintenance of labour power (reproductive consumption).
3. See George Ritzer, 'The "New" World of Prosumption: Evolution, "Return of the Same," or Revolution?', *Sociological Forum*, Vol. 30 (2015), No. 1, pp. 1–17.
4. See Sebastian Sevignani, 'Facetten der Debatte über das digitale Arbeiten. Herausforderungen für eine kritische Theorie des informationellen Kapitalismus', *Prokla*, Vol. 47 (2017), No. 186, pp. 43–62.

Notes

5. Karl Marx, *Economic Manuscripts 1857–1858*, in Karl Marx and Frederick Engels, *Collected Works* (MECW), Vol. 28, New York 1986, p. 530; Marx, *A Contribution to the Critique of Political Economy*, in MECW, Vol. 29, New York 1987, p. 97.
6. Marx, *Capital, Volume One*, p. 132.
7. Claudia von Werlhof, Maria Mies and Veronika Bennholdt-Thomsen, *Women: The Last Colony*, London 1988.
8. Herbert Marcuse, *Eros and Civilization: A Philosophical Inquiry into Freud*, Boston 1974.
9. Raymond Williams, 'Means of Communication as Means of Production' (1978), in *Culture and Materialism: Selected Essays*, London/New York 2005, pp. 50–63.
10. L. S. Vygotsky, *Mind in Society: The Development of Higher Psychological Processes*, Cambridge 1978.
11. Valentin M. Vološinov, *Marxism and the Philosophy of Language*, Cambridge, MA 1986 (1929); Ferruccio Rossi-Landi, *Language as Work and Trade: A Semiotic Homology for Linguistics and Economics*, Westport 1983.
12. Michael Hardt and Antonio Negri, *Empire*, Cambridge, MA 2000; Tiziana Terranova, 'Free Labour: Producing Culture for the Digital Economy', *Social Text*, Vol. 18 (2000), No. 2, pp. 33–58; Yann Moulier Boutang, *Cognitive Capitalism*, Cambridge 2012.
13. Andreas Boes and Tobias Kämpf, 'Informatization as Force of Production: The Informatized Mode of Production as Basis of a New Phase of Capitalism', in Klaus Dörre, Nicole Mayer-Ahuja, Dieter Sauer and Volker Wittke (eds.), *Capitalism and Labor: Towards Critical Perspectives*, Frankfurt am Main 2018, pp. 283–301; Sebastian Sevignani, 'Historisch-Materialistische Medien- und Kommunikationstheorie 2.0', *Maske und Kothurn*, Vol. 64 (2018), pp. 59–88.
14. Marx, *Capital, Volume One*, p. 284.
15. Rudi Schmiede, 'Informatisierung, Formalisierung und kapitalistische Produktionsweise. Entstehung der Informationstechnik und Wandel der gesellschaftlichen Arbeit', in Rudi Schmiede (ed.), *Virtuelle Arbeitswelten. Arbeit, Produktion und Subjekt in der "Informationsgesellschaft"*, Berlin 1996, pp. 15–47.
16. William Henning James Hebblewhite, '"Means of Communication as Means of Production" Revisited', *Triple C*, Vol. 10 (2012), No. 2, pp. 203–13.
17. To my knowledge, no Marxist media theory exists to this day. See my preliminary work in Sevignani, 'Historisch-Materialistische Medien- und Kommunikationstheorie 2.0'.
18. Luc Boltanski and Eve Chiapello, *The New Spirit of Capitalism*, London 2005, p. 360.
19. Mark Andrejevic, 'Exploitation in the Data Mine', in Christian Fuchs, Kees Boersma, Anders Albrechtslund and Marisol Sandoval (eds.), *Internet and Surveillance: The Challenges of Web 2.0 and Social Media*, New York 2012, pp. 71–88.
20. Karl Marx, *A Contribution to the Critique of Political Economy*, Preface, in MECW, Vol. 16, New York 1980, pp. 465–78, here: p. 469.

21. On this, see the global reach of the most widely used internet services as calculated by alexa.com: google.com (41.724%), youtube.com (43.036%), facebook.com (21.489%), baidu.com (9.847%), wikipedia.org (8.921%), yahoo.com (8.198%) (as of 21 October 2017).
22. Oscar H. Gandy, *The Panoptic Sort: A Political Economy of Personal Information*, Boulder 1993.
23. Sebastian Sevignani, *Privacy and Capitalism in the Age of Social Media*, New York 2016.
24. By distinguishing between the real and formal subsumption of labour under capital, Marx emphasises that the concrete labour process is influenced by the capital relation. Formal subsumption means that work activities, which originally did not occur within the capital relation, are subordinated to it, albeit without the activity itself being transformed. This transformation occurs only in the case of real subsumption. The theory of cognitive capitalism postulates – in contrast to Marx, who saw a tendency towards real subsumption – that there is a reversal of this tendency during the informational stage of capitalism. According to this notion, the mode of the appropriation of values fundamentally changes as a result: profits become rents, i.e. the value transfer from workers to capital today mainly takes place externally and subsequently, without the organisation and control over the actual labour process. See Carlo Vercellone, 'From Formal Subsumption to General Intellect: Elements for a Marxist Reading of the Thesis of Cognitive Capitalism', *Historical Materialism*, Vol. 15 (2007), No. 1, pp. 13–36.
25. Sebastian Sevignani, 'Privatheit, Entfremdung und die Vermarktung persönlicher Daten', *Forschungsjournal Soziale Bewegungen*, Vol. 30 (2017), No. 2, pp. 170–9.
26. Tithi Bhattacharya (ed.), *Social Reproduction Theory: Remapping Class, Recentring Oppression*, London 2017.
27. Nancy Fraser, 'Behind Marx's Hidden Abode: For an Expanded Conception of Capitalism', *New Left Review*, No. 86, 2014, pp. 55–72.
28. Bob Jessop, 'Knowledge as a Fictitious Commodity: Insights and Limits of a Polanyian Perspective', in Ayse Bugra and Kaan Agartan (eds.), *Reading Karl Polanyi for the Twenty-First Century: Market Economy as a Political Project*, New York 2007.
29. Massimo de Angelis, *Omnia Sunt Communia: On the Commons and the Transformation to Postcapitalism*, London 2017.
30. Simon Mohun, 'Does All Labour Create Value?', in Alfredo Saad-Filho (ed.), *Anti-Capitalism: A Marxist Introduction*, London 2002, pp. 42–58.
31. Ibid.
32. See, for example, Stuart Hall, 'Race, Articulation and Societies Structured in Dominance', in *Sociological Theories: Race and Colonialism*, UNESCO 1980, pp. 305–45.
33. Translator's note: see Chapter 14, note 33, above, p. 308.

34. Marx, *Capital, Volume One*, p. 486.
35. Ursula Huws, *Labor in the Global Digital Economy: The Cybertariat Comes of Age*, New York 2014, pp. 149–81, here: p. 167.
36. Fraser, 'Behind Marx's Hidden Abode'.
37. Klaus Dörre, 'The New *Landnahme*: Dynamics and Limits of Financial Market Capitalism', in Dörre et al. (eds.), *Sociology – Capitalism – Critique*, pp. 11–66.
38. Christian Fuchs, *Digital Labour and Karl Marx*, London 2014, pp. 115–16.
39. Christian Fuchs has calculated for 2007 that only around 12.4 per cent of the total profits generated by the world's 2,000 largest companies were in fact in the information sector. The latter, however, goes far beyond those companies that exploit prosumption (including telecommunications, the semiconductor industry, software and hardware production, all media companies, etc.). See Christian Fuchs, 'Capitalism or Information Society? The Fundamental Question of the Present Structure of Society', *European Journal of Social Theory*, Vol. 16 (2013), No. 4, pp. 413–34.
40. Something that is not uncommon for the tradition proceeding from Marx. For an early critical discussion of this aspect, see Dallas W. Smythe, 'Communications: Blindspot of Western Marxism', *Canadian Journal of Political and Social Theory*, Vol. 1 (1977), No. 3, pp. 1–28.
41. See, for example, Jodi Dean, 'Communicative Capitalism and Class Struggle', *spheres: Journal for Digital Cultures*, No. 1, 2014, pp. 1–16; Oskar Negt and Alexander Kluge, *Public Sphere and Experience: Toward an Analysis of the Bourgeois and Proletarian Public Sphere*, London/New York 2016.

16 ARTIFICIAL INTELLIGENCE AS THE LATEST MACHINE OF DIGITAL CAPITALISM – FOR NOW

1. Alex Hern, 'Elon Musk Says AI Could Lead to Third World War', *The Guardian*, 4 September 2017; Vera Günther, 'Jürgen Schmidhuber: "KI kann Männer ersetzen"', *Horizont*, 26 September 2018.
2. See, for example, Ray Kurzweil, *The Singularity is Near: When Humans Transcend Biology*, New York 2005.
3. John McCarthy, Marvin L. Minsky, Nathaniel Rochester and Claude E. Shannon, 'A Proposal for the Dartmouth Summer Research Project on Artificial Intelligence', 31 August 1955.
4. Pat Langley, 'The Cognitive Systems Paradigm', *Advances in Cognitive Systems*, Vol. 1 (2012), pp. 3–13.
5. Hector J. Levesque, *Common Sense, the Turing Test, and the Quest for Real AI*, Cambridge, MA 2017.
6. Arthur L. Samuel, 'Some Studies in Machine Learning Using the Game of Checkers', *IBM Journal of Research and Development*, 1959, pp. 210–29.
7. Ethem Alpaydin, *Machine Learning: The New AI*, Cambridge, MA 2016, p. 166.

8. Andrew Ng, 'Artificial Intelligence is the New Electricity', Medium.com, 28 April 2017.
9. Kenneth C. Laudon and Jane P. Laudon, *Management Information Systems: Managing the Digital Firm*, Upper Saddle River, NJ 2002.
10. Evgeny Morozov, 'Digital Democracy and Technological Sovereignty. Panel Discussion', opendemocracy.net, 13 December 2016.
11. The term 'platform' comes from software development and denotes a base technology on which certain services are based.
12. Nick Srnicek, 'Ich bin derzeit etwas pessimistisch', Interview, *OXI. Wirtschaft anders denken*, October 2018.
13. The phrase 'as a service' is used in the context of cloud computing to denote a function that is offered as a service and no longer purchased as actual software.
14. Karl Marx, *Capital: A Critique of Political Economy, Volume One*, translated by Ben Fowkes, London 1976, pp. 129, 134.
15. Stanisław Lem, *Summa technologiae*, Minneapolis/London 2013, p. 96.
16. Karl Marx, *A Contribution to the Critique of Political Economy*, in Karl Marx and Frederick Engels, *Collected Works* (MECW), Vol. 29, New York 1987, p. 92.
17. Nick Dyer-Witheford, *Cyber-Proletariat: Global Labour in the Digital Vortex*, London/Toronto 2015.
18. Yann Moulier-Boutang, *Cognitive Capitalism*, Cambridge, MA 2012, p. 57.
19. Tessa Morris-Suzuki, 'Capitalism in the Computer Age and Afterword', in Jim Davis, Thomas A. Hirschl and Michael Stack (eds.), *Cutting Edge: Technology, Information Capitalism and Social Revolution*, London 1997, pp. 57–71, here: p. 64.
20. Slavoj Žižek, *The Courage of Hopelessness*, London 2018, p. 65.
21. Maurizio Lazzarato, *Signs and Machines: Capitalism and the Production of Subjectivity*, Los Angeles 2014, p. 44.
22. Félix Guattari, 'Capital as the Integral of Power Formations', in *Soft Subversions: Texts and Interviews 1977–1985*, Los Angeles 2009, p. 254.
23. Michael Hardt and Antonio Negri, *Empire*, Cambridge, MA 2000.
24. Paul Mason, *Postcapitalism: A Guide to Our Future*, New York 2017.
25. Joseph Schumpeter, *Capitalism, Socialism, and Democracy*, New York 2008; Clayton M. Christensen, *The Innovator's Dilemma: When New Technologies Cause Great Firms to Fail*, Boston 1997.
26. Jason W. Moore (ed.), *Anthropocene or Capitalocene: Nature, History and the Crisis of Capitalism*, Oakland 2016.
27. Tessa Morris-Suzuki, 'Robots and Capitalism', in Davis et al., *Cutting Edge*, pp. 13–28, here: pp. 18–19.
28. Ibid., p. 18.
29. Morris-Suzuki, 'Capitalism in the Computer Age', p. 60.
30. V. Keller, 'LG IFA 2018 Keynote Speech: Evolve, Connect & Open with AI innovation', *LG Magazine*, 31 August 2018, at https://www.lg.com/uk/lg-magazine/brand-story/ifa-2018-keynote-speech-evolve-connect-open.

31. Ernst Bloch, *Heritage of Our Times*, Los Angeles 1991, p. 3.
32. Marx, *Capital, Volume One*, p. 134.

17   FORCES AND RELATIONS OF CONTROL

1. Philipp Frey and Simon Schaupp, 'Futures of Digital Industry: Techno-Managerial or Techno-Political Utopia?', *Behemoth*, Vol. 13 (2020), No. 1, pp. 98–108.
2. See Will Steffen et al., 'Planetary Boundaries: Guiding Human Development on a Changing Planet', *Science*, Vol. 347 (2015), No. 6223.
3. Shoshana Zuboff, *The Age of Surveillance Capitalism*, New York 2019.
4. Georg Jochum, *Plus Ultra oder die Erfindung der Moderne. Zur Entgrenzung der okzidentalen Welt*, Bielefeld 2017, p. 544.
5. Karl Marx, *The Poverty of Philosophy*, in Karl Marx and Frederick Engels, *Collected Works* (MECW), Vol. 6, New York 1976, p. 166.
6. Dudenverlag, *Das Herkunftswörterbuch*, Mannheim 2000, p. 631.
7. Karl Marx, *Capital: A Critique of Political Economy, Volume One*, translated by Ben Fowkes, London 1976, p. 287.
8. Karl Marx, *A Contribution to the Critique of Political Economy*, in MECW, Vol. 16, New York 1980, p. 469.
9. Norbert Wiener, *Cybernetics, or Control and Communication in the Animal and the Machine*, second edition, Cambridge, MA 1985 (1948, 1961), p. 11.
10. The term governance goes back to the Latin word *gubernare*, which – like the Greek *kybernan* – originally referred to the steering of a ship. Cicero transferred this term to the techniques of government (see Jochum, *Plus Ultra*, p. 409). Therefore, we could call the cybernetic technologies 'forces of governance'. Correspondingly, the term '*Steuerungswende*' used in the original German version of this article could be translated as 'governance transition'. However, the term governance today is predominantly used in a purely politological sense. To avoid misunderstanding, we therefore use the term 'control' to refer to both the technical and the political act of steering. In this, we build on Wiener's (1948) understanding of cybernetics as science of 'control and communication'.
11. Tiqqun, *The Cybernetic Hypothesis*, London/Cambridge, MA 2020; Nick Dyer-Whiteford, *Cyber-Proletariat: Global Labour in the Digital Vortex*, London 2015.
12. The second revolution does not replace the consequences of the former, but overlays them. In the current social-ecological crisis, the negative ecological side effects of the appropriation of nature caused by fossilistic-industrial modernity merge with the negative social impacts of the digital-cybernetic revolution.
13. Marx, *A Contribution*, MECW, Vol. 16, p. 469.
14. Akademie der Wissenschaften der UdSSR, *Grundlagen der marxistisch-leninistischen Philosophie*, Berlin 1972, p. 310.
15. Paul Mason, *Postcapitalism: A Guide to Our Future*, London 2016, p. xix.

16. Jeremy Rifkin, *The Zero Marginal Cost Society: The Internet of Things, the Collaborative Commons, and the Eclipse of Capitalism*, New York 2014, p. 333.
17. Jürgen Habermas, *The Theory of Communicative Action, Volume 2*, Boston 1987, p. 171.
18. Karl Polanyi, *The Great Transformation: The Political and Economic Origins of Our Time*, Boston 2001 (1944).
19. Simon Schaupp and Ramon Diab, 'From the Smart Factory to the Self-organisation of Capital: "Industrie 4.0" as the Cybernetisation of Production', *Ephemera*, at http://www.ephemerajournal.org/contribution/smart-factory-self-organisation-capital-%E2%80%98industrie-40%E2%80%99-cybernetisation-production.
20. Wiener, *Cybernetics*.
21. Ronald R. Kline, *The Cybernetics Moment: Or Why We Call our Age the Information Age*, Baltimore 2015.
22. Georg Jochum, 'Kybernetisierung von Arbeit – Zur Neuformierung der Arbeitssteuerung', *Arbeits- und Industriesoziologische Studien*, Vol. 6 (2013), No. 1, pp. 25–48.
23. Jochum, *Plus Ultra*.
24. Simon Schaupp, 'Measuring the Entrepreneur of Himself: Gendered Quantification in the Self-tracking Discourse', in Stefan Selke (ed.), *Lifelogging: Digital Self-tracking and Lifelogging – Between Disruptive Technology and Cultural Transformation*. Wiesbaden 2016, pp. 249–66.
25. Wiener, *Cybernetics*, pp. 159–62.
26. Eden Medina, *Cybernetic Revolutionaries: Technology and Politics in Allende's Chile*, Cambridge 2011.
27. Luc Boltanski and Eve Chiapello, *The New Spirit of Capitalism*, London/New York 2005.
28. Friedrich A. v. Hayek, *The Fateful Conceit: The Errors of Socialism*, Chicago 1988, p. 7.
29. Ibid., p. 15.
30. Fredric Jameson, *Valences of the Dialectic*, London 2009, pp. 420–5.
31. See also Leigh Phillips and Michael Rozworski, *People's Republic of Walmart: How the World's Biggest Corporations are Laying the Foundation for Socialism*, London 2019.
32. Zuboff, *Surveillance Capitalism*, p. 8.
33. Regine Kalka, 'Dynamic Pricing: Verspielt Amazon das Vertrauen seiner Kunden?', *Absatzwirtschaft*, 16 February 2016, at www.absatzwirtschaft.de/dynamic-pricingverspielt-amazon-das-vertrauen-seiner-kunden-75271.
34. A blockchain is a continuously expandable list of datasets chained together via cryptographic processes, thereby protecting them from manipulation.
35. See the chapter by Franza Drechsel and Kristina Dietz in this volume.
36. Pat Mooney, 'Blocking the Chain: Industrial Food Chain Concentration, Big Data Platforms and Food Sovereignty Solutions', 2018, at https://www.etcgroup.

org/sites/www.etcgroup.org/files/files/blockingthechain_english_web.pdf, pp. 30–31.

37. Hayek, *Fateful Conceit*, p. 8.
38. Translator's note: see Chapter 14, note 33, above, p. 308.
39. Frey and Schaupp, 'Futures of Digital Industry'.
40. Elinor Ostrom, *Governing the Commons: The Evolution of Institutions for Collective Action*, Cambridge 1990.
41. Algorithmic trading is a method of automated trade in stocks by computer programs.
42. Gosplan was the Soviet Union's planning authority.
43. Nick Dyer-Witheford, 'Red Plenty Platforms', *Culture Machine*, Vol. 14 (2013), pp. 1–27, here: p. 12.

Index

3D printers 63, 105, 215
99designs (online design service) 199

Abbott, Andrew 15
absolute surplus value 36, 42
abstract human labour 28, 29, 31
Acemoglu, Daron and Pascual Restrepo
    Robots and Jobs 105–6, 107, 112
Activity Theory 230
Adidas Speedfactory, Germany 156–7,
    158
affective labour 185, 189, 190, 192, 195
Agile Manifesto (2001) 186, 187, 196
Agile Manufacturing Enterprise Forum
    (AMEF) 186
agile work 6, 185–9, 196, 201
agrarian question 139–40, 141
agriculture 9–10, 140–2
    employment in 146
    digitalisation in 138–9, 145, 146–51
    use of machinery in 142–4
Airbnb (accommodation platform) 16,
    218
algorithms 16, 89, 151–2, 199, 207
Alibaba (e-commerce company) 160,
    161, 165–6, 245
Alpaydin, Ethem 244
Alphabet Company 245
Altaver, Elmar 141
Amazon Corporation 19, 148, 151, 159,
    245, 263–4
Amazon Mechanical Turk 10, 19, 100,
    218, 222, 223–5
    Turkomatic 223, 227
Andersen Consulting 102
Apple Company 163, 245
    Apple Siri 14

artificial intelligence (AI) 11, 14–15,
    109, 156, 162, 242–5, 253–4
    applications 250–1, 253
artificial neural networks 14, 15, 244
Ashby, Ross 261
Association of German Engineers
    (VDI) 74
Australia: cattle farming in 143
automated factories 49, 57–8
automation 1, 3, 6, 65–6
    definitions of 94
    impact on employment of 13, 26, 84,
        97, 103–5, 172
    impact on skills of 52–3, 59–60, 61,
        77–9, 162–3, 184
    investment in 107–8, 118
    methodology of research into 71–4
    post-WWII debates on 59–61
Automation and Qualification project
    (PAQ) 9, 67, 91–2, 94, 174
    *Automation in the Federal Republic of
        Germany* 67, 70
    'Educational Reform from the
        Perspective of Capital' 71
    fieldwork for 76–82
    Politics Around Work 67
    *Theories on Work in Automated
        Processes* 75
    'Theses on the Relationship between
        Science and Trade Union Politics'
        76
    Zerreissproben 82
automobile industry 6, 106–7, 112, 118

Babbage, Charles *On the Economy of
    Machinery and Manufactures* 50
Baidu (search engine) 245

banking: impact of computerisation on 102

batch size 1: 158, 159, 165, 168

Baukrowitz, Andrea and Andreas Boes 174

Bayer Company 151

Beer, Stafford 262

Benjamin, Walter 'Angel of History' 21

Benkler, Yochai 220, 221, 227

Bergmann, Joachim 95

Big Data 14, 97, 104, 148, 162, 165, 215, 220, 244, 246, 253, 265

Bloch, Ernst 253

blockchains 144–5, 148, 264, 265

Boes, Andreas 200, 213

Boltanski, Luc and Eve Chiapello 262

Bosch Company 161, 162

Boston Consulting Group 106

Botwinick, Howard 112

Bourdieu, Pierre 238

Brain, The (computer progamme) 138

Braudel, Fernand 66

Braverman, Harry 92, 94–5

Brazil: sugarcane production in 146

Brödner, Peter 62

Brookings Institute 106

Brown, John and Eric Leaver 'Machines Without Man' 59

Brynjolfsson, Erik and Andrew McAfee 18, 19, 101, 111, 130, 176

The Second Machine Age 2, 3, 16–17, 110

Brzeski, Carsten and Inga Burk 179

Burckhardt, Richard 63–4

Bureau of Economic Analysis *Concepts and Methods* 117

Burghardt, Manfred 172

Canadian Business 115

Čapek, Karel *Rossum's Universal Robots* 1

capital 132

constant capital 32–3, 37

fetishisation of 34

fixed capital 40, 89, 112, 114

productive capital 32–3

valorisation of 26, 28, 33–5, 36–7, 52, 254

capital accumulation 9, 37, 102, 103, 114, 139–40, 235, 238, 240

capitalism 5, 82, 111–2, 237, 247, 251

Cargill Company 144

Center for Contemporary Cultural Studies 82

Chile 262

China 157–8, 165–6, 245

Christensen, Clayton 251

class struggle 27, 237

Clickworker (crowdsourcing platform) 26, 199, 204, 218, 227

cloud-based platforms 2, 199

coal mining 45

competition 4, 112, 114, 181, 251

Computer Typesetting Conference (1965) 64

computer-integrated manufacturing (CIM) 56

computerisation 169, 171–2, 175

impact on employment of 104–5, 117, 178–80

management of 180–1, 183

computerised numerical control (CNC) 125, 129

computers 10, 95–6, 109–10

construction industry 45–6, 48

consumer price index (CPI) 36

contest platforms 209–12

contract manufacturing 160, 163–4

control transition 11, 256, 266, 267

cooperation 169, 170

and capitalist production 132–3

in labour process 177–8

corporate debt 118

corporations 147, 151

'creative destruction' theory (Schumpeter) 104, 114, 137, 251

creative work 174–5, 218
Crowdflower (microtask platform) 218
CrowdMed (crowdsourcing platform) 209
crowdsourcing 10, 26, 209, 223
crowdwork 10, 182, 199–200, 203–8, 212, 214, 218–9
cybernetic capitalism 258, 262, 263, 265–6, 267
cybernetics 98, 257–8, 260–3, 265–6

Dartmouth Conference (1956) 243
data
    access and control of 147–8
    integration of 161, 166, 167
    processing of 160–2
data collection 148, 161–2, 246
deep learning 244
Defense Advanced Research Projects Agency (DARPA) 110
Deleuze, Gilles 250
demand: unpredictability of 47–8
Demuth, Helena 51
Diebold John 63–4
digital capitalism 200, 216, 236, 242, 246, 248, 249–50, 253
Digital Labour Debate 229
digital platforms *see* platforms
digital technology 8, 55, 96, 150, 166, 215, 228, 256, 264, 266
    use in agriculture 138–9, 147, 149
digitalisation 4–5, 7, 231
    impact on society of 98, 255–6
    investment in 7
division of labour 2, 50, 169–70, 171–2, 178–9
drones 142, 143, 146
Drum, Kevin 'You Will Lose Your Job to a Robot - and Sooner Than You Think' 2–3
Dyer-Witheford, Nick 248, 267

e-commerce 159, 164–5

East Germany 61, 69–70
Eastern Europe: automation in 157–8
Economic Policy Institute 105–6, 117
economic recessions 105, 115, 172
    impact on employment of 101, 102, 108
Economist, The 110
electronics industry 164
European Court of Justice 144
European Manufacturing Survey 123
European Union General Data Protection Regulation 195–6
exchange value 3, 29–30
expertise 15, 17
exploitation 170, 232, 233, 240
    forms of 250

Facebook 11, 160, 219, 228, 229, 233–4, 238–40, 245, 263–4
factory system 43–4, 49, 50–1
feudalism 169
Figure Eight (AI company) 204
FinTech (financial technologies) 144–5
Fitbit (tracking system) 191, 194
Flextronics Company 160
Food and Agriculture Organization (UN) 145–6
food production 45, 138, 140–1, 144
Ford, Martin 15, 101, 107, 109, 111
    The Light in the Tunnel 114
    The Rise of the Robots 13–14
Ford Motors 112
Fordism 95, 200, 260
Fourier, Charles 230
Fourth Industrial Revolution 7, 55, 57, 97, 103, 104
Foxconn Company 160, 163
Frankfurter Rundschau 'The Factory Without People Will be a Reality in Ten Years' 61
Free Software movement 227
Frey, Carl and Michael Osborne 14, 104, 179

Fuchs, Christian 97
fully developed human beings, theory
    of 53, 73

general intellect 89, 247, 248–9, 250
General Motors 106, 112
General Motors-Toyota NUMMI plant
    108
general purpose technologies 130
genetic engineering technology 143
genome editing 144
German Economic Institute 179
German Sociological Association 75
German Trade Union Federation
    (DGB) 178
Germany 57, 163, 166
    automated factories in 59–61
    automobile industry 125
    ICT industry in 172–3, 174
    Nazi era 60
    post-WWII 90
    strategy for AI in 156
    use of robots in 123
    see also East Germany; West
        Germany
gig economy 218, 220
Global Financial Crisis (2008) 105, 172
Global North: agriculture in 140, 146
global sourcing 158, 159, 167
Global South: agriculture in 140–1, 146
Google 11, 16, 19, 148, 151, 160, 164,
    219, 229, 233, 249, 263–4
Gordon, Robert J. 109, 111, 116
Gormley, Antony *Another Place*
    (sculpture) 21
Gramsci, Antonio 82
Great Exhibition, London (1851) 48
Gröndahl, Boris 182
Guattari, Félix 250
Günther, Hans 59

Habermas, Jürgen 260
Haraway, Donna 19

Hardt, Michael and Antonio Negri 89,
    250
Harvey, David 137
Haug, Frigga 97
    *Theories on Work in Automated
        Processes* 75
Hayek, Friedrich 262–3
Helpling (cleaning service platform)
    218
Heβler, Martina 56, 66
Hirsch-Kreinsen, Hartmut 56, 91
Hirsch-Kreinsen, Hartmut and Beate
    Seitz 172
human beings 16–17
    in relation to machines 189, 196
human intelligence task (HIT) 26,
    223–4
Huws, Ursula 237

IBM Corporation 245
    IBM Watson 14
IF DruPa (German printing union) 62
immaterial labour 2, 6, 89
immediate labour 3, 136
Indonesia: surveillance in 143
industrial capitalism 169, 180, 247, 249
industrial internet platforms 156, 161,
    166–7
Industrial Revolution 17, 39–40, 44–8,
    47, 111
    labour force in 47
    introduction of social reforms 42–3
    see also Fourth Industrial Revolution;
        Third Industrial Revolution
Industry 4.0: 2, 7, 55, 80, 96, 135, 155–6,
    158, 159, 164, 265
    and automation 2, 84, 124, 128, 132,
        134, 166, 228
information and communications
    technology (ICT) 9, 95, 103,
    172–3, 199, 228
information processing: investment in
    107, 117

information technology (IT) 2, 6, 13,
14, 19, 54, 159, 172
innovation 174–5, 182, 251–2
perpetual innovation 252
Institute of Critical Psychology 68–9,
70
Institute for Employment Research
(IAB) 179
Institute of Labour Economy 131
Institute of Psychology, Free University
of Berlin 67, 70
Institute for Social Research (IfS) 91
Institute of Social Scientific Research
(ISF) 91
intellectual labour 73, 96, 180, 200
intellectual property 181–2
International Federation of
Robotics (IFR) 105, 123
World Robotics report (2017) 106
internet 15, 228, 229, 233, 234
Internet of Things 2, 7, 97, 155, 159,
161, 164
investment 54, 107, 115–6, 118
invisible labour 190
Iron Ox (agritech start-up) 138

Jameson, Frederick 263
Japan: agriculture in 143
Jasanoff, Sheila 20
Jovoto (innovation platform) 208, 209,
218
Jugendweihe (coming-of-age ceremony)
61

Kahn, Moritz 60
Kern, Horst and Michael Schumann 75,
90, 95
Klöckner-Humboldt-Deutz Company
60
Klopotek, Felix 27
Krotz, Friedrich 136
Kuczynsky, Jürgen 70, 88
Kuka Company 163

labour
exploitation of 236–7, 247, 249
productive power of 4, 5–6, 170–1
reserve army of 6–7, 94, 105, 107,
114, 203
subsumption of 216–7, 221
labour costs 157, 158, 182–3
labour force 31, 32, 47
labour process 199, 200, 257
management of 202–3
Labour Process Debate 92–3, 202
Landes, David *The Unbound
Prometheus* 43
Landnahme (land grabbing) 227, 236,
265
Langley, Patrick 243
Law of the Tendency of the Profit Rate
to Fall (LTPRF) 37
Lazonick, William 49
Lazzarato, Maurizio 188, 250
Lee, Kai-Fu 244
legal profession: impact of technology
on 16
Leibniz Institute for European
Economic Research (ZEW) 54
Lem, Stanisław 247
Levesque, Hector J. 243
LG Corporation 252
Lighthill, Sir James 244
long waves theory 5
Lucas Aerospace Corporation 226
Luddites 75, 87
Lutz, Burkart 92

machine learning 162, 243–4
machines and machinery 33, 40–3, 47,
54, 57–8, 86–7, 113, 131–2
in relation humans 16–17, 72–3, 124,
128–9, 188–9, 196
macrotask platforms 208–13
Malaysia: surveillance in 143
manufacturing industry 108, 123
near-shoring of 167
re-shoring of 156, 157

Marcuse, Herbert 88, 92, 230
Marx, Karl 86
   Capital 5, 27, 236–7
   Critique of Political Economy 27, 258
   Economic Manuscript 40, 51
   'Fragment on Machines' 3, 39–40,
      88–9, 136, 189, 247, 248
   Labour Theory of Value 28
   'Machinery in Large-Scale Industry'
      113
   The Poverty of Philosophy 88, 256–7
   for specific topics discussed by
      Marx *see* the topic, e.g. machines;
      surplus value
Mason, Paul 89, 97, 250
   Postcapitalism 259
McKenzie, Donald 52
McKinsey Global Institute 104–5
means of communication 231–2, 233,
   234
means of production 32, 170, 171, 231,
   257
mechanical engineering 46, 172
Metallarbeiter-Zeitung 58
metalworking industry 126–7
MHP Company 163
microelectronics industry 7, 172
Microsoft Company 245
microtask platforms 204–8, 212, 218,
   220–1
Mill, John Stuart 41
Minsky, Marvin 243
modes of production 88, 98, 141
money: role of 260
Monsanto Corporation 151
Moody, Kim 7, 9
Mooney, Pat 148
Moore's Law 14, 109, 116
Moravec's paradox 110
More, Thomas *Utopia* 19
Morozov, Evgeny 246
Morris-Suzuki, Tessa 248, 251–2
Moulier-Boutang, Yann 248

Munich Re Group 163, 164
Musk, Elon 242

Nasmyth, James 42
nature: and capitalism 141–2
neoliberalism 115, 181, 195, 259, 261,
   264, 265
networked factories 165
New Scientist 14–15
Ng, Andrew 245

Oracle software 161
Ostrom, Elinor 266

Park, I.P. 252
Parker, Sharon K. 187
planning 20, 168
platform capitalism 10, 97
platform economics 215–6, 217–8
platforms 10, 26, 161, 200–1, 203,
   218–21, 246, 250
   allocation by 221–5, 226
   collection of data by 219
   discrimination by 16
   functions of 204
   management of 20–24
   monitoring of data by 162
Pollock, Friedrich 94
Poppe, Johann Heinrich *History of
     Technology* 50
post-capitalism 215, 259
predictive maintenance 162
pricing: dynamic pricing 264
PriceWaterhouseCoopers (PWC) 174
printing industry 62–5
   women in 79–82
privacy 192, 234, 237, 240
private capital 181
private users data 160
   surveillance of 233–4
production
   customised producton 158–9
   forms of 44
   proximity to end customers of 157,
     158

production networks 155–6, 167, 181
productive forces 4–5, 25–6, 38, 93–4
    and relations of production 7, 82, 90,
        257, 258
professions and professionalism 15–16,
    17
profit motive 18–19, 30, 52, 54, 114–5
profits: internal investment of 116
prosumers and prosumption 11, 228–9,
    232, 234, 235–6, 237–40

Quantified Workplace project 190,
    191–6

radio frequency identity tags (RFID)
    263
railways 46–7
rationalisation 9–10, 53, 58, 92, 121,
    155, 217, 220, 251
regulation theory 5
relative surplus value 34–5, 36, 42
Rescuetime tracking system 191
Rethink Robotics Baxter robot 110
rice production 147
Rifkin, Jeremy 102, 115, 259
    The End of Work 101–2
Roberts, Michael 115
Robotic Challenge (DARPA 2014) 110
robots and robotics 105–6, 110, 112,
    115, 122–3, 124, 173
    collaborative robots ('cobots') 110,
        120, 128–9, 132
    division of labour in 125–6
    exhibitions of 58
    impact on employment of 105, 107,
        123
    industrial robots 103, 109, 110–1,
        123, 125, 126–7, 173
    investment in 107–8, 130
    lightweight robots 9, 120–3, 124,
        127–8, 132, 133–4, 135
    non-production of value by 26, 31,
        32, 34

programming of 129–31
service robots 173

Samuel, Arthur 243–4
Samuel, Raphael 43–7, 50, 53
SAP projects 54, 161, 177
Schaupp, Simon 168
Schmidhuber, Jürgen 242
Schmiede, Rudi 95–6
Schumpeter, Joseph 5
    and 'creative destruction' theory 104,
        114, 251
Schwab, Klaus *The Fourth Industrial
    Revolution* 17
self-employed workers 182–3, 214
self-service checkout points 25–6
servant class 51–2
service sector 112, 114, 175
    impact of digitalisation on 173, 175,
        178–9
Sève, Lucien 73
SFOUR (Russian self-service system) 25
Shaikh, Anwar 115, 116
shipbuilding industry 46
Siemens Company 71, 161, 162, 246
Silicon Valley 16, 21, 243, 245
Singularity University 13, 15
Six Sigma system 108
skills 52–3, 78, 162–3, 175
    de-skilling 65, 162–3
    soft skills 175
    specialist skills 176–7
    upskilling 61, 75–6, 84
smart factories 97, 163, 164, 166
smart farming 264
smartphones 233
Smith, Adam 50
social media 220, 228, 229, 238–9
Sociological Research Institute (SOFI)
    75, 90–1
software 172, 173, 175–6, 180
    'killer application' in 132
    licensing of 182

sponsored stories 240
Srnicek, Nick 97, 246
Standish Group 54
start-ups 115, 135, 147
steam power 44, 46, 48, 88, 111, 245
Stein, Helmut 59–60
subsumption 91, 96, 97, 212, 225
Suchman, Lucy 19
sugarcane production 146
supply chains 155, 160, 164, 263
surge-pricing algorithm 222, 224
surplus knowledge 252
surplus labour 28, 32, 33, 35–6, 113–4
surplus value 28, 29, 31–7, 155
surplus-value-creating labour 200, 202
surveillance 97, 143, 233, 234–5,
    239–40, 256, 261, 264
surveillance capitalism 97
Susskind, Richard and Daniel Susskind
    The Future of the Professions 15,
    16–17
synthetic biology (Synbio) 143–4, 151

'Taobao villages' 165–6
Taylor, Fredrick W. 58, 185
Taylorism 58, 95, 96, 109, 133, 188, 195,
    201, 202, 205, 212, 220
techno-futurism 101, 102–3, 111–2,
    117, 118, 248
technological determinism 55, 88, 90,
    92, 96, 111
technology 86–90, 92, 93
    fetishisation of 3, 27, 28–9
    impact on employment of 56–7, 97,
    102, 107
    investment in 113, 116–9
    see also digital technology
technology corporations 245–6, 251
Telechiric (remote control device) 226
Tencent (holding company) 160, 245
textile industry 45, 49
Thailand: production of rice in 147
Third Industrial Revolution 7

Toffler, Alvin 237–8
Topcoder (software development
    platform) 218
tracking technology 185, 191
    self-tracking 195, 261
trade unions 183–4
Trautwein-Kalms. Gudrun 183
Triple Revolution, The (1964) 101, 115
Trumpf Company 161, 162
Twenty-First Century Manufacturing
    Enterprise Strategy 186
Twitter 19
typesetting 79, 80

Uber (online service provider) 10, 218,
    219, 220, 222–3, 224
Ullrich, Otto 88, 92
United Automobile Workers (UAW) 108
United States
    employment rates in 47, 102
    robots in 105, 106
universal basic income 18
Unsere Welt von Morgen (children's
    book) 61
Upwork (employment platform) 199,
    208, 209
Ure, Andrew 57
    The Philosophy of Manufacture 48–9
    Technical Dictionary 48–9
Urry, John *What is the Future?* 12, 13,
    14, 19–21
use value 29, 32

value 28, 112, 236
    see also exchange value; surplus
    value; use value
value chain 41–2, 44, 166
value creation 6, 34, 112, 156, 166, 167
Varian, Hal 116
Victorian architecture 45–6
Vie Ouvrière, La 58
Volkischer Beobachter 'Factories
    Without People' 59–60

Volkswagen Company: investment in China by 158
von Neumann, John 261

Wallichs, Adolf 58
Walmart Corporation 263
warehouse work 102, 113
waterfall system 186
West Germany 61–2
  agriculture in 140
  automation in 70, 75, 77–9
  educational reforms in 68–9
  printing industry in 62, 64–5
  trade unions in 61, 75–6
Wiener, Norbert 257, 260–2
Wikipedia 16, 233
Williams, Raymond 231–2
Windolf, Paul 125
women
  and affective labour 190
  discrimination at work of 16, 78, 79–82
  office work by 95
  in printing industry 80–2

Wood, Ellen Meiksins 111–2
work
  concept of 229–31
  de-qualification of 96
  group work 187
  monitoring of 107, 108–9
  organisation of 92–3, 107, 108, 171, 173–4, 178, 225–6
  sociology of 93, 202
workforce
  self-management of 189, 192, 196
  self-organisation of 169, 175, 176, 177, 180, 181, 183
World Economic Forum (WEF) 104, 114
  The Future of Jobs 104–5
World Trade Organization (WTO) 104, 114

YouTube 233

Žižek, Savoj 249
Zuboff, Shoshana 264
Zuckerberg, Mark 251

Thanks to our Patreon subscriber:

Ciaran Kane

Who has shown generosity and
comradeship in support of our publishing.

Dedicated to our beloved teacher

Gurunanak

Who has shown the needs of, and
scholarship in appreciation of our traditions.

a reflection of spirit and wisdom, rising
in our midst as the present generation seeks
discerning growth of its own.